REUTERS' CENTURY

REUTERS

THE STORY OF A CENTURY OF NEWS-GATHERING

GRAHAM STOREY

Foreword by Lord Layton

GREENWOOD PRESS, PUBLISHERS
NEW YORK

First published in 1951
by Crown Publishers

Reprinted by permission
of Crown Publishers

First Greenwood Reprinting 1969

Library of Congress Catalogue Card Number 78-94619

SBN 8371-2571-5

PRINTED IN UNITED STATES OF AMERICA

FOREWORD

by Lord Layton

REUTERS' CENTURY IS IN ITS EARLY PHASES A TYPICAL success story of the nineteenth century. It is a colourful and adventurous one. But the development recorded in these pages is much more than this. It is also the history of the evolution of a unique international institution.

The merchants and manufacturers of the Industrial Revolution and the shippers who carried their goods into the farthest quarters of the globe dealt mainly in material things. The stuff in which Julius Reuter started to trade a hundred years ago was of a different kind. His merchandise was news – commercial, political and general news. His market was in the minds of men. Since that time, knowledge and the rapid and worldwide distribution of information have done more than anything else to weld mankind into a single community and have speeded up almost beyond belief the pace of change in human affairs.

We have learned, however, by bitter experience that news is a commodity that may be tainted, that thinking may be distorted and millions misled by suppression of the true and dissemination of the false. If freedom of the Press and of expression is an essential condition of a free way of life, the unfettered flow of objective information is its life-blood. It is at once the privilege and the heavy responsibility of the great news agencies to be the purveyors of that vital commodity.

Mr. Storey tells us that the founders of Reuters realised in their wisdom that the reputation of the Agency depended on the accuracy, objectivity and independence of their political as well as their commercial services. It paid to be good!

Yet no news agency can possibly carry all the news of the world; and every newspaperman knows how easily the picture can be affected by selection and emphasis. As Governments extended their interest ever more deeply into fresh aspects of daily life, it was natural that they should take an increasing interest in the distribution of international news. Economic and political rivalry and the development on a vast scale of the technique and apparatus of mass persuasion have given rise to one of the major social and political problems that face democratic peoples in our time – namely to keep propaganda out of the news.

This issue has inevitably become acute in a half-century which has seen two world wars and many minor ones. In the First World War the British Government sought to use Reuters as an instrument for stating Britain's case to the world. But by the time the Second War broke there had emerged a clearer understanding, even among Governments, of the lesson that Julius Reuter learned when he launched his competitive enterprise a hundred years ago.

It is reasonable that Governments should wish to state their case – and, indeed, in these days when humanity is deeply engaged in an ideological war, propaganda in the best sense of the word is literally a matter of life and death. Yet it is vital that those who distribute the news internationally should not presume to pick and choose but should present as fair and complete a picture as possible.

How to carry this out in practice has been the background of the later phases of Reuters' history. In these years a few clear principles have emerged. Here are three of them:

(1) The greatest safeguard against distortion is free access to the news, and competition not only between newspapers but between the Agencies themselves. There must be no territorial monopoly either internally or in the form of exclusive 'empires' such as those which arose from the arrangements between Havas, Wolff and Reuters in the forty years or so before the First World War.

(2) There should be no Government subsidies. You can never prevent those who pay the piper from calling the tune.

(3) The most suitable form of control is that news agencies should be owned co-operatively and controlled by the Press itself. If Governments must stand aside the enforcement of the highest standard can best be left to the users as a whole.

In recent years these principles have been applied in the case of Reuters. All attempts at territorial monopoly have long since been abandoned; during the Second World War it eliminated from its accounts all traces of subsidy both direct and indirect, and in 1941 a partnership arrangement between the provincial and London Press made it the property of the British Press as a whole.

But Reuters and Reuters alone among news agencies has carried the concept of a co-operative Press-controlled agency to its logical conclusion. An international Press service should be a service to the Press of all nations. Since the war the newspapers of Australia, of New Zealand and of India have become shareholders in Reuters, with directors on the Board; and its international character is further emphasised by the presence of journalists on its staff not only from these members of the

Commonwealth but from many other countries who are in contractual relations with the Agency.

The job of these men is not, of course, to slant the news for the benefit of this or that country, but to bring to headquarters in London a knowledge of each country, its Press, its politics and its general interests.

On the integrity and competence and on the international outlook of such a staff rests in a very special degree the responsibility for keeping clear and clean the news channels of the world. This is a challenge to the qualities of the journalistic profession at its very best, for in a free world there is no other profession to whom the task can properly be entrusted.

The responsibility is of course shared with many Press organisations throughout the world – including the great American agencies who have long fought for 'free trade' in news. Reuters only differs from these organisations in the fact that it has developed within itself an international control and an international staff. It is that fact which makes the New Reuters a unique international institution.

Contents

CONTENTS

Plates in Gravure

Reproduced in facsimile in the text are the first of Reuter's
'Electric News' telegrams (p. 25), and the announcement of
President Lincoln's assassination, an early Reuter success, as
printed in the *Daily Telegraph* of April 26th, 1865 (p. 38).

Acknowledgments

IT IS UNFORTUNATELY IMPOSSIBLE TO ACKNOWLEDGE by name all those who have helped me in the preparation of this book. But I want particularly to thank the many past and present members of Reuters' staff, both in London and abroad, who have given me indispensable material; Sir Roderick Jones (whose own reminiscences of his career in Reuters are being published this year), Mr. Alexander McLean Ewing, Mr. Philip Napier, son of the late Mark F. Napier, and the management and past and present Directors of the Press Association, for most helpful discussions and information; Mr. R. Austin Harrison, for permission to quote from two private letters to his father, the late Austin Harrison, from Baron Herbert de Reuter; Mr. Charles Marriott, for use of the valuable record of Reuters compiled by him in 1919, of great help to me; Mrs. W. H. G. Werndel, for making available her late husband's unpublished reminiscences; and Reuters' office in Frankfurt, for carrying out research into various German archives. The present management of Reuters placed at my disposal every document in its possession which I wished to see; and I should like to record here my appreciation of the free hand I was given to work upon all Reuter records, from the earliest preserved until the present day's, and the generous help I was accorded by the staff of Reuters at all times.

I wish also to thank the Royal Librarian, Windsor Castle, for permission to quote from the Royal archives; the Keeper of the Public Record Office, the Foreign Office Librarian, and the Librarian of *The Times*, for access to their respective archives and for permission to quote from them; Mr. Francis Williams and Messrs. William Heinemann Ltd., for a quotation from *Press, Parliament and People*; Dean Carl Ackerman for extracts from his Annual Reports of the School of Journalism, Columbia University, New York; and Mr. Kent Cooper and Messrs. Farrar and Rinehart, New York, for quotations from *Barriers Down*.

Among books consulted, I am especially indebted to *The History of The Times*, Volumes II and III; Henry M. Collins, *From Pigeon-Post to Wireless*; Valentine Williams, *The World of Action*; and Louis E. Frechtling, 'The Reuter Concession in Persia', an article published in the *Asiatic Review*, July 1938.

I am more grateful than I can say to my friend Professor Erich Heller, for the time and care he devoted to helping me with revision.

Finally, I wish to thank Lord Layton, of the *News Chronicle*, one of the representatives of the Newspaper Proprietors Association on the Board of Reuters, for his kindness in reading my manuscript and writing the Foreword.

G. S.

CAMBRIDGE: MARCH 1951

The publishers are grateful to the following for the illustrations contained in this book: Picture Post Library; the *Illustrated London News* (Plates 1a, 2a, 2b); Reuters Ltd. (page 25, Plates 1b, 3, 8b); Agence France-Presse (Plate 4a); C. Arthur Pearson Ltd. (Plate 6a); William Heinemann Ltd. (Plate 6b); Cecil Beaton (Plate 8a).

PART I

THE BARONS

1851–1915

During the building of the line from Aachen to Verviers in Belgium [in 1850] . . . I met a Mr. Reuter, owner of a pigeon post between Cologne and Brussels, whose lucrative business was being relentlessly destroyed by installation of the electric telegraph. When Mrs. Reuter, who accompanied her husband on the trip, complained to me about this destruction of their business, I advised the pair to go to London and to start there a cable agency . . .

WERNER SIEMENS:
PERSONAL RECOLLECTIONS

Mr. Reuter's office . . . the first centre of that organisation which has since gathered up into the hands of one man for all general and public purposes the scattered electric wires of the world.

ANDREW WYNTER, M.D.:
OUR SOCIAL BEES (1861)

One idea that Reuter conceived made his name famous. That was that all newspapers which printed his telegrams had to agree to carry his name at the end of each published message. This accomplished two things: it made the name famous and it let the public know who was responsible for the information in the message. In other words, Reuter was the first individual to let the public know 'who said so' as respects the origin of news dispatches. Englishmen saw the name in their newspapers, wondered 'who is Mr. Reuter?'; also they wondered how to pronounce the name.

KENT COOPER:
BARRIERS DOWN (1942)

I

Pigeon Postman

THE EARLY HISTORY OF REUTERS IS THE LIFE-STORY OF its founder, Paul Julius Reuter. The archives of his birthplace, Cassel, capital of the old Electorate of Hesse in Western Germany, contain no birth certificate bearing that name. They do, however, record that on July 21st, 1816, a third son, Israel Beer, was born to Samuel Levi Josaphat, then provisional Rabbi of Cassel; and nearly thirty years later the records of baptism in Berlin show that in 1844 Israel Beer Josaphat became a Christian and adopted the names of Paul Julius Reuter.

Other records – the memoir of a friend, some fragmentary notes from a Cassel antiquarian – throw a little more light on the Josaphat family. They tell of Samuel Levi's early days in the small town of Witzenhausen near by, where his father was judicial adviser to the Jewish community, and of his father's and his own reputation for learning. They tell also of the bad times under Napoleon's soldiers, and of the family's move to Cassel in 1814, a year before the battle of Waterloo.

But this is not an isolated story. The Josaphats were among the many families of European Jews who were then leaving their own communities and going out into the world. It was a movement which included such eminent Jewish thinkers as Moses Mendelssohn, who, at the end of the eighteenth century, saw only one hope for his race in Europe: the Jews must abandon their old exclusiveness and become full citizens of their adopted countries. With them they took their traditional intellectual training and a genius for assimilation. It was the

3

beginning of their unique position and strength in modern European life.

Some gave up their faith altogether, others only its more stringent commands. Samuel Josaphat himself remained a rabbi, and one of his sons followed him. Two cousins were university professors, one of Classics at Berlin, the other the distinguished Sanskrit scholar Theodor Benfey, at Göttingen. Other members of the family had already turned to commerce, including one of Samuel's nephews, settled as a banker in Göttingen. It was to him that young Israel Josaphat was sent on his father's premature death in 1829.

The thirteen-year-old boy was intended for a business career, but during the ten years that he spent here he first seems to have become attracted to the possibilities of a different profession. Göttingen was then the scene of some of the first experiments in electro-telegraphy. In 1833, Karl Friedrich Gauss, one of the greatest mathematicians and physicists of his age, succeeded, in collaboration with Weber, in sending electric signals to a neighbouring town through a wire fixed high up on the Johannis Tower of Göttingen. This caused a considerable stir. Gauss and young Josaphat certainly met in the 1830's. The story goes that the young man, employed then in his cousin's bank, attracted Gauss's attention by pointing out a serious mistake the mathematician had made in a money-exchange calculation. Was there anything else about him to arouse Gauss's interest? He was thin and his face gave the impression of considerable intelligence. Some noticed in his features a resemblance to the French composer Offenbach. Yet a friend of his family, who often met him during these years at Göttingen, says that, playing whist with him, he would not have dreamed of one day being entertained by that modest young man in one of the most palatial houses in the West End of London.

Gauss, however, must have found him sufficiently interesting to discuss with him the future of the telegraph. It is said that from these conversations sprang the young banker's vision of a telegraphic Agency. But, if this rather melodramatic story be true, it took many years for the vision to be realised, and even then it was along rather devious lines. Pigeons at first played a greater part in Reuter's schemes than the electric telegraph.

We next find him in Berlin, where he settled in the early 1840's. It was there that he was baptised and in 1845, as Paul Julius Reuter, married Ida Maria Magnus, the daughter of a Berlin banker. In appearance she was the opposite of Reuter himself. A Viennese friend of a few years later, in Paris, takes obvious pleasure in describing the two Reuters together: Julius, short, vivacious, energetic, with bird-like piercing eyes, in conversation always succinct and to the point; and his far bigger wife, with her long fair hair, *gemütlich*, rather sentimental, her manner of speaking often vaguely poetical. He also says how much she later helped Julius in his work. Assisted by his father-in-law's capital, Reuter took a share in an established Berlin bookshop and publishing business which now became known as 'Reuter & Stargardt'. Financially the venture itself was clearly a success: the bookshop still existed in Berlin up to the persecution of the Jews in Germany of the middle 1930's and, as 'J. A. Stargardt', exists in Hamburg today. But there were reasons, more compelling than commercial considerations, which made Reuter leave Berlin for Paris at the end of 1848.

In Germany, more than in any other European country, 1848 marks a year of revolutionary unrest and frustration. The failure of the Monarchy was even surpassed by the failure of the Revolution. During the year, Reuter and Stargardt published a number of political booklets and pamphlets then described as 'democratic'. It was soon a risky epithet. Stargardt himself was cautious and reserved: later members of the firm were convinced that Julius Reuter was the driving force in this enterprise. Whether Reuter was personally or only commercially implicated, Berlin was clearly no climate to suit him, and at the end of the year he joined the numerous political Radicals and men of letters from Berlin and Vienna who emigrated to Paris, taking his place among their circle. In this unstable atmosphere there was an increased demand for information, and above all for political news. Political journals cropped up all over Europe, particularly in those centres where the freedom of opinion was least impeded. Thus it was in Paris that Julius Reuter first embarked upon his career of news-gathering.

His first months in Paris he spent as a translator in the lithographic office set up by a certain Charles Havas in 1835. Havas, a rich merchant from Oporto, had bought up one of the first 'news bureaux' in existence, the 'Correspondance Garnier', and turned what was mainly a translating-office into an Agency which collected extracts from all the great European papers and delivered them daily to the French Press. By 1840 it catered for subscribers outside France as well, running a regular pigeon service between London, Brussels and Paris, and supplying news of Paris to the Francophile court circles of St. Petersburg. Between 1835 and 1845, under Charles Havas's directorship, this Agency established correspondents in most of the capitals of Europe. To work under Havas was an invaluable apprenticeship for Julius Reuter, but his temperament would not allow him to remain an apprentice for long. He was determined to become his own master. With inadequate means, and at the risk of complete financial disaster, he began in the spring of 1849 to publish his own rival news-sheet in Paris.

The vivid picture given of the enterprise by a Viennese exile in Paris named Gritzner shows Reuter's courage and perseverance: it also shows the squalor he and his wife were prepared to endure when odds were against them. Working on the same lines as Havas, they translated extracts from articles, social gossip and commercial news from the leading French journals, and then sent them to what subscribers they could muster among the provincial papers in all corners of Germany. Reuter himself was the sole editor, printer, administrator and accountant of this new firm, assisted only, as Gritzner says, 'by his pretty wife who worked away quietly, translating and copying with her faultlessly neat handwriting'. Their one living-room was their office, or rather the office their living-room, 'its curtains', to quote from Gritzner, 'damp and mouldering; the fireplace filled with remnants of hastily eaten meals, ashes, half-burnt pieces of wood and pieces of paper; a cracked mirror over the damaged marble-covered fireplace; cobwebs on the plaster mouldings on the ceiling, a rocky table under which a scarred dog used to sit with one leg perpetually out of action; and a dark background of heaps of paper and a press'. Despite all their hard work, one day, in the late summer of 1849, the dilapidated office had to be closed for good and Reuter and his wife disappeared.

It is impossible to say whether this failure of Reuter's first attempt at founding his own independent news agency was due to premature and ill-advised ambition, or to the steady worsening of the prospects in France for a free Press. Reaction in Paris had already led to a ruthless tightening of censorship. In a few years *The Times* was going to join bitter issue with Napoleon III on his muzzling of all political criticism; and French Liberals were to point to England as the only home of a free newspaper Press. What market there was on the Continent for a political news service seemed safely in the hands of the rapidly expanding Havas.

Such were the vagaries of political fortune, that, while Reuter was being disillusioned about the possibilities of a free Press in France, the chances in Germany were considerably improving. The concessions of the Frankfurt Diet had freed the newspapers of the most cumbersome restrictions, though the new Parliament's more liberal legislation did not affect some of the smaller States which had remained outside the

7

Frankfurt Confederation. In many parts of Germany every issue of a newspaper had still to be approved of by the police before it could appear. Yet even in these States one aspect of news freedom had been kept intact all the time: the economic liberty of commerce. As commercial enterprises grew and, through industrial expansion, became more intricate, they needed more reliable international information. Political police supervision was, even in the sphere of news, defeated by the sanctity of economic freedom.

From the days of the Fuggers, the Medici, and the House of Thurn and Taxis, with its ramifications through Central Europe, news-gathering to serve the ends of commerce and speculation had remained completely free. The Fugger agents had sent their regular news-letters from one end of Europe to the other, from Amsterdam to Venice, from Antwerp to Madrid, all to be collected and edited by their two central news-agents at Augsburg. It had paid the Hapsburgs not to interfere with them. The Princes of Thurn and Taxis had, at the end of the eighteenth century, added a profitable news service to their vast postal activities, by an auspicious habit of opening the letters and noting their contents before sending them on to their destination. By sharing with the German Emperor this simple method of gaining intelligence, they had been left in full enjoyment of their monopoly.

Stories about the Rothschilds' ingeniously basing their speculations on a complex system of intelligence, with its couriers and pigeons, were current throughout Europe. Legend had already transformed the Ostend boat to London which Nathan Rothschild's agent just caught after Waterloo into a specially chartered schooner. *The Times* had its own efficient service of market prices; Havas was already making his reputation by supplying the Bourse with the European exchange rates.

It was in supplying commercial news that Julius Reuter now saw his only hope. The pace and fever of financial speculation throughout Europe had increased wildly since the Napoleonic Wars. Violent fluctuations in the money market had followed the revolts and Carlist intrigues in Spain in the late 1820's; and the pre-1848 political agitations in Austria-Hungary, Germany and France produced an anxious demand for day-to-day news of investments and market conditions. The need for a speedy, accurate and reliable commercial news service was there to be met.

The opening to the public of the Prussian State telegraph line from Berlin to Aachen on October 1st, 1849, gave Reuter his chance. But someone else had seen it before him. Bernhard Wolff, a German-Jewish physician, with a strong subsidiary interest in the money market, founded 'Wolff's Bureau' in Berlin – the first telegraphic Bureau proper in Europe – almost on the day the line opened. He was joined by a successful Berlin lawyer (a cousin of Werner Siemens, the electrical engineer), and the two of them were soon using this new method of speedy communication for sending commercial messages from Berlin. Reuter himself, with Berlin monopolised by Wolff, made for the other end of the telegraph at Aachen, and established there his own small telegraphic office – or, as he called it, his 'institute'. Here he supplied local clients, bankers and merchants, with financial information, extending his service soon to nearby Cologne where, for a short time, he had an office too. He even ventured further afield, bringing news of stock-exchange and market prices from the main European countries to Antwerp and Brussels, with as much speed as the mail trains from Aachen would allow. From the very first he established his reputation with his clients by insisting on the principle of absolute equality between them. Reports still exist of how his subscribers at Aachen were locked in his office to receive the messages, so that all should receive 'Mr. Reuter's prices' simultaneously.

Throughout the winter of 1849 Reuter worked in Aachen

on the basis of this slightly awkward combination of telegraph wires and railways. Then, the following spring, the French Government opened its own telegraph line from Paris to Brussels for general public use. Reuter's sense of enterprise suddenly found wider scope. Private telegraphic communication was now possible from Berlin to Aachen, and from Paris to Brussels. Only a gap of about a hundred miles – the distance from Aachen to Brussels – had to be bridged to link telegraphically the greatest commercial centres of the Continent, Paris and Berlin. The mail train between Brussels and Aachen took up to nine hours. Carrier-pigeons would cover the distance in under two.

Carriers of military messages since Roman times, pigeons had, with the increase of financial speculation in the cities of Europe, come into their own as a rapid means of carrying despatches between these new battlefields. *The Times* had established a pigeon post between Paris and Boulogne in 1837, to speed up the publication of the latest European market prices; Havas was using them three years later. By 1846 twenty-five thousand carrier-pigeons were being kept in Antwerp alone and were proving an extremely sound investment.

On April 24th, 1850, Julius Reuter made a verbal agreement with a Herr Heinrich Geller – a brewer, baker and pigeon-breeder – in Aachen, to supply him with forty well-trained birds 'suitable for the establishment of a pigeon carrying service between Aachen and Brussels'. The contract, finally committed to writing on July 26th of the same year, laid down the most stringent conditions for maintaining absolute secrecy in the handling of messages. Herr Geller seems to have shown a considerable measure of generosity to his enterprising but by no means wealthy client. He first accommodated Reuter and his wife at his house in Aachen, and then acted as their guarantor when they took rooms in a local hotel.

Every afternoon, once the Brussels Bourse had closed, or

the last messages had arrived by telegraph from Paris, Reuter's agent in Brussels copied the latest stock prices onto thin tissue paper and placed them in a small silken bag secured under the wing of one of Geller's pigeons. For safety, three different pigeons were normally despatched with the same message. Six or seven hours before the daily mail train arrived, the pigeons were circling over their dovecot at Geller's house in Aachen, where a full team, consisting of Reuter and his wife, Geller and his thirteen-year-old son, Franz, caught them, extracted their messages, copied out the prices by hand and distributed them to their local circle of subscribers. Where the messages had to go further down the line, Reuter would run with them in person to the station telegraph office.

For eight months Reuter continued his activities as both pigeon postman and telegraphic agent; but soon the Geller pigeons and their ingenious postman were threatened with unemployment. The telegraph wire from Berlin to Aachen made its way as far as Verviers, and then to Quiévrain on the Franco-Belgian frontier, to be all but met by the Paris–Brussels line which was soon extended to Valenciennes. The two telegraph systems were now separated by only five miles. Julius Reuter gave up his pigeons and, in their place, installed relays of horses.

This narrowing of scope came most inconveniently. For Reuter had just begun all the necessary preparations for setting up a political news service as well. He now had agents in most of the main European cities: there was no reason why they should not supply him with political news. He had even improved upon the Havas way of offering the world extracts from journals. His correspondents were appointed with a view to their competence in gathering their own information at the centres of political activity. There seemed little point now in continuing with these costly plans, when the gap over which he had his only monopoly of operation was dwindling daily before his eyes. To bridge the Channel would be more in keeping with Reuter's vitality. Why should not both he and London benefit from his capacity to gather reliable European news?

Reuter followed the telegraph wire to Verviers, his pigeon post, as Siemens said, 'relentlessly destroyed' by the expanding electric telegraph. In November 1850 he wrote to Mowbray Morris, Manager of *The Times*, proposing that his 'institute' should 'receive and forward to England all despatches which may be telegraphed to Verviers for *The Times*'. He had not reckoned with *The Times*' conservatism. Morris's reply was polite but cold: Reuter's proposal 'deserved consideration' and Morris would communicate again 'if it should eventually appear expedient to accept it'.

Just after Christmas 1850 the gap of five miles was closed by telegraph wire. It meant, in fact, that Paris was linked with Berlin. Reuter and his relays of horses were redundant. The owners of the wires, the earliest German 'Magnetic Telegraph Companies', would not have him exploiting *their* invention. He had shown news-collecting to be a more profitable business than railway-signalling, for which the lines had originally been built; they had learned the lesson and wanted the new business for themselves. Director of the chief of them – the Berlin Telegraph Company – was Bernhard Wolff, clearly going to hold the field in North Germany.

Werner Siemens had already on a previous occasion advised Reuter to make a start in London. That summer Julius Reuter left for England. Sixty-five years later, in 1916, when the Germans saw Reuters as one of their deadliest enemies, it was a German authority on journalism, Arthur Jung, who noted that Reuter after all was a German; and that Siemens's advice, given to his countryman, 'would finally cause Germany irreparable harm'.

2

Foothold in London

JULIUS REUTER ARRIVED IN ENGLAND AMONG THE
crowds of foreigners coming to admire and be caught up in the
mood of the Great Exhibition. It was a peculiarly well-timed
arrival. The multitudes of every nationality who thronged the
Exhibition during the five months of that summer of 1851 were
paying homage to the two forces that made London the true
birthplace of Reuter's Agency: English tolerance, with all that
this meant to the Europe of Reaction in the middle of the
nineteenth century; and English commercial enterprise, with
its insistence on making London the world's financial hub and
the centre of the world's communications.

The Reuters went straight to London and took rooms in
23, Finsbury Square, the home of Herbert Davies, a physician. He was Julius Reuter's first friend in England; and when
six years later Reuter was granted naturalisation, it was Davies
and three medical friends who guaranteed his good affections
to Her Majesty the Queen's Person and Government.

On October 14th, Reuter rented two rooms in No. 1, Royal
Exchange Buildings, in the City of London – as near as he could
to the Stock Exchange – and set up his first 'telegraphic office'.
For some time, his only helper was a twelve-year-old office
boy, John Griffiths, whose lone responsibility in these precarious days was fourteen years later rewarded by the Secretaryship
of the newly formed 'Reuter's Telegram Company'.

Reuter's prospects were not so bleak as they perhaps looked:
he had some capital (although, as he always insisted, very

little) from his venture in Aachen; goodwill with merchants all over Europe who had profited by his pigeon service; and undoubtedly *some* relations with 'gentlemen connected with most of the European Governments', as he was careful to tell James Grant of the *Morning Advertiser* later. More important, he had his agents who had worked for him in the past in the chief European cities, and a good chance, now he was off their own grounds, of coming to terms with both Havas and Wolff.

There was another, and certainly a strong, motive in Reuter's mind for moving his headquarters to England: he was following the cable. This was the beginning of a policy which, within ten years, was to make his Agency straddle the globe. Well ahead in the laying of land lines – by 1848, nearly two thousand miles of English railways were equipped with the telegraph – British electrical engineers were now turning their attention to the sea. Submarine cable experiments had begun in Portsmouth harbour as early as 1846. Then, on a stormy day in early March 1849, 'the clatter of the electric alarum, in the far distant London station', as *Chambers's Journal* put it, told the Chairman of the South Eastern Railway Company that telegraphic contact had been made from a point two miles out at sea to the end of the land line at Dover. A line was soon laid to France. There were, of course, vicissitudes: one wire had its insulation scraped off by rocks under water, another apparently provided a catch for a French fisherman; but, while Reuter was opening his office in Exchange Buildings, Thomas Russell Crampton laid the first successful cable between Dover and Calais. A month later, on November 13th, 1851, it was, with great ceremony, taken into use – and Reuter had his unique chance.

What this meant to England can be best appreciated by remembering that it had taken nearly two months for the news of Napoleon's death to reach London – as long as for the news of Nelson's victory of the Nile. The *Morning Chronicle* had created a record by announcing the victory of Waterloo – 240 miles away – only four days after the battle.

Yet the newspapers were far from receiving the new cable as an unmixed blessing. Mowbray Morris, Manager of *The Times*, thought it 'a great bore'; he pointed out how untrustworthy and expensive it was, how easily it could cause unaccountable delays, and, altogether, how very much more reliable and respectable was the steamer. *The Times*, far and away the leader of the British Press in foreign news-gathering, preferred to continue its 'Extraordinary Expresses'. Yet Morris paid some sort of homage to the new Dover–Calais cable connection: he transferred *The Times'* special steamer from Boulogne to Calais.

If the newspapers were slow in adapting themselves to the new situation – and certainly in accepting 'Mr. Reuter's cabled messages' – the financial world was not so particular. One of Reuter's first agreements was with the Stock Exchange, which saw the extreme advantage in receiving the speediest news of the latest developments on the Continental Bourses. Within a short time, 'Mr. Reuter's Office' was twice a day providing his business clients – brokers and merchants in London and Paris –, for a fixed annual payment, with the opening and closing prices of the Stock Exchanges of both capitals. Virtual monopoly undoubtedly made the payment high; and soon he was extending the service to the other great European commercial centres: Amsterdam, Berlin, Vienna, Athens. The merchants of Eastern Europe, trading round the Black Sea and through the Danube basin, soon accepted him as their London agent; and the earliest Reuter telegrams preserved, of August 1852, have a markedly Eastern flavour. They are all short commercial messages, very much to the point; and when on occasions they seem to slip unwittingly into news of a wider character, it is merely the bearing on the market that matters. A potato disease is reported from Eastern

Germany: the concern is only for the effect on prices. Good news comes from the siege of Sebastopol in September 1855: there is no Reuter telegram in the Press, but an early Reuter messenger-boy, taking the message to the Stock Exchange, is put on a chair, cheered, and a collection made for him. The City is the centre of Reuter's activities.

At the same time he was still trying hard to break down *The Times'* indifference. It appears to have remained unaffected. Mowbray Morris kept on writing the type of letter designed for people who disturbed him. 'The Proprietors of *The Times* are not prepared to enter into arrangements with you', Reuter was told two months after establishing his office in London. In 1852 they were not interested in the exchange-rates of Brussels, Amsterdam and Vienna 'at a cost of eight guineas per month'. In May 1853, the answer to an offer to supply political news was just as clear: 'Your telegraphic summaries of foreign intelligence will not be used by *The Times*'.

Many men of lesser perseverance would have been content with leaving it at that, concentrating instead on the easier success which the commercial service had already achieved. But Reuter had his agents waiting in most of the European capitals, all of them ready to give him political news. Chief of these, a kind of 'General Agent' in Europe, was one of the most colourful personalities among Reuter's early colleagues. Sigismund Engländer was a Viennese who had fought on the side of the people in the 1848 revolution, and escaped from a death-sentence to Paris. There he met Reuter as a fellow-translator in Charles Havas's Bureau. In character he was very different indeed from the single-minded and austere Reuter: imaginative, Bohemian, full of ideas, some brilliant, others disastrous, and, as F. W. Dickinson, a great but not over-indulgent later Reuter Chief Editor, put it, 'a viveur sans peur, and with plenty of reproche'. Reuter early realised that he was just the man he would need for the struggle ahead to set the Agency going

16

in Europe. Engländer had an extraordinary instinct for political news, and an entrance to most of the Radical and progressive political societies on the Continent. There are no records of his correspondence at this period; but his voluminous letters to Herbert de Reuter thirty years later reflect his sustained ambition ever to enlarge Reuters' news service. His boasts that he was the co-founder of the Agency fit in with his imaginative exuberance rather than with the known facts; but later Reuter correspondents used to look to him for guidance as the doyen of the Agency; and there is no doubt that during these first uncertain years he was constantly pressing Reuter to turn to political news.

Reuter soon had small offices established at Calais and Ostend to supervise his Continental cable service, and to prevent delays as the telegrams were passed from one Administration to another; and by 1856, provisional arrangements for a common collection of news had been made with Havas and Wolff.

Meanwhile, something in the nature of a revolution was taking place in English journalism; and its results almost demanded that Reuter should begin supplying political news. *The Times'* campaign for a free Press, for the right to criticise public men where justice and truth demanded it, was provoked by parliamentary strictures on its attacks on Napoleon III. Its effect was an increased demand, felt throughout the whole Press and its public, for a more adequate system of political reporting. When *The Times* declared, in February 1852, that 'the first duty of the Press is to obtain the earliest and most correct intelligence of the events of the time, and instantly by disclosing them to make them the common property of the nation', it knew that it had the wherewithal to obtain that intelligence. The rest of the Press felt the same need; and Reuter was on the spot to satisfy it. It was the last thing that *The Times* intended; but, ironically enough, this campaign helped considerably to make Reuter the first great agent of political news in London. The ice which Reuter had been unable to melt was broken by the thundering of *The Times* itself.

There was, during the 1850's, another movement for what was also characterised as a 'free Press' – a demand for newspapers that the common man could afford to buy. This soon took the form of a movement against the then fivepenny *Times*. To destroy what Lord John Russell called *The Times*' 'vile tyranny', the campaigners for cheaper newspapers were in search of allies. The abolition of the Fiscal Stamp on June 30th, 1855 – one of the climaxes in the Radical campaign for the abolition of the 'Taxes on Knowledge' – gave the awaited impetus to English journalism. New provincial dailies were published – from now onwards papers like the *Manchester Guardian*, the *Liverpool Post* and the *Scotsman* appeared daily – and in London the competition to *The Times* began with the founding of the *Daily Telegraph*. The latter's reduction from 2*d*. to the first London 1*d*. paper in September 1855 was followed in the next year by the first issues of Cobden and Bright's 1*d*. dailies – the *Morning Star* and *Evening Star*. All these new papers, intent on keeping down the costs of production, were soon glad to accept Reuter's services. He saved them the formidable expense of keeping numerous foreign correspondents abroad.

More important still, this new journalism catered for, and created, a vastly increased and changed reading public. In 1854, the total circulation of daily papers throughout the United Kingdom was under 100,000 copies per day, of which *The Times* accounted for 51,000; sixteen years later, in the Franco-Prussian war, the *Daily News* alone reached 150,000. The sympathies of the majority of this new reading public were far more in tune with the 'spot' news and short political messages, in which Reuter was to specialise, than with the longer and more reflective 'correspondents' letters' of the

conservative *Times* and *Morning Post*. And the desire for foreign
news at home seemed met by events abroad. W. H. Russell's
despatches to *The Times* in the Crimean War had shown the
country something of the power of the Press. The Risorgimento
was gathering pace in Italy; Great Britain was at war in China;
and in May 1857, units of the Bengal army mutinied.

This demand for news expressed itself in still more ambitious submarine cable projects. Charles Bright had laid the
first cable in deep water between Scotland and Ireland; and
in 1856 he and Cyrus Field organised the Atlantic Telegraph
Company. After two vain efforts to cross the Atlantic, a cable
was spliced in mid-Atlantic on an August day in 1858. Queen
Victoria and James Buchanan, the President of the United
States, sent congratulatory and fervently hopeful messages to
each other, inspired by this new link between the two countries.
Cyrus Field became an American national hero, and plans were
made for a nation-wide celebration throughout America on
September 1st. The sense of buoyant optimism in England
seemed reflected in the contents of the first cable news message
to cross the Atlantic: '. . . Settlement of Chinese question;
Chinese Empire opens to trade; Christian Religion allowed.
Mutiny being quelled, all India becoming tranquil.' This was on
August 27th. Within a week, while the September celebrations
were at their height in America, the current failed and the
cable went dead.

Mowbray Morris records that during the three weeks' life
of this first Atlantic cable he had considered using Reuter for
a *Times* American money-market service. Owing to the break-
down of the cable connection, this intention was not realised,
but *The Times'* resistance was gradually giving way.

Julius Reuter's plans were now complete. Since March 1857,
he had been a British subject, and had announced his intention
of remaining permanently in England. Soon afterwards, Lord
Clarendon, the Foreign Secretary, promised him the privilege

of receiving copies of the Foreign Office's telegrams from India, a concession that had already been made to the Telegraph Companies. He had truthfully written to Clarendon that his office, as the 'Continental Telegraph, under the direction of Mr. Julius Reuter', was supplying almost all the leading papers on the Continent with London news and official despatches. Now, as 'Mr. Reuter's Office', he urgently needed this news to supply the needs of the Press in London.

Frontal attack on *The Times* had failed; so Reuter decided to take his chance with the rest of the metropolitan Press. He chose first the *Morning Advertiser*, founded in 1794 by the powerful Licensed Victuallers' Association. James Grant, its Editor, describes the interview in *The Newspaper Press*, published in 1871:

In October, in the year 1858, one morning, a gentleman called on me. His accent, though he spoke English well, at once indicated his German nationality.

'Have I,' he said, 'the pleasure of speaking to Mr. Grant?'

I said that Grant was my name.

'Would you favour me with a few minutes of your time, as I have what I regard an important proposal to make to you?'

'Oh, certainly,' was my answer. 'Take a seat,' and so saying I handed him a chair.

'My name," he continued, 'is Reuter. Most probably you have never heard of it before.'

I said I had not had that pleasure.

'I am,' he resumed, 'a Prussian; and have been employed for many years as a Courier to several of the Courts of Europe, from the Government of Berlin; and in that capacity have formed personal intimacies with gentlemen connected with most of the European Governments. It has occurred to me that I might, therefore, be able to supply, by telegraph, the daily press of London with earlier and more accurate intelligence of importance, and, at the same time, at a cheaper rate, than the morning journals are now paying for their telegraphic communications from the Continent. But,' Mr. Reuter added, 'before bringing under your consideration my proposals and plans, it is right I should mention, that previous to coming to you, I called on the manager of *The Times*, as the leading journal, to submit my views to him.'

"That was perfectly proper,' I observed. '*The Times* is not only the leading journal of Great Britain, but of Europe and the world. Did the manager of *The Times*,' I inquired, 'entertain your proposals?'

'He listened to them,' said Mr. Reuter, 'and to my exposition of the grounds on which I felt I could carry them out, and said that he had no doubt I felt confident I could accomplish all that I was willing to undertake; but, he added, that they generally found they could do their own business better than any one else. That, of course, I regarded as a negative to the proposals I had made to *The Times*, – I have therefore come next to you, as Editor of the *Morning Advertiser*, to lay my plans before you, and to submit my proposals for your consideration.'

Mr. Reuter accordingly entered into full particulars relative to what he proposed to do, the grounds on which he expected to be able to carry out his plans, and the arrangements he had already made by which he could immediately furnish a proof of the practicability of all he was prepared to undertake.

On carefully listening to all that Mr. Reuter said, I remarked, as the manager of *The Times* did, that I had no doubt whatever that he was fully persuaded in his own mind, of his entire competency to accomplish all he was prepared to undertake. I added that I would go even farther than that. I had, I said, no hesitation in saying that after attentively listening to his statements I had faith in his ability to carry out all he was ready to engage to do; but, I added, that as certain arrangements existed which I had made some time before with our Continental correspondents to receive telegraphic information of anything of importance which transpired in any of the European countries, I should think it unwise to break up those arrangements until absolutely certain from experience of the success of Mr. Reuter's plans. I should here remark, that before this he knew, because I had told him, that the average sum we were paying monthly for our telegrams from the Continent was £40, and he had offered, while pledging himself to transmit to us, as a rule, 'earlier, more ample, more accurate, and more important information from the Continent,' to charge only £30 per month for it all. Of course, this was a great consideration; but though I told Mr. Reuter that the difference in the expense was a very important

21

matter, yet even that consideration must give way to the efficiency of the manner in which that department of the *Morning Advertiser* must be conducted. If, I said to Mr. Reuter, I had any absolute guarantee that he could accomplish all that he undertook to do, I would at once accept his proposals, in connection with the terms which he mentioned, but that while renewing the expression of my belief that he would be able to do all which he undertook to accomplish, still that was only my opinion; and that I would not feel justified in giving up the existing arrangements to a mere opinion, however firm my faith might be in its soundness. Mr. Reuter, I saw from a single word he said, heartily responded to the reasonableness of this representation of the case, characterizing it as a business-like view of the matters under our joint consideration. His countenance brightened up on my saying that if I were satisfied that all he proposed was practicable, I would at once agree to his terms; and like one who had full faith in his ability to do all that he had undertaken, he immediately answered, – 'Nothing could be more reasonable than that you should not think of giving up your existing arrangements for receiving telegraph communications from the Continent, until you were furnished with practical proof that better arrangements could be substituted for them; but so thoroughly satisfied am I that my plans would be found better as well as cheaper, that I am willing to make this proposal to you, – that I shall send you daily for a fortnight my telegraphic communications from the Continent without making any charge for them, and you can in the meantime, go on receiving your own as before. In this way,' Mr. Reuter added, 'you will be able to institute a comparison between the value and the number, as well as the relative cheapness of my telegraphic messages from the Continent, and those which you receive from your correspondents under your existing arrangements.'

I not only at once admitted the liberality of this offer, but intimated my acceptance of it. Mr. Reuter, on my doing so, expressed the greatest pleasure, and added, 'As I am going to make the same proposals to all the other papers – the *Telegraph*, the *Morning Herald*, and the *Standard*; the *Morning Chronicle*, the *Morning Star*' – both the latter journals being at that time in existence – 'and the *Morning Post*, – will you permit me to say to the respective managers of these journals that you have accepted my proposals? Because,' he continued, 'that may have the effect of inducing them also to accept my offer.' 'With great pleasure, on the understanding,' I answered, 'that you state to them the conditions on which I have done so, – that is, provided that after receiving your telegrams for a fortnight without any charge, I am satisfied that you do the business much better as well as cheaper, than it is done under the existing system as worked by our own private correspondents.'

Mr. Reuter renewed the expression of his gratification at the result of our interview, and before leaving said to me – and this is the great point to which I wish to direct attention – that if I had declined to accept his proposals as *The Times* had done, he would not have called on the managers of any of the other papers, but have abandoned the idea altogether of organizing a system of telegraphic communication from abroad, because, he added, if the *Morning Advertiser*, or any one of the then existing morning papers, had declined to accept his proposals, the acceptance of them even by all the others, would not have sufficed to meet the expenses which it would be necessary to incur in the efficient carrying out of his plans. But all the other morning papers, except as I have said, *The Times*, accepted the same conditions as those to which I agreed, namely, that if they were satisfied, after a fortnight's trial, that his organization was superior to their own, they would permanently adopt his.

Mr. Reuter, in terms of the understanding not only come to between him and myself, but between him and the other managers, with the one exception I have mentioned, – at once applied himself to the carrying out of his engagements; and most certainly the result of the comparison between his organization and that of the morning papers at the time proved the very great superiority of his. Not only did I at once give a permanent acceptance to Mr. Reuter's proposals, but the managers of the other journals did the same; and from that day is to be dated the wonderful organization now known throughout the world as 'Reuter's Agency.' *The Times*, I ought to mention, soon after joined the other morning journals in accepting Reuter's telegrams.

The simple facts which I have stated will, I am sure, be regarded as constituting one of the most striking illustrations which ever were furnished of the saying before alluded to, that great events sometimes spring from causes which seem to be of the most trivial kind.

No one can read what I have thus written without being struck with the fact, that not only one's reputation in the world, but his fortune sometimes depends on the slightest conceivable incident. That was the turn of the tide in Mr. Reuter's fortune; and since then the tide has flowed with an increasing and rapid power, until he has become, as he deserves to have done, the possessor of a magnificent fortune, – one too whose proportions are still daily growing greater.

In mentioning these facts I have said nothing which Mr. Reuter would not himself say; for on one occasion, when I was dining at his house, several years after his system was in full and successful operation, he stated in the presence of a large company, among whom were Sir Charles Wheatstone, Dr. Gull, and several other eminent scientific and literary men, what I have just stated, – that had the proposals he made to me in the interview between us which I have described been rejected, his name would never have been heard of by the world in connection with an organized system of telegraphs.

I am very desirous, in narrating these facts, that no one, as I have before remarked, should for a moment suppose that I claim the slightest merit in the part I performed in the matter. I was merely courteous to Mr. Reuter, just as I would have been to any one else, when, as a perfect stranger, he called on me. I listened to what he had to say, and decided on conditionally accepting his proposals, on purely business principles, – as I would have done to any other proposals made to me which I might have deemed adapted to promote the interests of the morning journal I have mentioned, which was then under my sole editorial control and managerial superintendence.

This interview was indeed 'the turn of the tide in Mr. Reuter's fortune'. Reuter promised to give the *Advertiser* a fortnight's free trial of his telegrams from the Continent, and, if they proved satisfactory, to supply a regular service, at a cost to the paper of £30 a month: a saving to it of over £100 a year. Encouraged by the hope of having secured a first newspaper subscriber, he now went the round of the remaining London papers, making the same proposal to each. All were prepared to give him a trial; and the first telegram of the new service, on October 8th, 1858, was available to almost every London newspaper: the *Telegraph*, the *Daily News*, the *Morning Star*, the *Evening Star*, and the rest.

ELECTRIC NEWS.

—◆—

The following Telegram was received at Mr. REUTER's Office, October 8th.

BERLIN, October 8th, 4.7. PM.

The official Prussian Correspondence announces that the King recognizing the necessity has charged the Prince of Prussia to act as regent with full powers, according to his own views, until the re-establishment of his (the King's) health.

The necessary publications of this resolution is expected.

The Chambers will probably be convoked on the 20th inst.

Printed at Mr. REUTER's Office,
1, Royal Exchange Buildings, City.

During this first fortnight Reuter distributed short political despatches from Berlin, Vienna, Paris and Madrid, and telegrams from Marseilles bringing 'advices by the last steamer' from Constantinople and Athens up to the previous week. He reported 'fermentation in Crete', and the Turkish mob's loudly announced desire to 'massacre all the Christians'. From Marseilles a report from the *Bombay Times* was circulated, showing that, despite the optimism about the end of the Mutiny of two months before, the Central Provinces were still holding out. On October 18th came the news, of particular interest to Reuter himself, that Ceylon had been connected with India by submarine telegraph.

The fortnight's trial was a success; and by the middle of October 1858, almost exactly seven years since he had first set up his office in London, Reuter had won a permanent foothold in the English Press. Even *The Times* had succumbed at last. There is no more reliable testimony to the quality of Reuter's early news service than this note, entered in his diary for October 13th, 1858, by the distrustful and long-resisting Mowbray Morris: 'Saw Reuter about telegrams of foreign news. He agreed to send all to us and to charge us only for what we publish for 2/6 for 20 words if his name is quoted, and 5/– if not quoted.' For six weeks, *The Times* seems to have paid for the luxury of not acknowledging Mr. Reuter. The first acknowledged telegram in its pages was quoted as received at Mr. Reuter's office on December 7th, 1858. It was a message from Marseilles that King Ferdinand of Naples 'has offered to the Western Powers to re-establish diplomatic relations by sending Ambassadors mutually'. Of not perhaps striking importance in itself, it was one of the first of a series of despatches which began to focus attention on the clouds gathering in Italy. Cavour's secret negotiations with Napoleon about expelling the Austrians from Italy had already begun; and the lull in European affairs since the end of the Crimean War was rapidly drawing to a close.

On January 4th, 1859, Reuter received and published news of certain words addressed by the Emperor of the French to Herr Hübner, the Austrian Ambassador, during the New Year's Day celebrations in the Tuileries. 'Commented on in public,' Reuter reported, 'they produced a certain agitation.' The Emperor had said: 'I regret to say that my relations with your Government are not so friendly as formerly. However, I beg you to inform your Sovereign that my sentiments on his behalf have not changed.' Anxiety at the sinister undertone of this speech rose high in England; London was full of rumours about the contents of Napoleon's forthcoming speech to the French Legislative Chambers on February 7th. Reuter seized on the chance of making a dramatically quick report of it, and prepared his plans with characteristic thoroughness. The French authorities acceded to his unusual request for an early copy of the speech: it was not in the nature of Louis Napoleon to object to publicity of this sort. The only stipulation was that Reuter's agent in Paris should not open the sealed envelope until the Emperor had begun to speak. The Submarine Cable Company was prepared to sell an hour of its time exclusively to Mr. Reuter. As, at noon exactly, the first sentences of the Emperor's startling declaration of France's new power began to ring out, the same words were being cabled to London. By one o'clock, after a short delay on the cable, Napoleon's flamboyant peroration was being translated into English in Reuter's office in London: '. . . he who ascends the steps of the throne supported by the voice and feeling of the people . . . the first motives of his actions, as his last judges, are God, his conscience and posterity!' An hour later special editions of the London papers were on sale in the City. The Stock Exchange was beginning to panic; the Paris Bourse was in a state of great excitement. 'The Imperial speech', as another Reuter message said with some restraint, had 'not removed fears of an approaching war'. The substance of the speech could indeed only be regarded as an open threat to Austria: '. . . the Cabinet of Vienna and mine, I say it with regret, have often found themselves at variance on questions of principle. . . . In this state of affairs, there is nothing extraordinary in the fact that France should draw closer to Piedmont. . . .'

It was Reuter's first dramatic success. The war between France and Austria that followed on April 16th, 1859, faced him with the new problem of organising war correspondents. Until now, his service had been used mainly to supplement the more detailed messages sent by the leading newspapers' foreign correspondents. As Mowbray Morris, Manager of *The Times*, put it, not without a touch of irony, Reuter was at least good for news 'known to persons of average information'. War suddenly put his despatches on a different footing. Military commanders found it convenient to give their reports to an Agency, rather than to a number of rival war correspondents. A habit of discrimination in favour of Reuter set in, sometimes officially acknowledged, sometimes just brought about by the whim of a particular commander: a habit which increasingly aroused the indignation of the wealthier London newspapers which were jealously guarding the interests of their own war correspondents. Yet favours given to the Agency continued and became more and more obvious. While the Sardinian Commander-in-Chief was threatening to hang any newspaper agent he found within his lines, the altogether different status of Reuter's agents was openly acknowledged. That June, while the remnants of the Austrian armies were being chased out of Magenta and Solferino, Reuter had agents encamped with each of the three armies; and British neutrality meant that on more than one occasion the English public could read separate Reuter telegrams on the same action sent respectively from the Austrian, French and Sardinian headquarters. By the time of the armistice of July 8th, 1859, and the meeting of the two Emperors at Villafranca, Reuter's reputation for impartiality was made.

On the whole, Reuter had used his advantages fairly and kept to his own function of giving the short *facts* of a situation. He was sensible of the consequences of trespassing on the newspaper correspondents' prerogative of presenting the graphic details; speed and accuracy remained his agents' watchwords; and his despatch even of the great battle of Solferino ran to only a dozen lines. Equally important was the principle of equality on which he insisted in his dealings with the newspapers at home. From the very beginning, he had applied the same rule to his newspaper subscribers as to the clients of his financial service: simultaneous publication of his news to each.

The earliest news-carriers to the provincial newspapers had been the 'Electric Telegraph' or 'Magnetic' Companies first established in 1846. These had made a bid to act as *collectors* of news as well; but they mostly collected it from reports already published in the London papers, and the provincial Press was bound to be that much time behind. From 1855, one of these Companies, through a judicious contract to receive *The Times*' European telegrams and sell them in the provinces, had been acting virtually as a '*Times* news agency'. But, here again, the provinces would not have their news until at least a day later than *The Times*' morning edition.

By 1860, Reuter was sending his telegrams both to individual provincial papers and to the 'Electric and International' Telegraph Company, which distributed them throughout the provincial Press, for a composite fee. Had it not been for the inevitable time-lag due to primitive telegraphic equipment, the provinces would have received their foreign news as speedily as the London newspapers; and the smaller provincial papers in particular had reason to be grateful for Reuter's insistence on equal availability of his news to all subscribers.

There were, of course, struggles fought by those papers

which considered they could do their own business best, against what they felt as Reuter's encroachment; nor was the Agency without criticisms of its efficiency. Hardly a month passed without some complaint, from *The Times* in particular: it is certainly not surprising that Mowbray Morris should express himself at times very angrily. 'I have had frequent occasion', he wrote in 1861, 'to remonstrate against the flimsy, stale and even ridiculous character of some of the intelligence which you send to *The Times*. I call this stuff "intelligence" by a great stretch of courtesy: but it is in fact neither intelligent nor news . . .' Once he remarked to Reuter: 'I dare say you know that the public says freely, concerning your telegrams, that most of them are compiled in the City from newspapers and private letters.' And although he admitted that the suggestion was obviously untrue 'with respect to most of the news', Reuter had to be perpetually on his guard against charges of this kind, only too readily made by editors, who resented their dependence on him for the supply of news. This also accounts for the fact that Reuter had often to fight for the accurate reproduction of his telegrams, against the editors' inclination to preserve at least the appearance of their individual originality by chopping and changing mercilessly what he gave them. From the beginning he had insisted on having his name quoted at the head of his messages. In early days, it was convenient for editors to comply with his wish: it freed them of responsibility for their contents. Soon, however, the public regarded Reuter's name as a token of reliability, thus strengthening his position in his dealings with the newspapers.

This situation soon enabled him to raise the terms of subscription. As the field of his activities widened, to include news from America, Australia and the Far East, he could more than meet his rising expenses by doubling and then almost trebling the annual subscription rate. The London daily papers, which had received Reuters' service for £30 per month in 1858, found themselves paying £1,000 a year ten years later. As James Grant wrote, most of the papers grudged these various advances, and would rather have been content with the amount of news which they had first received: 'but they could not help themselves, unless they had combined together. They were driven into a corner. When one agreed to accept Mr. Reuter's telegrams, at an additional cost, from new parts of the world, the others were compelled to follow at any cost . . .' Reuter's principle of equality proved a two-edged weapon.

By 1859, 'Reuter's Telegrams' had their unchallenged place in the British Press. The public were not certain how to pronounce his name – or, since he was a foreigner, resolutely refused to be certain. A writer in the *St. James's Gazette* did his best to settle this problem for them:

> *I sing of one no Pow'r has trounced,*
> *Whose place in every strife is neuter,*
> *Whose name is sometimes mispronounced*
> *As Reuter.*
>
> *How oft, as through the news we go,*
> *When breakfast leaves an hour to loiter,*
> *We quite forget the thanks we owe*
> *To Reuter.*
>
> *His web around the globe is spun,*
> *He is, indeed, the world's exploiter:*
> *'Neath ocean, e'en, the whispers run*
> *Of Reuter.*

*

Reuter was now a pronounced, and occasionally mispronounced, British Institution.

3

New York to Norderney

ON APRIL 13TH, 1861, THE UNION GARRISON OF FORT Sumter outside Charleston, South Carolina, surrendered to its Confederate besiegers, and the American Civil War had begun. The world was soon clamouring for information. It was a busy time for Julius Reuter. War correspondence had to be organised on a far larger scale than during the short war in Italy of 1859; moreover, it had to be transmitted entirely by mail-boat. As his special correspondent, to establish a system of war reporting, Reuter sent a certain James McLean. It was a most successful choice.

Editorial organisation at home needed more attention. The London staff had grown considerably; and the separation of the commercial from the political news department of the Agency was becoming urgent. A first move was made by opening a second office, exclusively to deal with the American news. The messages from America had a habit of arriving by night; and the new office in No. 2, King Street, just across the garden of Julius Reuter's own house in Finsbury Square, was organised for work during the late hours. Reuter's habit of looking in on the Night Editor the last thing at night and first thing in the morning, and occasionally at almost any hour in between, became an uncomfortable ritual of the night's business. Two young men now joined the staff who were later to play important parts in the building-up of the Agency: Henry Collins, who became Reuters' chief pioneer in the Far East and Australasia; and George Douglas Williams, who was to be one of the Agency's most successful Chief Editors.

Apart from the successfully expanding commercial service, full attention was now focused on the incoming news from America. The war suspended every hope of renewing the cable experiments; and it needed McLean's organising skill to work to the strict schedule imposed by the time-table of the transatlantic mail-boats. Soon after the outbreak of war, as public excitement in England grew at every fresh American despatch, both Reuters and *The Times* chartered special fast steamers to meet the mail-boats outside Southampton Water. Wooden cylinders containing the American mails were thrown down to them, and the two boats then raced to the shore, to be the first in getting their messages on to the London telegraph.

New competition from the Telegraph Companies soon forced the Reuter boat further out into the Atlantic Ocean. Charles Bright had, in 1853, laid the first cable between Scotland and Ireland for the 'Magnetic Telegraph Company'; and both the Magnetic and a new Company called the 'Telegraphic Despatch', were now making a new bid at being acknowledged as news-gatherers by the Press. They were using tenders to intercept the American mail-boats at Roche's Point off Queenstown, on the south coast of Ireland, and, by telegraphing their news via Cork and the Irish cable to London, beating Reuter by several hours. It was a situation that demanded the same initiative that he had showed at Aachen. He secretly obtained permission to erect a telegraph wire of his own between Cork and the little harbour of Crookhaven, sixty miles away on the extreme south-western tip of the Irish coast. The line was laid and run by two German engineers; and a team of three men was given a small tender, the *Marseilles*, to intercept the mail-steamers when they were first sighted off Crookhaven. McLean, in New York, placed his despatches in canisters; and George McCall, one of Reuter's intercepting team, describes how the picking-up of the canisters was done. They were caught with long netted poles; and

33

at night lit up with phosphorus before being lowered from the ship. Ninety miles' sailing-time to Roche's Point was thus saved, and Reuter's messages were now eight hours before his rivals' in London. 'Mr. Reuter', as McCall put it, 'had staggered the news-men of his time.'

At the end of 1861, this ingenuity had its reward. In November, the Confederate Government sent two Commissioners to present their case to Europe: James Mason, destined for London, and John Slidell for Paris. They were taken on board the British mail-packet *Trent* at Havana, to cross the Atlantic. On November 8th, the *Trent* was stopped and boarded by the United States sloop *San Jacinto*; and, in defiance of protests from the British naval officer in charge of the mails, the two envoys removed by force. They were now being held prisoners by the North. Passions in England rose high. A Cabinet meeting decided that refusal to free the Commissioners would be an 'unfriendly act'. By December 2nd, a note from Lord Palmerston, the Prime Minister, demanding the immediate release of the prisoners, was on its way to Washington. But it was not until three and a half weeks later, on December 27th, that Lord Lyons, the British Minister in Washington, received a favourable reply from Lincoln's Government. Meanwhile the country was in the grip of war fever. A Tenniel cartoon in *Punch* expressed the public mood: the British lion glared from his island ramparts across an empty waste of waters; the caption beneath read, 'Waiting for the Answer'.

When it did come, early in the New Year, Reuter was the first to receive it. The message was cabled to him from the Irish coast on a Sunday. The newspapers themselves had it in time for the Monday morning editions. Reuter decided to take it personally to Palmerston, in Downing Street. He obtained an immediate interview, and, beating the official despatch, was the first to give him the news. The Commissioners were to be released at once; and, as *The Times* of January 9th put it: 'The Old World is no longer at enmity with the New'.

The privilege Reuter had requested and won, early in 1857, of receiving copies of Foreign Office telegrams from India, lasted only ten months. In December, he was accused by the new Conservative Foreign Secretary, Lord Malmesbury, of distorting a statement on the situation in Naples, and the Foreign Office telegrams stopped. As his own service grew during the next ten years, he began to send his most important telegrams to Ministers free of charge. It was a courtesy he already performed for the Queen and the Prince of Wales. But the Foreign Office remained suspicious; and, despite the considerable value of Reuter's early information of the American Civil War, he obtained little official news in return. His prompt dealing with the United States' answer to the '*Trent* Note' now gave him credit where he needed it.

But, ultimately, Reuter stood or fell on his reputation with the Press. Generally, there was satisfaction: McLean's service from America was proving an undoubted success. Yet Reuter's ambitions soon went beyond the field open to him with the available technical means. By 1861, there were Reuter agents in the Far East, South Africa and Australia, as well as his special representative in America. Their methods of communication, however, were hazardous. The furthest point the cable from England had reached was Malta; and the Malta line was notoriously badly worked. *The Times*, in particular, once so suspicious of the telegraph, was now always ready to reproach Reuter for slowness. 1861 – the year of the outbreak of the American Civil War – saw Reuter's subscriptions doubled, 'due to telegraphic expenses with the Far East'. Even then, without adequate cables, news from these countries only trickled in, with very long gaps in between. In September, Mowbray Morris wrote exasperatedly that news from the Far East and Australia, 'with very rare exceptions, has been meagre and vague', and pronounced his extreme dissatisfaction. But the real hostility from the Press had been overcome; the battle now was with communications. Before Reuter could turn to them, more serious worries were arising out of the Civil War in America.

English fury over the *Trent* affair had only been an exaggeration of hostility to the North among a large section of the more articulate public. The upper classes disliked Lincoln's democracy. The commercial community, and particularly the Lancashire cotton industry, saw themselves being ruined by the blockade of the Southern ports. John Bright, at his mass-meetings, was accusing – not without justification – the English Press of being partial in favour of the South. W. H. Russell, *The Times*' correspondent, was virtually driven out of the North in 1862 for his unfavourable comments on its Army. The *Standard* was raising its circulation by 20,000 copies a day, thanks to the passionately pro-Southern 'Manhattan letters' of its Editor, Captain Hamber.

As we have seen, Reuter's first clients in London were in the City; his links with the cotton industry had grown closer through his recently founded service of market quotations to merchants trading in India and the Far East. His first subscriber in the Press was the conservative *Morning Advertiser*; and his most zealously pursued one *The Times*. There is little doubt that at that time the Agency reflected to some extent the upper-middle-class attitude and prejudices of the City and of some of its newspaper subscribers. It was not altogether surprising, therefore, that Reuter's news was, in some quarters, accused of having a pro-Southern bias. For some period his American telegrams were virtually boycotted by considerable sections of the Continental Press. Some of the French-influenced newspapers of St. Petersburg began to caution their readers 'against being deceived by Reuter's telegrams', and were inclined not to publish them at all. Germany, too, because of

Reuter's first news venture, in 1850,
included a pigeon post between Aachen
and Brussels. In 1944, Reuters' pigeons
brought news from the Normandy
beachhead.

The coat of arms of Baron de Reuter,
granted by the Duke of Saxe-Coburg-
Gotha in 1871, recognised by Queen
Victoria twenty years later.

Julius Reuter's chance came as the submarine cables spread. These contemporary prints show the Dover–Calais cable rolled up in a huge coil, and being paid out by the steamer *Goliath*.

her own aspirations for unity and religious liberty, was too much in sympathy with Lincoln and the North not to share this displeasure at Reuter's reporting. In 1863, political passion led to moral suspicion, and moral suspicion to straightforward indictment: the North Americans in Great Britain spread the rumour that Reuter was bribed by the South. It originated in the apparently genuine belief of Benjamin Moran, of the United States Embassy in London, ever on the watch for signs of partiality for the South in England. The slightest scrap of evidence in substantiation would have ruined Reuter's reputation. None was produced. Reuter counteracted the rumours by pointing to his arrangements for collecting his American news from both Northern and Southern agents.

Beginning in the summer of 1863, Reuter's 'special American telegrams' reported a sequence of Northern victories: Gettysburg, the battles of the Wilderness, the victorious advance of Grant's army of the Potomac from the scrub south of Washington to Richmond, Sherman's march to Savannah and the sea. On Palm Sunday, April 9th, 1865, Lee surrendered to Grant. It was the end of the war.

Five days later, in the evening of April 14th, President Lincoln was shot through the head by John Wilkes Booth in Ford's Theatre, Washington. He died early the next morning. Reuter reported the tragic event two days ahead of all other news of it. McLean, his American agent, overhauled the American mail-boat as it was leaving New York harbour, in a specially hired tug, and threw his report in a canister aboard. Its publication stirred intense sympathy all over England. *The Times* referred to an 'unexampled manifestation of feeling' among the British public. At the same time, it reprimanded its agent in Cork for again being beaten by Reuter.

That the Agency increased its reputation during the American War was due to the fact that Reuter's 'special American

AMERICA.

ASSASSINATION
OF
PRESIDENT
LINCOLN.

ATTEMPTED MURDER OF MR. SEWARD.

(REUTER'S TELEGRAMS.)

NEW YORK, APRIL 15 (10 A.M.).

At 1.30 this morning Mr. Stanton reported as follows :—

"This evening, at 9.30, President Lincoln, while sitting in a private box at Ford's theatre with Mrs. Lincoln, Mrs. Harris, and Major Rathburn, was shot by an assassin, who suddenly entered the box, and approached behind the President. The assassin then leaped upon the stage, brandishing a large knife and escaped in the rear of the theatre. A pistol ball entered the back of the President's head, penetrating nearly through. The wound is mortal.

"The President has been insensible ever since the infliction of the wound, and is now dying.

"About the same hour an assassin, whether the same or not is as yet unknown, entered Mr. Seward's apartments under pretence of telegrams' had shown a regular and speedy factual survey of events to be something more than a merely supplementary service to the Press's own correspondents. To enhance both regularity and speed, still better communications were needed. The cable was still the main problem.

With the war over, Cyrus Field's Atlantic Company made yet another attempt to lay a transatlantic cable. In the summer of 1865 Brunel's great ship, the *Great Eastern*, took a cable as far as two-thirds of the way across to Newfoundland; then it snapped. On June 30th of the next year, 1866, the fifth and final attempt began. The *Great Eastern* once more sailed with the cable from Valentia, off the coast of south-west Ireland; and this time, on July 27th, it reached Heart's Content in New-foundland without incident. A final triumph was the rescuing of the snapped 1865 cable in mid-ocean, from its grave of over a thousand fathoms. This old cable was reconnected; and by September 8th, 1866, Europe and America were joined by two separate telegraph cables. The devotions of many outstanding men were invested in this achievement: chief among them Cyrus Field, the American founder of the original Company in 1856, and Lord Kelvin, the Company's chief electrical engineer from 1857.

One of the first European despatches to reach America across the new cable – and paid for at the rate of £2 a word – was of extreme personal interest to Reuter. On August 13th, 1866, travelled the news of the signing of the Peace of Prague, which ended the seven weeks' war between Austria and Prussia. Among its less publicised results, it meant, as will be seen later, the closing to Reuter of one road of European expansion.

For some time the plan of laying his own cable to Northern Europe had been maturing in Reuter's mind. The centre of gravity of European news had moved eastwards: he wanted to create principal offices in Germany and Austria. At the same time he had still more extensive ambitions than this. The first overland telegraph to India, via Russia, Constantinople and the Persian Gulf, was completed during the last days of the American Civil War. With his own cable extended through North Germany, to link with this overland wire, he would possess a virtual monopoly of the quickest route from Great Britain to the East. With this prospect in mind, he began negotiations with the Hanoverian Government.

By the beginning of 1865, the King of Hanover had promised him a Concession to land a cable in the island of Norderney, in the East Frisians, off the north coast of Germany. The Hanoverian Government would then connect it with new land wires to be built first to Hanover, thence to Hamburg, Bremen and Cassel, to be used *solely* for Norderney cable messages. Reuter's return to his birthplace was to be a peculiarly exclusive affair.

'Reuter's Telegram Company' was the first child of this Concession. Fresh capital was essential; and Reuter had little difficulty in finding subscribers. On February 20th, 1865, under the recent Companies Act of 1862, the new Limited Liability Company was incorporated, with a nominal capital of £250,000 (10,000 shares of £25), of which £80,000 was paid up. Its immediate objects were to take over the Agency, and to acquire Reuter's rights in the Hanoverian Concession. For the business he had built up over nearly fifteen years the Company paid Reuter £65,000; and for more than fifty years this sum was treated as the equivalent of Reuter goodwill. The first Board consisted of Admiral Sir John Dalrymple Hay, Chairman, Colonel James Holland, Mr. Sydney Stopford, and Julius Reuter, Managing Director. Reuter kept this position until his retirement, and in the day-to-day running of the Company his authority stayed supreme. No ties with the past were broken: all the old staff at home and abroad were retained; and, to preserve continuity still further, John Griffiths,

Reuter's original office-boy of 1851, became the Telegram Company's first Secretary.

On November 15th, 1865, the Royal Hanoverian Government formally signed the Concession. Besides the cable privileges, Reuter was given the right to establish an office in Hanover. The 'English encroachments', as the King of Prussia soon called them in a formal letter to his Cabinet, had begun.

The cable was built at great speed, and in less than a year was ready to enter the sea. The laying of it, at the end of September 1866, was entrusted to Henry Fleeming Jenkin, a colleague of Lord Kelvin, and a great friend of Robert Louis Stevenson. Stevenson's memoir of his friend quotes a vivid letter from Jenkin to his wife, describing the *William Cory*'s laying of the cable from off Lowestoft to Norderney, where Reuter himself was waiting. It shows the hardships these first cable-engineers endured. Soaked to the skin, his arm in intense pain after the day's handling of the heavy cable, Jenkin writes how 'I went to bed early: I thought I should never sleep again, but in sheer desperation got up in the middle of the night, and gulped a lot of raw whisky, and slept at last. But not long. A Mr. F. washed my face and hands and dressed me; and we hauled the cable out of the sea, and got it joined to the telegraph station, and on October 3rd telegraphed to Lowestoft first and then to London. Miss Clara Volkman, a niece of Mr. Reuter's, sent the first message to Mrs. Reuter . . . They were all very merry, but I had been so lowered by pain that I could not enjoy myself in spite of the success.'

At Norderney, however, the situation had changed. In July the Prussians had occupied Hanover – Austria's ally – after defeating her army at Langensalza; and the annexation of the Kingdom followed. The formal Prussian attitude to Reuter was entirely correct. On August 3rd, the Prussian Ambassador in London, Count Bernstorff, wrote to him that the Prussian Government 'regarded with favour the Hanover Cable and confirmed without hesitation the Concession'. But this period of unreserved enthusiasm was short-lived: Prussia soon insisted on essential modifications 'made necessary by the lately altered condition of affairs'. On November 25th, 1866, a new agreement was signed in Berlin which 'in substance' recognised the Concession; but Reuter's proposed office in Hanover was to be given up, and its exclusive wire moved to Berlin. Moreover, the Prussian Government contracted the right to use it for an average of 70 messages a day to be sent to London.

The original Concession stipulated that Reuter should send representatives to reside in Germany. The new agreement made it quite clear that the Prussian Government would not insist on accommodating such visitors. From the Hanoverian Concession might have come a kind of *Pax Britannica* over the main supply of news to North Germany; the Prussian agreement was at best a favourable truce.

On the last day of 1866, the Norderney cable was opened for traffic. Within a year it was giving the Agency, from telegram fees paid by outside customers alone, a revenue of £2,000 a month. Of greater importance was the fact – foreseen by Reuter – that it was proving an immense help to his projects for wider expansion.

One of the Telegram Company's first acts was to send new trained representatives abroad. They went as pioneers, with much the same task in front of them as Reuter himself once faced in England. Commerce, then news, had been the order of Reuter's services in London. It was to be the same overseas. Optimism in the London office ran high. First goal was the Middle East. An experienced journalist named Virnand was sent to Egypt; and within a year he reported branches set up at Cairo and Alexandria. Suez was still the Eastern end of the European cable, and it quickly became a thriving centre for Reuter's service of private commercial telegrams to be mailed to and from the East.

With the completion of the first Indo-European overland line, India and the Far East lay open. In February 1866, the Company made one of its more important decisions: Henry Collins, now barely twenty-two, and with less than four years' experience in the Agency, was sent to Bombay, with authority to establish Reuter branches throughout India and Ceylon.

For three years his letters to London are full of despair at bad communications. The line invariably breaks down at the most critical moments in the news. It goes dead for ten days on the verge of the Austro-Prussian War. Then, with the war at its height, and the cotton market wildly perturbed, it fails again. Reasons are numerous. Deep snow is embedding the wires in the Caucasus mountains; or Persian nomadic tribes have used the telegraph poles as targets and carried off the wires. On one occasion, Collins exasperatedly reports that a whale has entangled himself up in the last stretch of cable laid in the Persian Gulf.

The New Year brought, through the opening of the Norderney cable, an improvement in speed; but breakdowns at the Eastern end of the line are still the bugbear of Collins's life. In March 1868, after a break in the Persian Gulf, he writes to Reuter: 'There will be no steamer available for repairs for at least two months, and it is believed that the monsoon will by that time have burst, and stop all operations. It is therefore the most serious break that has occurred since the establishment of this Branch . . .' But ingenuity and perseverance had their reward. When Collins returned home in the summer of 1872, he had laid the foundations of a Reuter Empire. From Bombay to Yokohama, Reuters was becoming another British institution in the East.

There were now two new and reliable cable routes. In 1869, the faithful *Great Eastern* had laid the Indian Submarine Company's cable across the Indian Ocean, from Bombay to Aden, in a single stretch of 1,800 miles. On the next New Year's Day, the new Indo-European overland line was opened. Through Bushire, on the Persian Gulf, Teheran and Russia it linked up with one wire of the Norderney cable in North Germany. But by this time the Norderney cable had finished its service for Reuters: in February 1870 it became the property of the British Government.

The Government project, of which the taking over of Reuters' Norderney cable formed a part, was one of the first instances of large-scale nationalisation in English history. It directly affected every organisation then concerned with collecting and carrying news within the British Isles. Its effects on Reuters were indirect, but also important.

For nearly twenty years the country's telegraph installations were the private property of the Telegraph Companies. Their first use by the Press, in the 1840's, was spasmodic. On August 6th, 1844, *The Times* declared itself 'indebted to the extraordinary power of the Electro-Magnetic Telegraph' for being first to announce the birth of Queen Victoria's second son, Alfred Ernest. Three years later, Queen Victoria's own words, as she opened her Parliament of 1847, were telegraphed to the provincial journals. Within a quarter of a century, the new invention was immortalised in this couplet (on the illness of the Prince of Wales in 1871), attributed to Alfred Austin, the future Poet Laureate:

> *Across the wires the electric message came:*
> *'He is no better, he is much the same.'*

– lines that have at least the distinction of being among the worst in the English language. The Electric Telegraph had clearly come to stay.

The private Telegraph Companies meanwhile flourished by collecting for themselves the news to be communicated along their own lines. By the early 1850's, the Companies had a monopoly of supplying news for use by the provincial papers. For an annual subscription of under £200 a year, the *Glasgow Herald* or the *Manchester Guardian* or the *Belfast News-Letter* could buy a news-ration of up to 4,000 words a day: there would be a summary of the happenings in Parliament, the day's horse racing, the Stock Exchange prices. Very soon, Reuter's telegrams from abroad were included; but the distributing of these, as well as of all internal British news, was still in the hands of the owners of the telegraph wires.

The smaller provincial papers were quite happy with this method; but, by 1860, grumbles from some of the larger papers were percolating through the provinces. The private Telegraph Companies were accused of delays, inaccuracies and exorbitant charges: their 'intelligence department', which selected the news, certainly did not live up to its name. As a result of dissatisfaction, representatives of the provincial Press formed their own 'Press Association' in 1865, in Manchester. It was initiated by John Edward Taylor, the son of the founder of the *Manchester Guardian*, and its purpose was to gather the news from the provincial Press itself. This first blow to the news monopoly of the Telegraph Companies was, the next year, followed by a still more disquieting event: the Postmaster-General requested a report from the technical staff of the Post Office on the telegraph situation: would they be able to manage it if the telegraphs were taken over, lock, stock and barrel, and entrusted to them? The answer was that they could; and, after a certain amount of controversy and financial uneasiness, Gladstone's Liberal Government, authorised by the Electric Telegraph Acts of 1868 and 1869, made the entire internal telegraph lines of the country the property of the State. The Government paid substantial compensation to the private Telegraph Companies, and the original estimate of £4 million was ultimately almost doubled.

Reuter immediately saw the advantages of the State's taking over the Norderney cable as well. After his previous experiences with the Prussian Government he was afraid that, as the owner of a telegraph line on Prussian territory, he could become involved in a political struggle. And, in any case, the British Government seemed in a paying mood. He began negotiations with the Post Office to sell the cable; and, as his legal adviser, briefed William Vernon Harcourt, one of the ablest lawyers of the day. After long bargaining, and a resort to arbitration, Harcourt succeeded in fixing a price based on compensation for twenty years' profits; and, for an enterprise which had cost it £153,000, Reuters was paid £726,000. It was ironical that the man who was to be Gladstone's great supporter and ten years later his Home Secretary, should have been Reuters' chief counsel in a case which cost Gladstone's Chancellor of the Exchequer such a considerable sum of money. Ten years later, in a diary note of a visit with his father to Gladstone at Hawarden Castle, Harcourt's son Lewis records: 'There was some discussion about the telegraph system in England, and both Gladstone and W. V. H. agreed that when they were bought by the Post Office in 1870, the price which was given for them was unnecessarily large . . .'

It was certainly a windfall to the Agency, but it was treated with little regard for the future. A high proportion of the large profit was at once distributed to the shareholders: no proper Reserve Fund was created. The situation on the Continent quickly claimed the rest. For Reuter's position in Germany, weakened already by the unfavourable terms of the agreement with the Prussian Government, was becoming steadily worse. His German competitor, Bernhard Wolff, formidably backed by Bismarck and the King of Prussia, now threatened to oust him altogether. It was felt in Prussia that Reuter's ambition and organising skill would finally give London a monopoly of world news. In such a situation it was easy for Wolff to persuade the Prussian Government that the expansion of his own Bureau was in the national interest. He made plans for mobilising greater financial support. To obtain the money from trustworthy, 'patriotic financiers like the gentlemen v. Oppenfeld, v. Magnus and Bleichröder' (as they were called by King William of Prussia in a letter he wrote in 1867 in his own hand to Wolff), he sought patrons in the loftiest quarters; and, as the letter quoted shows, succeeded. 'I can', wrote the King, 'only applaud your plan to extend with the assistance of a share-holding company your telegraphic institution ... and I would be very pleased if' – here follow the names of the patriotic financiers – 'would come to an agreement with you over the business in question. It seems to me very important and necessary that such an institution should be created in Prussia, in order to counteract the influence of the English institution. – WILHELM.' As will be seen, Reuters finally reached a compromise with Wolff. But the struggle was expensive and taught Reuters what Government support of a rival news agency meant.

Although the British Government now owned the internal telegraph system, no State interference was contemplated with the business of gathering news. The collection of all British news – from both London and the provinces – was taken over by the Press Association, which was re-formed by the provincial papers in 1868, and sent out its first message, from its central office in London to its newspaper subscribers all over the British Isles, in February 1870. The Press Association naturally wanted Reuters' foreign telegrams for the provincial papers, and Reuters wanted the Press Association's British news for its foreign clients. Moreover, Reuters realised that a strong and independent domestic Press was the only reliable base upon which to build its foreign service; while the members of the Press Association, the provincial newspapers, saw in the Agency a source of foreign news to rival the wealthier London papers' 'own correspondence'. It was only natural that close collaboration between the Press Association and Reuters should soon come about. Contracts for the mutual supply of news began immediately, in 1870, and from then on each organisation became steadily more important to the other. This sharing in the supply of news to the Press by two separate and independent Agencies, the one collecting domestic news, the other foreign, was unique to Britain. By encouraging mutual stimulus and criticism, the system undoubtedly did something to strengthen both.

4

Power Politics in Europe

REUTER'S FIRST AGREEMENT WITH THE TWO POWERFUL
Agencies on the Continent, Havas and Wolff, was made in
1856, before his Office had become a news agency. It was
mainly a contract to exchange the latest quotations and market
prices between themselves. When Reuter entered the field, the
other two were well established and could afford to give him
a helping hand. Havas, under Charles Havas's more ambitious
son, Auguste, had no qualms about running an advertisement
agency concurrently with its news service. The smaller French
provincial papers began to pay for their news by giving the
Agency advertisement-space; and this Havas sold profitably
to third parties. It was this income from advertising which was
soon to make Havas the strongest news agency on the Continent. Wolff for some time confined himself to supplying commercial news, and was already monopolising almost the whole
of Central Europe.

Two years later, in 1858, Reuter had the English Press firmly
behind him. The next agreement with the two Continental
Agencies, made the following year, was for a reciprocal exchange of political news. Reuter would obtain most of his
news of France from Havas, and of Germany from Wolff,
supplying the other two with British news from London.

When Reuter was no longer merely Mr. Reuter, but
Managing Director of Reuter's Telegram Company, this neat
division between the three of 'spheres of interest' was disturbed. Reuter now had behind him considerably more capital,

49

and, above all, the increased reputation gained by his success in reporting the American Civil War. He decided, as we have seen, to expand into Europe. Fifteen years before, Brussels had been one end of his original pigeon post. It was to the Low Countries that he now offered his news and commercial reports. Together with Havas he set up a joint office in Brussels, which soon produced sub-agencies at Antwerp, Ghent and Bruges. In Amsterdam, Reuter bought the local Agency owned by a certain Alexander Delamar. The two brothers Delamar, who took charge of these new Reuter offices, Alexander in Amsterdam, Herman in Brussels, became the loyalest of Reuter servants; and Alexander's son Abraham, by then a redoubtable octogenarian, was still ruling the office in Amsterdam when it became an outpost of convenient neutrality fifty years later in the First World War.

Meanwhile, the King of Hanover had signed the Norderney Concession. Soon afterwards, however, with Reuter offices established in Hamburg, Frankfurt and Hanover, Bismarck's expansionist policy defeated not only the Kingdom of Hanover and Austria, but also Reuter's ambitious German strategy. As we saw, Bismarck, not surprisingly, preferred Wolff of Berlin to Reuter of London. Wolff wrote to the King of Prussia, the King of Prussia called upon his patriotic bankers, and in May 1865 – three months after Reuter's own incorporation in London – Wolff's 'Continental Telegraph Company' was formed in Berlin.

For a while, Reuter, still acting under his 1859 treaty of friendship with Wolff, carried on with his plans, and within a year added offices in Berlin and Vienna to those already set up in Hamburg and Frankfurt. But, with Bismarck's power behind Wolff, and the King of Prussia's declared intention to counteract these Press 'encroachments' from the London Agency, conflict was inevitable. It came in the following year. The 1859 contract had expired, and the fantastically high rates of the new American cable – £20 for ten words – made some form of combination between the three Agencies essential. Reuter proposed that they should all share in the early agreement he had made with Daniel Craig, the resourceful general agent of the New York Associated Press. The plan was that they should divide between themselves the cost and profits of Craig's transatlantic telegrams from New York. Wolff refused to pay the sum demanded, and made a contract of his own with a group of Middle West American newspapers which had split off from the New York Associated Press and, in rivalry to it, incorporated itself as the 'Western Associated Press'. Reliance on rival camps in America was a symbol of the struggle that developed in Europe.

With the exception of Hamburg, all the new Reuter offices were right in the enemy's lines. Against direct Prussian Government resistance they had little hope of survival. Wolff's Continental Telegraph Company in Berlin, and the semi-official 'Korrespondenz-Bureau' of Vienna, received a most important Government privilege. Their telegrams, containing political news, were treated as 'official correspondence'. This meant that they enjoyed priority of despatch over all private telegrams: the term 'private' including, of course, Reuter telegrams. This naturally put Reuter at an essential disadvantage with his German subscribers; he was bound to be late – perhaps even with his commercial information. And rumour had it that the privileged Agencies found devices to expand their official advantage to their Bourse quotations as well.

Nevertheless, all the Reuter offices held out, although mostly run at a loss. The Hamburg office even fought and won a battle of its own. The free Hansa city found Reuter particularly attractive. It saw in him an ally against Prussian nationalism. The traditional cosmopolitanism of the Hanseatic League had always displayed friendly sentiments towards anything English; in addition, neither Wolff nor any smaller local Agency could offer the Hansa clients anything to touch Reuter's overseas service of prices from America, the West Indies and the Far East. Two of the Hansa's five leading newspapers subscribed to Reuters almost at once; and soon the Agency won the custom of the Börsenhalle, the city's main commercial club. For a time, Hamburg was Reuter's most thriving overseas branch. Reuter prospered in the atmosphere of the city's Bourse; and, as it had been the Stock Exchange on which he had built up his early prosperity in London, he could now model his Hamburg activities on that of the parent office. The New York prices used to arrive in cipher between two and three o'clock every morning, demanding immediate decoding; and every day the Reuter messenger-boys in their grey London uniforms were seen distributing their telegrams among the multitudinous confusion of the Hamburg Bourse.

To defend and expand his one foothold in Germany, Reuter made an agreement with the local Agency of Bremen, another great port of the old Hanseatic League, and established contact with the earliest Scandinavian Agency, Ritzaus of Copenhagen. Finally, Havas was brought in on the side of Reuter, and by 1869, Wolff, besieged in his Prussian lair, was ready for negotiations.

The result was the first of a remarkable series of 'Agency Treaties' designed to prevent future conflict by ensuring to each Agency its appropriate territorial 'sphere of interest'. Through them, the 'triumvirate' – Reuter, Havas and Wolff – controlled the news channels of the world for the next fifty years. The three Agencies treated their wares – political news and commercial information – like any other commodity; and applied *laissez-faire* principles to their distribution. Wolff had, it is true, the undisclosed backing of the Prussian Government; Reuter and Havas were acting entirely on their own. Together they produced a plan to divide up the world between them, each Agency to have certain exclusive areas in which to collect

Julius Reuter at fifty-three, painted by Rudolf Lehmann.
He was a fighter of immense courage and a business man of genius.

The early struggle for news-monopoly in Europe was fought with the Agencies founded by Charles-Louis Havas (below) and Bernard Wolff.

and distribute its news. Within twenty years of the foundation of their little offices, Reuter, Auguste Havas and Wentzel, Wolff's successor as Director, were talking quite confidently in terms of empires.

Wolff received the exclusive right to 'exploit' – as these early agreements termed it – Austria, the Scandinavian countries and Russia. In return, a fairly considerable sum had to be paid annually to Havas and Reuter. Reuter agreed to close all his German and Austrian offices, with the exception of Hamburg. Here he stayed for two more years to honour his agreement with the Hamburg Bourse; and the Reuter interest in the city lasted, in name and profits, till 1900. The Reuter and Havas gains were more in the nature of *faits accomplis*. Practical monopolies were now formally assigned to them: to Reuter, the British Empire and the Far East; to Havas, the French Empire and the Latin countries of the Mediterranean – Italy, Spain and Portugal. There was soon to be a formidable move by Havas into South America, helped by the sympathy of the Latin republics, and perhaps reinforced by nostalgia for the shattered dream of a French Central American Empire.

On the last day of January 1870, six months before Louis Napoleon declared war on Prussia, the Agreement was signed. The small European Agencies were quick to align themselves with the triumvirate. Stefani of Rome (founded in Turin in 1854) and Ritzaus of Copenhagen were soon relying on the three for their world news from London, Paris and Berlin; and the Korrespondenz-Bureau of Vienna was considered important enough by the three Agencies to merit a separate Treaty.

With the problem of competition settled, Reuter could now devote his attention to further improvements in his real business: the gathering and supplying of news.

On July 4th, 1870, a Reuter telegram told the English Press: 'General Prim has sent a deputation to offer the Crown of Spain to a Prince of Hohenzollern, who has accepted the proposals'. *The Times* did not so much as comment on it. But within a few days the whole of France was in a state of excitement. Napoleon was convinced that it was a move by King William of Prussia, the head of the House of Hohenzollern, to bring Spain under Prussian influence. The candidature was withdrawn, but Louis Napoleon refused to be satisfied without a statement from King William that it would never be repeated. The notorious Ems telegram followed. 'Edited' by Bismarck, it turned William's refusal to make this statement into what the French read as an insult to their ambassador. Indignation in France mounted rapidly: Louis Napoleon decided on war. On July 19th, the Franco-Prussian War began.

Reuter's recent agreement with Havas and Wolff gave him the quickest possible access to the official communiqués of both France and Prussia. In addition, he had just moved G. D. Williams, one of his ablest young correspondents, from Florence to Paris. The telegraph was now entirely accepted as the normal medium of news transmission. Even Mowbray Morris, of *The Times*, instructed his correspondents abroad that 'the telegraph has superseded the newsletter, and has rendered necessary a different style and treatment of public subjects . . .' At the same time, it became obvious that neither public nor newspapers nor individual correspondents were in for a 'levelling down' of news, as had been often anxiously forecast by many people in the newspaper world. On the contrary, relying on the Agencies for reporting the facts, the newspapers' foreign correspondents were able to concentrate more on the description of details and on political comment. More than before, a correspondent could now make his own and his paper's reputation by the particular quality of his individual observations. During the Franco-Prussian War there were many instances of this: Archibald Forbes's reporting considerably raised the circulation of the *Daily News*; Henry Labouchere, caught in the siege of Paris, lifted it further still with his 'Letters of a Besieged Resident'; and Robinson, of the *Manchester Guardian*, the only staff correspondent in the town during the siege of Metz, proved so successful a reporter as to earn the remark from Shirley Brooks, the editor of *Punch*, 'You and Bismarck are the only persons who will gain by this war; *you* deserve it.'

While individual reporters distinguished themselves and their newspapers, Reuters' service was appreciated just because it eschewed sensation. It was invaluable to the host of smaller papers that could not afford their own correspondents. It gave the first news of the French catastrophe at Sedan; and immediately on Louis Napoleon's surrender, Reuters' correspondent, G. D. Williams, was back in Paris, which he had left at the beginning of the siege, to follow, with most of the other English correspondents, the French Government to Tours. Now he was present in the Palais Bourbon when, on a Sunday morning, the revolutionaries surged across the Pont de la Concorde, invaded the Legislative Body and, with Jules Simon at their head, proclaimed the French Republic.

During the siege of Paris, Reuters had been saved from silence by its invaluable agreement with Havas. The French Agency organised its own balloon service out of the increasingly restless and famine-stricken city; and Reuter-Havas's *nouvelles de Paris par ballon* became one of the few reassuring signs in the British and European Press of Paris' continued life.

On the Prussian side of the scene, however, Reuters became involved in an incident which showed, in a spectacular enough fashion, the dangers inherent in the new system of large-scale gathering and reporting of international news. By abusing it, unscrupulous politicians could succeed in utilising completely unwitting reporters for their own purposes and in reaching in the quickest way all the centres of public opinion. It seems no accident that Reuters should have learned this first lesson – remembered and acted upon throughout the subsequent history of the Agency – from Bismarck, who had set the pattern with his fatal editing of a political telegram.

Soon after Sedan, Bismarck saw a chance to use Reuters for venting his indignation in a quarrel with the Prussian Crown Prince. If it set Reuters and *The Times* by the ears at the same time, so much the better. After Louis Napoleon's surrender, W. H. Russell, *The Times'* distinguished war correspondent, sent a despatch to his editor, giving an account of the interview between the two Emperors. It was given to him by the Prussian Crown Prince. Three weeks later, on October 2nd, Reuters received the following telegram direct from Ferrières, Bismarck's headquarters: 'The report of the conversation between King William and the Emperor Napoleon, given by *The Times'* correspondent Russell, rests throughout upon pure invention. – BISMARCK.' Next morning, the same message reached London once more, this time from the Berlin Agency via Amsterdam. It was circulated to the Press. Russell, naturally furious, demanded an interview with Bismarck, now at Versailles. Bismarck denied that he had seen the telegram. Russell sent a strong note to Reuters in London. Reuter himself replied: 'All I can say in answer to your telegram is that I have published the despatch in question exactly as it came without adding, omitting, or altering a single word.' The situation could only be solved by Bismarck's publishing a denial himself that he had seen the telegram; called upon to do this, he temporised, was evasive and finally refused. Russell was unable to obtain redress. In a later letter to a friend, however, Russell showed that he had found out the true motive for the embarrassing incident: Bismarck's hurt vanity. The Crown Prince (the source of Russell's report) knew more of the King's talk with Napoleon than Bismarck himself; the King had confided more in the Crown Prince than in his Chancellor. *The Times* did its best to pour oil on the waters by suggesting that Bismarck must have wished to correct some slight inexactitude, and that some underling had usurped his name and issued the sweeping denial.*

It was partly Havas's need for stronger financial backing, intensely felt amidst the general French instability following upon defeat and revolution, partly anxiety lest Wolff should become over-ambitious in the wake of Prussia's victories, which brought Reuters and Havas closer together after the Franco-Prussian War. At one time Reuters even began negotiations to purchase a considerable share in Havas; but with the rapid recovery of France, and of Havas with her, this plan was soon dropped. Instead, the closest collaboration ensued and lasted for the next five years. A 'joint purse' agreement was made, stipulating that all profits from all sources should be shared. It was, unfortunately, this insistence on *all* sources of income which led a little later to a parting of the ways, when one of Reuters' sources dried up and Havas did not wish to become involved in the drought.

The 'joint purse' was first to pay for an expansion into South America. The cable from Europe to Brazil was completed in 1874; and the two Agencies followed it by setting up a joint Chief Office at Rio de Janeiro. The auspices looked bright. A Frenchman from Reuters' editorial staff was put in charge of it. Division of labour seemed easy. For political news, the South American Press was mainly interested in the Latin countries in Europe. This was Havas's orbit of influence. But London was, even for South America, a centre of commercial interest: Reuters' contribution was to run a commercial service between Rio de Janeiro and the great English and Continental markets: London, Liverpool, Antwerp, Hamburg, Genoa. Reuters had, however, another scheme as well; and it was its ambitions in this other venture which brought the new intimacy with Havas to grief.

* *The History of The Times*, Vol. II, pp. 429-31, gives a full description of the incident.

For some years past the Agency had been offering its special facilities to the public for the sending of private telegrams. It now planned to set up a complete private telegram service between South America, North America, the West Indies and Europe. The scheme was to be based on a special new Reuter branch in New York; and it needed a man of great capacity there, to deal with the complex coding involved. For some unaccountable reason, the post was given to an inexperienced man whose only capacity seemed to be for making mistakes. Within a year, the plan had to be abandoned as a complete and costly failure. Not unnaturally, Havas was far from pleased at having to bear half the costs of the enterprise; and in the face of what both Agencies agreed to call 'irreconcilable differences', the 'joint purse' agreement came to an end on June 30th, 1876. But friendly relations were unaffected. As a safeguard, a new agreement set out a long list of the two Agencies' 'territorial possessions'. South America appeared on it as exclusively Havas's. It was to remain the main centre of Havas's influence abroad for some considerable time.

Reuter's own orientation was now clear. With the balance of Agency power restored in Europe, and a strong and friendly Havas firmly embedded against any expansion by Wolff, he had a free hand to bring ever closer the scattered communications of the Empire. This was now to be the Agency's main policy abroad.

Twenty-five years after its opening in London, Reuters was known throughout the world. *Fraser's Magazine*, of June 1876, credits Reuter with the introduction of 'that supply of foreign telegraphic news which is now so prominent a feature of all English newspapers', and comments upon his 'large enterprise and sagacity'. It is surprising to find on what an unspectacular financial basis this 'large enterprise' rested. For a year or two Reuters had owned its own cable, the submarine line to Norderney. After this had been sold to the Government, the

Agency's total capital was reduced to £72,000. Of this, £65,000, the price paid to Reuter for his business when the Company took over, represented Reuters' goodwill. Outside its offices, mostly leased, the firm possessed hardly any substantial equipment of its own: until the late 1870's it had three private telephone lines – to *The Times*, to the Press Association, and to the American Associated Press office in London – and one of Professor Wheatstone's 'Universal private telegraphs', a rather primitive-looking object, used for service enquiries from the head office to the telegraph stations. That was all. As for profits, the news service itself could hardly pay its way; only the commercial department, and the still successful service of private telegrams to and from the East, kept the Company financially afloat. The annual profits from the Norderney cable gave the shareholders for two or three years a substantial increase in dividend; but the Company's average yearly profit during the 1870's was only about £7,000, with a usual dividend of 7½ per cent.

Reuters' real value was its name. The reliability and impartiality of the little news-gatherer who had founded his Office in 1851 was the Company's greatest capital. It could not be expressed in figures, and was hardly ever expressed in words. An incident, however, in the autumn of 1871 made it for once articulate. A London newspaper reported that Engländer, Reuter's early associate whom we have mentioned before, was involved in 'a new political and social movement', clearly of a Radical order. Engländer was summoned before the Board, which insisted on 'the necessity that all officials of the Company should carefully abstain from all public connection with political associations of any kind whatever'. The Chairman's words, 'Our character for impartiality, on which we mainly depend for success, would be seriously imperilled by any suspicion of political partisanship', expressed the unwritten Reuter doctrine. Seventy years later it was laid down in the

Reuter Trust: 'Reuters' . . . integrity, independence and freedom from bias shall at all times be fully preserved'. By 1941,
it had become necessary to be more explicit about such principles.

A series of moves of home showed the steady increase in
Reuters' importance. The Company, shortly after its formation, moved from Royal Exchange Buildings to a larger office
at 5, Lothbury. Now, in the spring of 1871, it decided to purchase a house in one of the most ancient streets of the City of
London: No. 24, Old Jewry. Fifty years before, the old mansion, dignified with age and begrimed with the soot of London,
had been advertised in *The Times* as 'a comfortable and desirable dwelling-house with a garden'. Like *The Times* itself,
which had taken over the old home of John Walter, its founder
and first of the remarkable family-dynasty of its rulers,
Reuters lost nothing by this aura of domesticity in its surround-
ings. Compared to 5, Lothbury, its new home was almost
palatial. The Elizabethan antiquary, John Stow, had written in
1598 of the 'merchants and persons of repute' who lived in the
old street. Before that, the King's servants kept a Royal Palace
on its site, and, in the far distant past, the Jewish merchants had
settled there when William the Conqueror invited them from
Rouen. Now this old rabbit-warren of a building, with its
low-pitched ceilings and steep staircases, was soon permeated
with the atmosphere of a Dickensian family-business. The
Board Room, particularly, on the first floor over the doorway,
where the reigning Reuters, father and son, often sat far into
the night poring over work in solitary state, gave the firm a
touch of patriarchal dignity.

That same autumn came the first formal recognition of
Reuter's achievement. On September 7th, 1871, Ernest II,
Duke of Saxe-Coburg-Gotha, conferred upon 'Paul Julius
Reuter, of London, in acknowledgement of his extraordinary
qualities', a Barony of his State, 'with the name of Paul Julius,

Baron von Reuter'. It was as Baron Julius de Reuter that the founder of Reuters now became universally known.

Twenty years had to elapse, however, before Reuter received the full privileges of his Barony in Great Britain. There is no doubt about Queen Victoria's personal trust in Reuter: she often mentions his telegrams in her diaries, and her confidence in him clearly emerges from an angry note she sent in 1878 to Disraeli. Her Government seemed to be taking too little notice of the Russians' interest in Constantinople. It was not a diplomatic despatch, but a Reuter telegram on the Russian army's moves which had stirred the Queen's anxiety. To her it was information, as she put it, from someone 'who generally knows'. But it was some time before the Government took steps to encourage Royal recognition of Reuter. The impulse finally came from the Marquis of Salisbury. 'Baron Reuter', Salisbury, as Prime Minister, wrote to the Queen in June 1891, 'has for a great number of years done his best to work with the Government for the time being: and his zeal in furnishing early information to Your Majesty personally deserves acknowledgement.' Acknowledgment graciously came; and a Royal Warrant of November 6th, the same year, gave Baron Reuter and his heirs the privileges of the Foreign Nobility in England.

The new Baron's coat of arms, granted by Duke Ernest II, shows on a blue shield the globe, broken by rays of silver lightning coming from its four corners. Over a flagstaff, horizontal above it, gallops a horseman, holding a spear in his hand. Underneath, a silver ribbon proclaims Reuter's ubiquity: '*Per Mare et Terram*'. It is still the crest of Reuters.

5

Eastern Ventures

REUTER'S FIRST AGENTS IN THE EAST, MEN LIKE HENRY Collins in India, had one immense advantage. In the British communities they found almost at once ready and enthusiastic subscribers. In India, long before the vernacular newspapers could afford Reuters' news, no British-owned or British-read paper could be without it. For British merchants in India, China, and throughout the Far East, Reuters' market prices and quotations became one of the necessities of existence. For the British in India, civil servants, Army officers, their families and appendages, Reuters' telegrams in newspapers and clubs soon became a direct link with home. For many years, it was this population – and, increasingly, the Indian and Chinese merchants themselves – to whom Reuters' Eastern services chiefly appealed.

There were numerous technical difficulties in making a start. Collins had a hard time before him for a while when, in March 1866, he set up the first Reuter office in Bombay. He had one Parsee clerk and a messenger as staff. There was as yet no regular cable service from England to India. Ferdinand de Lesseps – the 'great bore', *Punch* called him, as his endless negotiations with the British Foreign Office dragged on – was still boring his way to Suez. The opening of the Suez Canal should soon lead to cable-links between Alexandria and the East. To organise a news office in Bombay with a cable line from India to Alexandria at his disposal would clearly make all the difference to Collins's task. But for three years Collins could never be sure whether or not there was, or was to be, such a cable. Its unpredictable break-downs, even when there was one, still meant crisis after crisis; and when everything was all right with the cable, there was the anxiety of the expense of using it. In the absence of an International Telegraph Convention, each Government and Company concerned with the overland wire wanted to make the highest possible profits. At a charge of £1 a word and a minimum of £20 a telegram, Collins was complaining in one letter to London that an average of 77 words sent daily was greatly in excess of his budget. Fifty years later, in the First World War, an average of 4,000 words a day sent to India showed how cheap cable rates had helped to change the position. Technical difficulties aside, the service Collins offered was at first by no means popular with everyone. Among the larger newspaper subscribers, the Reuter principle of equality to all was always disliked. India was no exception. The wealthier merchants objected to a scheme that gave the same facilities to *all* merchants; the larger newspapers, which had formed themselves into a powerful Association and were organising their own commercial news service from England, felt the same kind of resentment.

When Collins arrived, the cotton market in Bombay was in a state of great agitation. The daily reports of cotton prices were awaited with feverish interest. Bombay was still under the intoxicating spell of the cotton boom which the blockade of the Southern States during the American Civil War had brought about. The city was full of stories of huge fortunes and of the Arabian Nights' entertainments of the successful speculators. Collins had the thankless task, before long, of reporting rapidly falling prices. His quotations were regarded as a sort of death-knell for the Indian cotton merchants.

He advertised a twice-a-day commercial service from Liverpool and other English markets to Bombay. To make it pay, a minimum of forty subscribers was needed. Response to his invitation was slow at first; but, after a month, the first Reuter message was delivered to over fifty subscribers. It quoted Bombay Dhollera cotton at 17*d*. per lb.; before the American Civil War it had stood at 4*d*.: by the end of this season it was down to 4*d*. again, and many fortunes had been lost.

By then the Agency had established its reputation for absolute reliability. Within a few weeks no native dealer would sell a pound of cotton before he had seen Reuters' overnight quotations. A dishonest employee in the Bombay office could have made his own fortune, and wrecked Reuters', within a very short time, by disclosing the overnight prices to an unscrupulous bidder in the open-air Bombay Cotton Green before business started at 7 a.m. the next morning. In not far short of a century's working, only one man, a Portuguese clerk from Goa, tried it; and despite his ingenuity, he was quickly found out. His method was simplicity itself. Every morning, as the clerks wrote out their multiple copies of latest Liverpool prices for simultaneous distribution, the Portuguese went to a window and spat outside. His fellow-conspirator, waiting below for the signal, rushed to the Cotton Green. Without a word or a note, he had his information: if the prices had risen overnight, the clerk spat to the right; if they had dropped, he spat to the left.

Collins, having established his commercial service, turned to political and general news. Ceylon led the way. This island, owing to its position on the main sea-route between Suez and Singapore, was rapidly becoming conscious of the new demands for European news; and the *Ceylon Observer* of Colombo became Reuters' first subscriber, to be followed, after protracted negotiations between Collins and the Indian Newspaper Association, by almost every newspaper in India and Ceylon. Firmly established in India by the end of 1866, Reuters began to spread its network through the whole of the peninsula. Offices were opened at Calcutta, Madras and

Rangoon; Karachi was made into a distributing centre. In England, Reuters distributed only foreign news; in India, it was soon supplying the Press with domestic information as well.

Collins also established direct relations with the Government at Calcutta. This proved easier than it had been in England. Collins was received by the Governor-General, Lord Lawrence, with warmth; Lawrence appreciated the help they could be to each other. The Governor-General would receive Reuters' telegrams; Reuters' Agent would obtain early intelligence of the Government's official news in return. It was the sort of relationship between Press and Government which successive great editors of *The Times* in the nineteenth century felt to be essential to the paper. It throws an illuminating light on the development of public ethics that people did not then seriously doubt the reliability of 'official information', and did not object to this sort of collaboration between Government and an independent news agency. In India, the Government occasionally paid for Reuters' transmission of official news to England, for instance in the case of the Viceroy's speeches. Today, it is a fundamental Reuter principle that *all* its news must be paid for at the receiving, not the sending, end. The advantage of receiving post-free official speeches had, in a later and much more propaganda-conscious age, to be sacrificed to this principle.

But in the 'sixties there was little time for expounding principles *about* news. Collins had a hard task to maintain a flow of news between England and the East at all. The break-downs in the cable during the financial crises of the summer of 1866 called for extreme ingenuity. When the line went dead for the second time, with the Austro-Prussian war at its height, he pulled off a brilliant *coup* by using the little-known and normally unreliable Turkish Government line via Fao, at the head of the Persian Gulf, and Constantinople, to make contact with the new Reuter office in Alexandria. For sixteen days, while the overland route was out of use, the secret was kept and the scheme worked perfectly. On another occasion, he chartered two special steamers to carry messages down the Persian Gulf, where a break had occurred, to get messages through about every three days. This 'Reuter Express' went on for two months, while Collins fumed at the absence of repair-ships. A final success was achieved by Julius de Reuter's own genius for obtaining secret concessions – a genius not always viewed kindly by rivals. He obtained a Concession from the Turkish Government, giving Reuter messages priority over 'that part of the route where the delays almost invariably occur'. They invariably occurred in Turkey; and soon the Agency's tele-grams were beating other messages by six to eight days. The annoyance of the Bombay Chamber of Commerce at Reuters' priority was not lessened by the fact that it had just made Reuter himself the Chamber's Agent in London.

Reuters' announcement in India of the victory by Austrian ironclads over the Italian fleet at Lissa created a record by taking less than twenty-four hours in transit. For some time the battle was regarded as a Reuter invention. Two years later, the message announcing Disraeli's resignation at the end of 1868, after an eight months' uneasy Ministry, took only seven-teen hours.

Bombay had meanwhile served as a base for a rather spec-tacular feat of Reuter reporting. King Theodore of Abyssinia had just imprisoned a number of British envoys and mis-sionaries in his capital, Magdala, and in the cool season of 1867 a strong punitive expedition under Sir Robert Napier set out from Bombay to rescue them. With the fleet of 400 sailing-ships went several Reuter correspondents. Their descriptions of the force's dash to Magdala, the release of the captives, and the King's suicide in his fort, caused great excitement in India as well as in England.

In these early Indian days there were mistakes as well as

successes. The high cable-rate made a code-system essential; and an expert was sent to Karachi specially to take charge of the decoding. Mistranslation of a mutilated keyword could bring disaster; and mutilation in one of the first messages sent from Bombay to Colombo nearly did. The victim of the mistake was, ironically, Reuters' first newspaper client in the East, the *Ceylon Observer*. A Reuter message, London to Bombay, read, 'Report Asiatic Bank shows loss £142,000'. Over the Indian Government line to Colombo, 'shows' became mutilated into 'shops'. It was during the financial crisis of the summer of 1866, when the banks' mortality-rate was high. The editor of the *Ceylon Observer* at once concluded 'shops' must be 'stops', and issued a Special Edition. Under the heading of Reuters' Telegrams the excited public read: 'It is reported that the Asiatic Bank has stopped payment with a loss of £142,000'. There was an immediate panic: the Colombo and Kandy Branches of the Bank were rushed; calm was only restored when the Bank's head office in London denied the report. Reuters was saved from legal action by producing the facsimile of the message it had sent to Colombo. The fact that the Bank *did* close its doors, for ever, only a few weeks later, did not detract from the Agency's temporary setback.

A one-word error in a Reuter message could be catastrophic. It could confound politics and upset international finance; and how easily reputations might be destroyed by the more insidious moods of the cable is shown by a telegram which a highly respectable Manchester cotton agent in Madras sent to his firm in Lancashire. He ordered a certain make of cotton goods much in demand in the Indian bazaars. 'Ship Turkey Red Forties', he telegraphed; and his employers found themselves instructed: 'Ship Turkey Maid for Vice'.

In 1869, plans for laying the Indian submarine cable were at last ready. Immense excitement greeted the *Great Eastern* as she slowly propelled her huge bulk of 23,000 tons into

Bombay. A luncheon on board, attended by the Governor and 300 guests, celebrated the occasion. The cable was laid the 1,800 miles across the Indian Ocean to Aden, without a hitch. A few weeks later it was opened by congratulatory messages between the Prince of Wales, from a special banquet at the Guildhall, London, and the Governor-General of India, the Earl of Mayo, at Simla. The conclusion of the exchange of telegrams in less than half an hour was regarded as an unprecedented feat at the time. Point de Galle, Ceylon, was for some time the terminus of the new cable. Reuters' Agent there, chief partner in one of the pioneer coffee firms, was soon busy dealing with a vast new influx of messages that came by mail-boat from Australia, the Straits and China, to be telegraphed to England by Reuters. Competition in this new local industry soon arose; and before long the mail-boats from Australia used to be intercepted, before they reached anchorage, by a regular fleet of fast native boatmen in their *catamarans*, racing to meet them first.

The outgoing service further East and to Australia was just as busy. The hardest task for the Reuter messengers was, in the late 'sixties, to take messages from Point de Galle to Colombo along the seventy-two-mile-long rocky coastal road, in a jolting coach pulled by mostly unbroken imported Australian horses. It was a throw-back to what was, thirty years before, the normal method of news-gathering in Europe.

Ceylon's importance to Reuters grew; and, before the extension of the cable further east to Singapore and China, Point de Galle prospered as the centre of Reuters' 'Eastern Private Telegram' service. Merchants and ship-owners used it regularly; and the Eastern Telegraph Company of London, far from being concerned at what looked like competition, was far-sighted enough to see its future benefits from this inevitable expansion of trade. By 1875, Reuters was handling between three and four thousand telegrams to and from the

East in a month; and it was relying on the revenue from these private telegrams to pay for the unprofitable news service.

With the Indian branches flourishing, Collins followed the cable, as it opened up yet more countries to the European telegraph. In 1871, while Reuters was obtaining the full benefits in Europe of its 'Tripartite Treaty' with the two great Continental Agencies, Collins was taking the Reuter service into the Straits Settlements, Singapore and Java. By the end of the year he was in Shanghai, setting up the first Reuter office in China which, after the customary initial difficulties, soon became the centre of the Agency's activities in the Far East.

The last stretch of the cable was to Japan. Within twenty years of Commodore Perry's reaching the bay of Tokyo (Yedo, as it was then) with his squadron of four American ships on July 8th, 1853, thus opening up Japan to the West, Collins was organising the first Reuter branches in Yokohama and Nagasaki. From a bridge in Tokyo he looked down on the building of the first Japanese railway.

Simultaneously with this drive to the East, Collins was doing his best to give a service of European telegrams to the thriving new Press in Australia. In the late 'sixties the telegrams from London to Point de Galle were sent on by steamer to King George Sound, Western Australia. It was a restricted service; and the Australians were soon demanding more than what they considered to be the mere skeleton reports of European events. In 1868, Collins was complaining that he could not give Reuters' Agents in Australia 'an accurate report of the progress of the Spanish Revolution in a summary of the latest news of 100 words only'. The next time the boat sailed, he took the bold step of extending it to 160 words. He also telegraphed to London 'to send the *very* latest news, so that the Australian newspapers would have no cause to complain about lack of information'. But they did complain, and the more spirited of them soon decided to take things into their own hands. Even before the cable was laid, the *Melbourne Argus* and the *Sydney Morning Herald* made special arrangements for Reuter telegrams to be sent to them independently from London. That was in 1872. The next year, the submarine cable from Java reached Port Darwin, and was taken overland across Australia to Adelaide. On the last day of the year, the proprietors of the *Argus* and the *Morning Herald* came right to the source of the news and attended a Reuter Board Meeting in London. They had appointed their own London correspondents, and they made it clear that they wanted Reuters' news on the spot in London, and not delivered to them through Reuters' Agents in Australia. They were made to pay highly for this: £2,000 a year each for copies of the Reuter telegrams sent to Australia, an average of 40 words a day. It was an expensive challenge; but the two Australian newspapers gained much prestige at home.

Three times during the next seventy-five years the Australian newspapers, or some of them, asserted their independence by rejecting proposals to change these arrangements. They insisted on their preference for taking news from Reuters at the source in London.

But the Agency was persistent. Collins's brother, who had been sent to assist him in India, followed the cable to Australia, and in 1874 became Reuters' Agent in Sydney. Three years later he succeeded in bringing about a new agreement. Reuters undertook to give a world news service to the entire Australasian Press. Cable rates were high – minimum charge for a telegram, at £1 a word, was £20 – and the cable had a habit of breaking down for ten or twenty days at a time between Java and Port Darwin. Much of Reuters' energy in Australia went into the more profitable channels of supplying market prices and a private telegram service. But the newspapers' demands, often taking the form of complaints, gave Reuters no chance to neglect its primary task of giving the day-to-day news of Europe to a continent isolated by thousands of miles of sea from the rest of the great news-centres of the world. The Agency had no little share in the achievement of the Australian and New Zealand newspapers in overcoming this isolation.

In the summer of 1872, Collins completed this first major piece of pioneering for Reuters, and returned home. He had travelled from Bombay to Yokohama, Northern China to Java; and wherever he had been he had set up Reuter offices and laid the foundations of Reuters' new domains in the East. Soon after landing in England, Collins found himself appointed special representative for Baron de Reuter's interests in one of the most remarkable foreign Concessions ever granted to a private citizen.

6

Reuter Khan

ON JULY 25TH, 1872, AT TEHERAN, THE PERSIAN CAPI-
tal, a Concession was ratified between Baron Julius de Reuter
and His Majesty Nasireddin Shah, the Shah of Persia. It contained, as Lord Curzon, in his *Persia and the Persian Question*,
put it, 'the most complete and extraordinary surrender of the
entire industrial resources of a kingdom into foreign hands
that has probably ever been dreamed of, much less accomplished, in history'. It gave Reuter virtual dominion over the
economy of the Shah's kingdom and of many of his subjects'
lives, for the next seventy years; and it promised a complete
opening-up of the country to the West.

This ambitious and exotic enterprise was not the Agency's,
but Julius de Reuter's own. The Persian Concession was given
to him personally. He obviously relied on strong backing; and
he began with the keen support of one of the partners in the
powerful Far Eastern trading firm of Jardine Matheson & Co.
He was so sure of success that he would not even launch a
special Company.

The Reuter Concession in Persia is an extraordinary story
of individualism; of a shrewd and energetic *entrepreneur*'s
venture into high politics and into a country then notorious
for its corruption and successful intrigue. The effective mixture
of imperialism and business sense which informed the project
is the key to at least one side of Reuter's character. And
although the story belongs to Reuter's biography rather than

to the history of Reuters, at the same time it reveals much of the driving-power which was behind the Agency's steady expansion.

It seems certain that neither the Shah of Persia nor Reuter was fully aware of the other's genius in the matter of Concessions. Either Reuter's researches failed to show him the fate of previous European projectors in Persia; or he was confident he would succeed where others had failed. The past was, in fact, strewn with victims. Five years before, Dr. Stronsberg, a Prussian, had lost £4,000 caution-money for failing to carry out a Concession couched in somewhat similar terms to Reuter's. Austrian and French concessionaires had paid the same penalty. All illustrated the remark of the British Minister at Teheran, that the European projects 'had been entertained principally as a means of profit to the Persian Ministers and the Agents employed by them'. On the other hand, the Shah did not perhaps realise that for the first time he was dealing with a man of extraordinary shrewdness, and absolutely determined to have his rights.

More than two years before, in 1870, the Persian Minister in London, General Mohsin Khan, had begun to interest Reuter in the idea of putting Western capital into Persia. The ancient country, despite the stories of its fabulous wealth, had still a primitive civilisation. The possibilities for British trade were immense; Persia's strategic importance, as an overland route to India, considerable. Reuter was excited and confident. In the late spring of 1872, he sent a confidential agent to the Shah's court at Teheran, to secure the Concession Mohsin had promised. There was – as there had been over previous Concessions – intense opposition from the fanatically conservative priesthood of the Shiah Moslems, who saw only catastrophe in giving rights over their country to an infidel; but, with the support of the Shah's Grand Vizier, the Concession went through. It was solemnly signed by all the Shah's Ministers, and formally ratified by the Shah himself, in the presence of his full Cabinet, on July 25th, 1872.

The next day, the full text of the Concession was telegraphed to Reuter in London. Its terms virtually placed the country in his hands. He was given 'the exclusive right to build a railway from the Caspian Sea to the Persian Gulf with such branches as he might afterwards determine', and to operate it for seventy years. He had further rights to carry out works of irrigation, develop the forests and mineral resources, to undertake roads and other public works for the development of the country, and to farm the State Customs for the next twenty years. As Lord Curzon said in the book already quoted, when news of this extraordinary Concession became known a year later, it 'literally took away the breath of Europe'. The Concession authorised Reuter to raise a loan on the London market of £6 million: the Persian Government nominally guaranteed a 5 per cent interest. Here the shrewdness of the Shah first showed itself. Conditions attached to the guarantee switched the real security from the Persian Government to the profits of the enterprise itself. As a guarantee of his own faith, Baron de Reuter had to deposit £40,000 caution-money in the Bank of England in the joint names of General Mohsin Khan and himself.

The Baron now set about his preparations with vigour. Collins, as his special representative, was ordered to collect a staff of British engineers and other technical advisers, and to make a preliminary survey of the route for the railway. The Shah's advisers had insisted that the first stretch of this railway was to be from Resht in the north, just inland from the Caspian Sea, to the Shah's capital, Teheran, in the central plains – some 150 miles. The Concession stipulated that the *commencement des travaux* should be made within fifteen months of the date of signature. When Collins and his party finally left England in February 1873, they had nearly nine months in which to make a start.

Reuter was meanwhile feeling his way in another direction. Apart from opening up Persia to Western civilisation and promising an immense new market for British trade, his Concession, he knew, offered great strategical advantages to Great Britain. He saw it as a vital link in a possible railway route to India, already advocated by many. Besides, it could serve as a counter to the southward advance of the Russians, who, as he wrote in September 1872 to Lord Granville, Gladstone's Foreign Secretary, were 'making great progress with their railway towards the Caspian Sea'. This same letter made clear his own hopes of at least moral support from the Government: 'I desire to serve this my adopted country', he wrote, 'by my enterprise under British auspices alone, and I shall have pleasure in doing so without soliciting a subsidy from Her Majesty's Government. I nevertheless desire to feel assured that in the event of difficulties arising between the Persian Government and myself, Her Majesty's Government will recognise the validity of my scheme, and protect my rights as a British subject, so far as may be in their power.'

But Reuter's judgment of the political scene was over-confident. Gladstone's Government was loath to undertake any new commitment that might end up by costing the Treasury money. The India Office, far from leaping at this new project, was coldly critical. Persia, it had been assured on expert advice, was 'effete and even more incapable than Turkey of adopting European habits of vigorous thought or moral sense'. The Persians, it seemed, were irrevocably damned. Even the hint about stopping the Russians fell on deaf ears. The Shah's insistence on beginning the railway in the north, instead of taking it up from the south first, from the Persian Gulf, had wrecked Reuter's 'vital link to India' plan. By cutting southward through Persia from the Caspian Sea, the railway would, in fact, at first be benefiting Russia.

The Foreign Office's reply came the next month. Her Majesty's Government would, of course, 'view with satisfaction the efforts of the Shah's Government to increase by means of railways and roads the resources of Persia', but 'they cannot bind themselves officially to protect your interests whilst carrying out your engagements with that Government'. It was stereotyped, correct and discouraging.

Full preparations for the railway continued. Collins's party reached Constantinople in the March of 1873; and, after a month's delay (due, Collins was convinced, to various undercurrents of Persian intrigue), reached Teheran in May. Here they were received and profusely entertained by the Grand Vizier and his Government colleagues. But the day before, the Shah himself with three of his wives and an immense retinue of mounted servants had left for the first peaceful visit of a reigning Persian Sovereign to Europe. With full pomp and ceremony, and all the sumptuous extravagance credited to him by tradition, he was to travel up the Volga from Enzeli, the port of Resht, and then visit St. Petersburg, Berlin and London. The Grand Vizier was to join him at Enzeli, leaving a deputy to deal with the details of the Concession. The deputy's lack of sufficient authority was the first disquieting sign that the Shah might, at the least, be playing for time.

A survey of the 150 miles from Resht to Teheran went ahead; a plan for cutting through the 8,000-feet Elburz mountain pass was completed; and the first consignment of rails despatched from England. Actual work on the railway itself, however, could not begin without agreement between the Persian Government and Baron de Reuter on the 'cahier des charges', the specification authorising the purchase of the mass of materials needed. The Shah now decided that the handing-over of this document must be a suitable ritual, and insisted that his new Minister to England, Malkom Khan, should bring the *cahier* with him, and hand it over *personally* to Reuter. With the deadline for the official 'beginning of work' on the railway only six months off, time was now vital. As the new Minister travelled westward in the spring of 1873, Reuter or his representatives met and besieged him in turn at Vienna, Berlin, Brussels, Paris and, finally, London. When Reuter did finally hold him down to an agreement about the *cahier*, it turned out that an embarrassing situation had arisen. Malkom Khan, it seemed, had retained for himself the title to a quarter of the original Concession, which, of course, he could dispose of to the Russians or to anyone he pleased. It cost the Baron £20,000 down, and a promise of a substantial share in all future profits, to regain full ownership of his own Concession. At last, on July 5th, he had his authority for the engineers to begin constructing the line from Resht. There were just three and a half months to go in which work had to begin. In early September, six weeks before the deadline, the ceremony of the turning of the first sod was performed in the presence of the British Consul and foreign residents.

Reuter was meanwhile doing his best to put his relationship with the Shah onto a more personal and more advantageous footing. To save transport of bulky Persian coin, and avoid exchange difficulties, he had loaned the Shah £20,000 towards the cost of the Royal train, to be made available in the European capitals. When, in return for a further loan, he tried to obtain certain assurances about his Concession, the Shah politely refused the new offer. As the Shah's triumphal tour approached England, and the Royal preparations for his reception became the talk of London, the news of Baron de Reuter's Concession was released. The timing was brilliant. The English public greeted it with enthusiasm, and applauded the new bonds soon to be drawn between this exotic Oriental monarch and itself. Among the Press, *Punch's* rhyming wit alone betrayed a touch of scepticism:

77

There's Reuter – let's hope 'twill be Reuter Khan
Instead of Reuter cannot –
Has set himself calmly the gulf to scan,
Which in Persia, since Kadjar rule began,
Hath yawned with wider and wider span,
'Twixt dried-up nature and dwindled man
Where the gold stream – for Nadir Shah that ran –
Again to Nadir has got.

Parliament, however, was worried, and in a rather more serious mood. In the Commons, questioners stressed Baron de Reuter's high honour and intelligence and his 'thoroughly English principles'; but they applied the words 'extraordinary' and 'dangerous' to the powers given to him under the Concession. Robert Lowe, the Chancellor of the Exchequer, answered them in the usual stereotyped fashion: 'We have no interest in the matter'. In the Lords, Granville, the Foreign Secretary, when asked whether the Concession was 'in the interests of Persia and in accordance with British policy', confined himself to admitting that the Concession existed. Here again, murmurs of 'dangerous' greeted the confirmation.

It *was* dangerous, though the dangers were different from whatever Parliamentary anxiety anticipated. Rumours were already circulating in Teheran that the Shah would denounce the Concession on his return. There had been demonstrations there against it in May, inspired by the Priesthood; and Russian disapproval of such a Concession being given to a British subject was an open secret. But work on the railway continued. By the deadline, late in November, a thousand men were employed, and the first mile of the earthworks had been completed. Collins received a letter from the Grand Vizier's deputy congratulating him on his successful start.

With the return of the Shah almost immediately afterwards, the whole atmosphere changed. The Shah rode past the works in the vicinity of Resht without even drawing rein; and the news was flashed to Teheran that the Grand Vizier, the chief favourer of the Concession, had been dismissed in disgrace. Rumour had it that he owed his downfall to sending the Shah's three wives home from Resht on the outward journey: he had doubted the eagerness with which they would be welcomed at European Courts – and the Shah had had to travel alone. The Vizier's later story to Collins, that the Shah dismissed him to save his own face when he later revoked the Concession, is far more probable. At any rate, despite the thousand workmen, the earthworks, and the consignment of rails on its way, complaints that the Concession had not been truly begun by the deadline in November began to arrive from the Persian Government.

Weeks passed. The labourers went on working; the Persian Government and the Baron's representative went on arguing. At the end of the year, the Shah's advisers decided that some portion of the rails should have been 'déposé', actually laid ready for use; and the *Teheran Gazette* officially announced that 'it is evident the Baron does not intend fulfilling his engagement or adhering to his Concession'. The next week the Reuter Concession was denounced as null and void. The formal reason given was obviously a quibble. The excuse given to the British Minister at Teheran was fear of the Priests. They were 'fomenting a disastrous political crisis', the Shah's Government said, and the stability of the Throne was in danger: sacrifice of the Concession was the only way to avert it. Behind the Shah's change of face was clearly another reason: one far more sinister to English minds.

Russophobes in England were ever ready to spin Russian plots around any failure of a British enterprise on the route to India; and the Shah was soon becoming notorious for playing off Great Britain and Russia against each other. He had a talent for making a profit out of it for himself. But in this case, Russian pressure on the Shah was certain. The British Ambassador to Russia had reported that the Shah was most impressed and flattered by his reception at St. Petersburg during his European journey; subsequent efforts by the Russian Legation in Teheran to have a new Concession granted to a Russian Company sufficiently explained the flattery. Apart from this, Prince Gortschakoff, the Russian Imperial Chancellor, later confessed to Reuter, at a meeting in Interlaken, that he had denounced the Concession to the Czar: it seems most unlikely that this denunciation did not reach the Shah. Later, in November 1874, the Persian Minister explicitly admitted to Lord Tenterden, British Permanent Under-Secretary for Foreign Affairs, that it was Russian insistence which had broken the Concession. The prospect of a British interest on the Caspian, Russia's 'closed sea', was anathema to the Russians; and the fact that the Reuter Concession was until now entirely innocent of any backing by the British Government, inconceivable to them.

But innocent it still was. Protests and appeals against the annulment of the Concession being alike unavailing, the workmen were dismissed in the spring of 1874, and the professional staff withdrawn. The failure of the Persian Government to make any attempt to claim the £40,000 caution-money from the Baron did not make its case any stronger. Sir William Harcourt, now Solicitor-General, stated his opinion that the annulment of the Concession could not be legally justified.

Of greater hope to Reuter seemed the result of the General Election of February 1874. The Conservatives came in with a strong majority; and Disraeli's foreign policy was far more likely to become involved in Persia than ever Gladstone's had been. But permanent Foreign Office officials remained permanent: Lord Tenterden, suspicious of Reuter, was now accusing him, to the Foreign Secretary, of 'laying verbal traps for the Government, into which he tries to get 'em to entangle themselves'; and the new Foreign Secretary, Lord Derby, was just as frightened of involving England with Russia as his predecessor had been. When Reuter asked that the British Minister at Teheran should use his good offices to end the *impasse* which had arisen, he was told that he could only expect the assistance given to 'any other British subject' in like position.

Nevertheless, the fate of the Concession was from now on to be decided as much in Whitehall as in Teheran. The struggle for rights over the industrial future of Persia had widened. It was no longer between a shrewd business-man and the advisers of an intriguing Shah. The contest became extended to Governments.

Twice more, in the last year of Gladstone's Ministry, Reuter had done his best to interest the British Government in his schemes. In the spring, he had dangled in front of the India Office's eyes the bait of an east–west railway across Persia, in place of his present one from the north. He wrote to Lord Granville that, with a contingent guarantee from the Government for half of the interest on a £10 million loan at 6 per cent guaranteed by Turkey, he would construct a further railway from Constantinople to the Persian frontier. He would then connect the Persian with the Turkish system, and thus establish a through railway line from Calais, via Constantinople, to Persia, with a view to its ultimate extension eastwards. This time the India Office was worried. The stakes on both sides – as a private Memorandum noted – were extremely high. Reuter was asking for a guarantee of £300,000 a year, a very considerable sum; but refusal might let Persia slip out of British hands completely, to become a Russian province. Worse still (the India Office was very realistic), Reuter might despair altogether of assistance, renounce British citizenship, and place himself under Russian protection. The consequences, the Memorandum thought, would be 'inconvenient'. The same week the whole question of railway communications came up in the Commons. Gladstone was pressed to reconsider his former negative policy.

If England did not co-operate with Turkey and provide a shorter route to India, Ferdinand de Lesseps, now free from his Suez Canal project, would. He had already proposed a route from Russia. But de Lesseps was no longer a red rag to the British Government: Gladstone was far more worried about paying out Treasury money. In any case, he had in front of him an expert opinion that any hopes of progress in Persia were 'visionary'. He saw no reason to reconsider his policy. Armed with the Prime Minister's veto, the Lords of the Treasury dealt shortly with Reuter: 'It would be contrary to established rule', Lord Granville wrote from the Foreign Office, 'for Her Majesty's Government to guarantee interest on the cost of a work undertaken in a foreign country'. The Government remained coldly indifferent.

An offer to give the Concession an international basis met the same lack of response. This time Reuter reached as far as an interview with Lord Granville. He came to it fresh from meetings with Bismarck, the Austrian Foreign Office and Prince Gortschakoff. Germany, Austria and, most significant of all, Russia, would all support a Concession 'in an international sense', to build a railway across Turkey and Persia. It was an extraordinarily far-seeing suggestion; and Granville was sufficiently impressed to send a special report to the Queen and to Gladstone. But the endless bickerings and bargainings over the Suez Canal International Company had been too painful a lesson. Her Majesty's Government foresaw the whole nightmare's taking place again; and once more Reuter was refused any Government assistance.

Positive plans for making the Concession serve British interests had found indifference. The first inkling of a rival Power on the scene galvanised the Foreign Office into action.

In August 1874, a few months after the Persian denunciation of the Reuter Concession, news was suddenly telegraphed to Lord Derby that a General Falkenhagen, a retired Russian

Officer of Engineers, had been granted a railway Concession in Persia. Under strong pressure from the Russian Legation, it had already been signed by the Persian Minister of Public Works. The Shah was too compromised with the Russian Minister to refuse to ratify it. Quite unknown to the public, the situation nearly became critical. No British Government could allow Persia to become a province of Russia. The Reuter Concession offered the obvious way out. There was no need for the Foreign Office to change its policy and actively *support* Reuter: Lord Derby could still remain as aloof as ever. But the Reuter Concession was an admirable weapon with which to confront other Concession-hunters in Persia. The granting of railway rights to another concessionaire would meet with Baron de Reuter's just complaint, and such complaint would have the approval of Her Majesty's Government. It was an ideal arrangement for the Foreign Office; for Reuter it was, in a way, even more frustrating than Whitehall's previous indifference.

He had already warned Lord Derby of the Russian Company's previous overtures to himself. In return for his Concession rights, the Russians had made him a most generous offer. They would pay for everything he had so far put out, and give him 20 per cent of their profits, for the full seventy years, from the railways, forests, mines and Customs in four of the Northern Persian Provinces. He had refused, because, as he told Lord Derby, he was 'yet in hopes of utilising the Concession in the interests of England'.

The Falkenhagen crisis settled any uncertainties in Derby's mind. For the first time, he took strong action. He supported Reuter's formal protest to the Persian Government at this granting of a new Concession, with his own rights outstanding; and he told the British Minister in Teheran to use all his influence to persuade the Shah to resist Russian pressure. This new toughness had its desired effect. The following May, despite all former Persian promises, General Falkenhagen finally withdrew his proposals; and any danger of British conflict with Russia was past.

Reuter now set about obtaining a favourable settlement of his own claims. He was prepared, if necessary, to surrender his Concession to the Persian Government, and fight for an indemnity to cover his outlay. He had still, however, high hopes for his more ambitious projects. In the summer of 1875, he pressed on Lord Derby the immense advantages to both England and India of a railway from Baghdad to Persia. He could promise, he told the Foreign Secretary, Turkey's full co-operation. Derby felt it would still commit the Government far more positively than it wanted to be committed. Proposals and withdrawals followed each other for another year: telegrams and despatches from Teheran to London piled up. At last a modified scheme was agreed on between Reuter and the Shah: a railway from the Turco-Persian frontier to Ispahan, the old capital of Persia; the working of certain mines and forests; and the right to establish a Persian Bank. The British Minister in Teheran strongly backed it, and added irrigation works and the reconstruction of an ancient dam. Reuter sent Collins out to Teheran again; Lord Derby gave the scheme the blessing of his 'unofficial support': it looked as though something concrete would finally come from the Concession. Then war broke out between Russia and Turkey. The Shah was afraid to negotiate, with fighting almost on his western frontier; and, after the Russian victories, he was more frightened still.

The pattern of failure seemed complete. In the summer of 1878, six years after his first arrival, Collins was finally withdrawn from Teheran. The same year Reuter's hopes flared up once more. In March, Lord Derby resigned from the Foreign-Secretaryship: Disraeli's aggressive policy to Russia had worried him for too long. His successor, Lord Salisbury, far more sympathetic to Disraeli's own brand of imperialism, took an immediate interest in the Reuter Concession. He was told of both Reuter's and Collins's conviction of the advantages that a railway in Persia would bring to Great Britain. In November, the Persian Government intimated that it was prepared to negotiate with Baron de Reuter for the building of a railway from the Persian Gulf to Teheran. Salisbury had clearly been active.

Disraeli's own private letters to the Queen at the time show how in general he was hoping to bolster up Persia. 'We may make arrangements with Persia', he wrote in October 1879 (in connection with the possible British occupation of Afghanistan), 'which may tend to the restoration of her influence in Asia, and save her from the ravenous maw of Russia.' The Reuter Concession was the sort of enterprise that appealed to him. As a question of policy, however, it was the concern of the India Office; and the India Office was still distrustful of any disturbances of the *status quo* on the route to India – and even more reluctant to pay for them. Reuter's request now for assistance towards the interest on the necessary capital met the same answer as the Lords of the Treasury had given before. The India Office was not prepared to help.

The last hope of the Reuter railway Concession in Persia was over. The Baron waited ten more years for a possible renewal of British interest. At last, in 1888, he sent his second son, George de Reuter, to Teheran, vested with full powers to settle his claims. Again, it looked as though negotiations would linger on; but a year later an Agreement was finally concluded. In satisfaction of his claims, the Baron was given the right to found the Imperial Bank of Persia. It was incorporated by Royal Charter the same year, with offices in Teheran and London, and Baron George de Reuter among the directors. Three years later it advanced a large loan to the Persian Government, and just before the First World War it was to play an important part in stabilising the country's finances. It was one of the few ironies in the story of the remarkable Concession that Julius de Reuter did not live to see.

It would be absurd to say that this outcome of Reuter's vast Persian plans was not a failure. How far it was a failure of British policy as well, is bound to be a matter of controversy. Energetic support of Reuter by the British Government would certainly have made Great Britain the paramount influence in Persia. As it was, the Reuter Concession had successfully kept the other Powers away. By the turn of the century, a ten-mile line from Teheran to a nearby shrine – built by a Frenchman – was the only Persian railway that Western capital had been able to construct.

7

Baron Herbert

WITHIN TWENTY-FIVE YEARS OF ITS FOUNDATION, despite all the trouble its founder was having in Persia, Reuters was an accepted institution. Julius de Reuter had realised his dream of a world-wide telegraphic Agency, overcome prejudices, and made his creation indispensable to newspapers all over the world. But a faint scent of the aroma of the counting-house still clung to it. Its first clients had been merchants, and its market reports were as well known as its political news. To its founder, the reporting of accurate financial intelligence was every bit as important as general news.

The second generation of the Reuters saw a change. The functions of the Agency remained the same. Its services expanded in every direction, it continued its tradition of sending out Agents to explore new territories. But the next forty years saw a complete revolution in English journalism, brought about largely by the influence of America and by a new popular Press read by a different class of reader: in every sort of news a more personal note was demanded. To this change Reuters was forced to respond, although some of the Old Guard in the Agency would have preferred to ignore many of these new demands. In the long run, resistance was impossible. Reuters' internal correspondence during this period reflects a great deal of uncertainty and irritation. Were correspondents to confine themselves to the reporting of solid facts, or were they to pay homage to the new popular 'impressionism' by adding 'colour and light' to their news?

Herbert de Reuter, Julius's eldest son, born in 1852, was a very different man from his father. Julius was a man of remarkable imagination, who had the ability and qualities to realise most of his vast schemes: he was a pioneer, a fighter of immense energy and courage, a business-man of genius. Herbert was more sensitive, more complex; a keen, but not nearly so shrewd a business-man; a good judge of talent, but less of character, than his father. He had many of the qualities which go to make the great editor of a newspaper, and thus a far better understanding of editorial problems than Julius had. Like the rest of the Reuter children, he was educated in the English tradition, which in his case meant Harrow and Balliol College, Oxford. His own choice added Paris, where he went to study music, one of the chief passions of his life.

This interest already showed a temperament markedly unlike his father's. Julius de Reuter was sociable, restless, active, an insatiable traveller, kept open house at No. 18, Kensington Palace Gardens, and showed an almost patriarchal attitude towards his staff: he loved to gather them around him at family parties, where, with enormous zest, he insisted on playing Christmas games at any season of the year. His own love of music he indulged by being a frequent visitor to the opera at Covent Garden; he gave musical parties in his home; he arranged lavish receptions for famous musicians and singers, among them a great favourite of his, Adelina Patti, then at the height of her fame. Herbert, on the other hand, never went to the theatre or opera. He too often stayed up late into the night; but it was always alone, either solving advanced mathematical problems – a fascination that lasted his life – or reading the musical scores that filled his study and sometimes found their way into the great Board Room at 24, Old Jewry. By inclination a recluse, he was a voracious reader, and on a multitude of subjects. He rarely travelled, and never outside Europe. Yet with his apparently shy manner he combined great kindness, an unusual charm, and an animated enthusiasm for serious discussion: in everything that interested him his erudition was immense.

At first he was extremely reluctant to give up his music and enter the Agency. But by 1875, the negotiations and intrigues of the Persian Concession were taking up a great deal of his father's energies; and in November he was persuaded to enter the firm as 'Assistant Manager without salary'. With his long fair hair and his retiring manner, the young man of twenty-three presented an odd contrast to the sprightly, Parisian elegance of his father; in their one surviving photograph together, Herbert looks the artist, Julius the man of affairs. For a year, as Dickinson, the later Chief Editor, said, 'he sauntered', apparently uninterested. Then suddenly he seemed to accept the Agency as his heritage. On Julius's resignation, in May 1878, he was entirely qualified to take over his duties as the new Managing Director: from now on, Reuters was to be his chief interest in life.

The Reuter staff, scattered through the world, would have noticed Herbert's succession from the mere change of tone in the letters they received. Although the correspondence of Julius de Reuter with his staff had been official (all his surviving letters are business letters in the strictest sense), he was by no means formal when he suddenly turned up to visit them on his innumerable trips round Europe. Relations with Herbert were maintained through a regular and almost courtly personal correspondence. He loved words; and, except for the official communication, had a horror of the bare fact. A letter to his Manager in Cape Town gives some impression of his style: he is thanking him for a present of a box of grapes. 'It has arrived,' he writes, 'with its precious contents in such excellent condition as to make decision difficult whether to award the palm to Nature for a masterpiece, or to Man for his triumph over time and space. If it be permissible to interpret perceptions

89

through the senses as the analogues of ideas conveyed in language, the exquisite aroma of this luscious fruit can assuredly claim to inspire a feeling of enjoyment akin to the æsthetic satisfaction derived from the Odes of Anakreon and Hafiz, and I thank you sincerely for this delightful gastronomic translation of Greek and Persian song.'

Nor did this sense for the occasion desert him in the office: when a youthful secretary, drafting a letter in French, showed himself a little weak in spelling, Herbert's only comment was, 'I suggest a little redistribution of the alphabet'.

The last years of Julius de Reuter's reign were marked by financial anxiety; this was to recur again and again. News itself, political and social news, was, as the Press had long realised, a far from profitable commodity. There were only two ways for a news agency to keep its head above water. It could accept direct help from its Government and become an out-and-out official Agency, as many of the smaller European Agencies were doing. (Wolff itself, as has been seen, had already succumbed to the temptation of the Prussian Government's aid in its struggle against Reuter in the late 1860's; and it turned to the same source for help in its financial reorganisation after the Franco-Prussian war. This meant an obvious increase of domestic power; but the days of its international acceptance as a world Agency were numbered.) The other way was to develop subsidiary interests and live off those. For some time to come, Havas was able to thrive on its enormous advertisement revenue. But it is dangerous for the moral integrity of an Agency to mix news with advertisements. It was better in the long run for Reuters that its two ventures into advertising – both during Baron Herbert's reign – proved disastrous; the first through incompetence, the second through vehement and united hostility from the Press.

Fostering of subsidiaries was the way Herbert de Reuter chose. Neither he nor Havas was above accepting a few subventions to help towards their overseas transmission bills. Luckily again (in view of the principle later involved), Reuters obtained very few. For twenty-five years, until the end of the century, the two Agencies were paid a thousand pounds each a year by the Khedive of Egypt towards the expenses of cabling messages to and from the Egyptian Government; and, as mentioned before, the Viceroy of India used to pay Reuters the transmission costs for some of his speeches to be telegraphed home to England. But such help was pitifully small. To pay for the great improvements he intended to make in the news service, Herbert de Reuter relied on the faithful backing of the clients of the old commercial service, on the Agency's service of private telegrams for the public, and on various other subsidiary schemes he later embarked upon.

The gloom that overshadowed the few years before he succeeded Baron Julius was caused by a large drop in the private telegram profits. The Cable Companies were formidable competitors, and in England itself the Post Office was for many years prepared to serve the public at an annual loss of £300,000 on its telegrams. By the beginning of 1877, the new and cheaper word-tariff of the St. Petersburg International Telegraph Convention was ruining Reuters' telegram service to the East. However, when Herbert took over, the Company was well on its feet again. Griffiths, the Secretary, had saved the Agency's Eastern Department by a new and even more elaborate code, which cut down the wording of private telegrams by almost a half: the development of such codes and intricate methods of 'packing' telegrams was soon to become one of Reuters' most successful ways of adapting itself to precarious financial situations.

Herbert de Reuter began office with quite a considerable Reserve Fund to draw upon. He soon needed it. He had great ambitions for the news service, and he showed initiative and sound intuition in carrying them out. The whole tone of

Reuters' foreign service was improved by his appointment of British correspondents to take the place of many of Julius's original Agents, who were often nationals of the country of their appointment. Many of the best, and later well-known, Reuter correspondents dated their careers from now: W. H. G. Werndel, who was to become one of the leading journalists in the Balkans; Fergus Ferguson, later a very successful war correspondent; David Rees, who became the intimate friend of Kitchener and Cromer and the leaders of all parties in Egypt.

Cheaper telegraph rates made possible a great increase in the Reuter outward service. 'Omnibus' telegrams, covering a multitude of news-events, were now sent round the world direct from London, instead of being retransmitted by Paris and other branch offices. The gain in speed and personal control was immediate; and Griffiths was sent off on a number of world-wide missions – to Egypt, India, Australia, and later the United States – to improve the news service on the spot. More significant was Herbert's creation in 1880 of the post of Chief Editor. Until then, the Reuter Editorial had had a scattered, rather rambling existence, without any final authority outside Julius de Reuter himself.

Engländer, before he took up his post again as the Agency's general politician in Europe, and James Hecksher, later Head of the Parliamentary service, were two of the oddly assorted men who had taken a hand in running the Editorial office. Herbert de Reuter now wisely decided to make it an autonomous department, directed by one man. From now on, the Agency adopted for its own set-up one of the principles on which a newspaper is organised, thus justifying what J. D. Symon, in *The Press and Its Story*, said about it at this time: 'Reuters has, in fact, become a newspaper that appears vicariously'.

The new post was given to G. D. Williams, who had been recalled to London several years before, after his successful reporting of the Franco-Prussian War. During the twenty-two years of his office, he controlled a news service that was rapidly being expanded to cover vast new areas, and he succeeded in strengthening it in face of many of the far-reaching changes demanded. Conservative and utterly loyal to the Reuter tradition in which he had grown up, he left a strong mark on the character of the Agency.

During the first decade of his Editorship he had to grapple with the varied exigencies of war-reporting. Events soon showed the advantages of having a permanent correspondent at least somewhere near, whenever political disturbances occurred. Immediately on the declaration of the second Afghan War in the winter of 1878, Harry Williams, the new Chief Editor's brother, was sent from Lahore to the North-West Frontier. Within a fortnight of the British attack, he was being congratulated for his speed in announcing General Roberts's first victory. It was a chance to develop Indian political news, and Herbert de Reuter at once took it. 'This Afghan War has created such an interest in India,' he wrote to Williams the same December, 'that we cannot afford to let Indian politics drop . . .' He gave him authority to send extra messages after the war was over. A report of the Indian Telegraphic Administration of the following year, that its increased revenue was due mainly to 'the length and frequency of Reuter messages', throws into relief the change of emphasis in Reuters' Eastern service from commerce to political news.

In South Africa, too, Reuters' first correspondents were almost entirely taken up with wars. There had been an Agent in Cape Town since 1876; but with no cable, the Press had paid little attention to his mailed news. The almost complete lack of English interest in the Zulu War of 1879 showed how, as early as that, 'news' was being equated with speed. It was a Reuter message which shook the public out of its apathy. It came by cable via St. Vincent, whither Sir Bartle Frere, the new Governor of the Cape, had diverted the mail-steamer so as to hasten the ill news to England. It announced the disaster of Isandhlwana, where the Zulu King Cetewayo's warriors had raided and annihilated most of Lord Chelmsford's camp. The next year a cable was laid to East Africa, and within a year a special correspondent was in Natal, reporting the first Transvaal War. Once again, a Reuter message sent the first news of another British defeat: this time the death of Sir George Colley, Governor of Natal, in the battle of Majuba Hill, soon to become a symbol to the Boers of the impotence of British South African policy at the time.

Herbert de Reuter was just as anxious to improve the service nearer home. His correspondents did send him news from Europe; but the 1871 Havas-Reuter-Wolff Treaty blocked any hope of distributing a service to any subscribers outside the 'sphere of influence' allotted to Reuters. Direct service to any European newspaper was barred. The same Treaty had made Turkey an exclusive field for the French Agency, leaving Egypt to Reuters and Havas jointly. It was a very precise reflection of British and French foreign interests. Disraeli's return to power in 1874, however, brought a new and more aggressive British policy in the Near East. His dramatic purchase of the Khedive's shares in the Suez Canal made closer relations with Egypt essential and inevitable; while, further east, he centred everything on the bolstering-up of Turkey. The new political orientation set the pace for the two news agencies. The British and French struggle for influence in both Turkey and Egypt was from now onwards echoed by competition between Reuters and Havas.

In Egypt, Reuters' emphasis had been on political rather than commercial news, from the first. Perpetual political disturbances gave plenty to report. Reuters' first Agent had set up an office in Alexandria in 1866; and for the next decade a service of bulletins in English and French was distributed by

Reuters and Havas jointly. One of the earliest subscribers to the service was the Egyptian Royal House; the few early newspapers joined in the 1870's, and in 1882 followed the *Egyptian Gazette*, under whose first contract Reuters was to receive 25 per cent of the proceeds of all sales of the paper. In the same year, the revolt of Arabi Pasha broke out against the Khedive, and soon British troops, supporting the Khedive, were involved.

The next twenty years saw Reuters' Agents in Egypt driven to a variety of expedients to cope adequately with the constant wars and expeditions in the Sudan, and not least with the temperaments of some of the commanding officers involved. More than once they had to protect themselves and their offices. During the Arabi Pasha revolt of 1882 Joseph Schnitzler, who, as Chief Agent, had moved Reuters' head office from Alexandria to the capital, Cairo, left the city by the last heavily sandbagged train, to continue the service to London from the cable-head at Alexandria. He arrived to find Alexandria in a state of panic and tension, with a British fleet of warships in the harbour. While the British were bombarding the rebels in the town, he kept touch with London from the cable-ship off shore. News of the bombardment itself was the first important announcement to be *telephoned* from Reuters' head office in London to the Press Association. The speed of transmission added to the shock.

The final defeat of Arabi Pasha came with Lord Wolseley's victory at Tel-el-Kebir in September, two months later. By that time, the Reuter service had been reorganised, and J. Piggott, one of the most active of the Reuter war correspondents during the Sudanese wars, sent an almost hour-to-hour service of the battle to London. The Queen, whose son, the Duke of Connaught, was leading the Brigade of Guards, received personal despatches from Reuters at Balmoral. 'Had a telegram that the army marched out last night. What an anxious moment!' was her diary entry for Wednesday, September 13th; then 'Another telegram, also from Reuter, saying that fighting was going on, and that the enemy had been routed with heavy losses at Tel-el-Kebir. Much agitated'; and finally a wire that her son was safe and well, which she at once took to 'Louischen', the Duchess of Connaught.

The new situation in Egypt, with British influence rapidly taking the place of the old British and French 'dual control', brought a gradual preference in the country for the British news agency over the French. Reuters was soon to be the main *internal* Agency within Egypt as well. In August 1881 the fanatical Mahdi, Mohammed Ahmed, had proclaimed his mission to conquer Egypt, throw out the Turks, and convert the world to his faith. Three years later his conquest of the Eastern Sudan began: the menace to Egypt appeared very real indeed. For the next sixteen years, until the final British victory of Omdurman and the death of the Khalifa and his Chiefs which followed, Reuters' correspondents had the task of reporting, first to Cairo and then to London and the world, the vicissitudes of the Mahdi campaign.

It exercised all the Agency's ingenuity. When Gordon was cut off in Khartoum in May 1884, dromedaries had to be used to carry bulletins through some parts of the Sudan. The reports of the expedition that raced to rescue Gordon – the expedition that arrived two days too late – were rushed back to Cairo by relays of horses. J. Piggott, Reuters' special correspondent, setting off on one Marathon ride, was entrusted with the expedition Commander's despatches as well. The Reuter Agent in Cairo wrote rightly to London: 'The work of a War Correspondent appears to be journalism no longer, but simply horsemanship.'

Lord Kitchener, who, the following autumn, began his long series of campaigns up the Nile, was one of the first Commanders to see the immense benefits to the morale of his troops, of regular news from home. On his orders, a daily Reuter news-bulletin was sent from Cairo, addressed 'Army up the Nile'. When things went badly at the beginning, the news service was one of the few things that pleased him. After exasperation at 'the Government's shilly-shallying about what is to be done out here', in a letter of May 1885, he acknowledged the value of Reuters: 'The troops are pretty well tired already of their summer quarters, and are kept on though by Reuter telegrams'.

His trust in Reuters at times proved embarrassing. When, at the end of 1897, the special desert railway was being built for the Berber expedition, he suddenly announced that 'in view of the great difficulty of transport' he would allow no newspaper special correspondents with him, but only 'one Reuters' Agent, who must not be a military officer'. For a short time Reuters' special correspondent gave exclusive reports of Kitchener's moves. The correspondent chosen was H. A. Gwynne, who had been with Kitchener to Dongola two years before, and had then distinguished himself as a war correspondent in the Turkish-Greek War. Later, Kitchener's confidence recommended him to General Roberts, and he became Reuters' chief representative in the Boer War. Exceptionally strong physically, capable of any endurance, and in many ways a soldier by nature, he had an outstanding career as a Reuter war correspondent, before he gave his energies to Tory politics and the fighting editorships of the *Standard* and the *Morning Post.*

For some campaigns Reuters employed Army officers to send occasional despatches: Major Wingate, later, as Sir Reginald Wingate, Governor-General of the Sudan, was congratulated on 'an excellent service'; and the Agency's success in reaching London with early messages of the victories of Atbara and Omdurman certainly owed something to Wingate's position as Kitchener's Chief of Intelligence and Press Censor.

Reuters' Omdurman message was the first Press news of the battle to reach England. The young Reuter correspondent, Lionel James, had used an ingenious trick. He simulated authority to an orderly, and his message was taken by special steamer up the Nile – with Kitchener's official despatch.

By the turn of the century the Reuter position in Egypt looked permanent. Havas had acknowledged the change in the political situation, and had left the Egyptian news-market entirely to Reuters, for a financial compensation and the promise that Reuters' telegrams both in Alexandria and Cairo would now be headed – as the old joint ones had been – 'Reuter-Havas'.

Egypt was Herbert de Reuter's first major addition to his news service. Turkey and the Balkans – and news from these regions was soon to become very important indeed – offered a far harder task. While the European Powers scrambled with each other to get news out of Turkey first, the Sultan's Government – the *Sublime Porte*, so called – did its level best to suppress most of it. When, in 1877, Sigismund Engländer arrived in Constantinople as Reuters' correspondent, he found all the apparatus of suppression in full swing. The June before, Sir Edward Pears had sent to the *Daily News* the horrifying account of the Bulgarian Atrocities, in which the Turks had massacred in cold blood 12,000 Christians. The Sultan's reaction to European horror and fury, and still more to the English Foreign Secretary's warning that 'any renewal of the outrages would be more fatal to the *Porte* than the loss of a battle', was not reform, but an even more stringent censorship. Engländer was soon sending nine-tenths of his telegrams in a special code across the frontier into Bulgaria, to be transmitted to England by agents he employed there. As far as he succeeded in getting despatches out of the country, he had plenty to report.

Turkey had been at war with Russia since April 1877; and in June panic seized Constantinople as the Russians swept south over the Danube. By the Armistice of the following January, the Russians were only a few miles off Constantinople, all wires had been cut, and Reuter messages to England, together with official despatches, had to travel via Bombay. Queen Victoria, as determined as Disraeli that Constantinople should not fall, was in a state of extreme agitation. 'The Queen writes her third letter, the third on one day,' she wrote to Disraeli on February 7th. '. . . Whether the Russians have got to Constantinople (for in spite of Gortschakoff's answer and denial the Queen is sure they are there, or are nearly so, for Reuter states it, who generally knows) on an agreement with Turkey or in spite of the *Porte*, it is equally a case of breach of faith and We have told them again and again so.'

The British Fleet was ordered to Constantinople. The chain of events was begun which led to the Congress of Berlin, insisted upon by Disraeli as the vindication of his foreign policy. By the 'Treaty of peace with honour', Russia accepted a considerably diminished Bulgaria, and Constantinople was safe again. And a private Convention with the Sultan gave Great Britain Cyprus, in return for a military guarantee of Asiatic Turkey against any further Russian aggression.

It was a Reuter message – a verbal one, gained in very unusual circumstances – which, during the Berlin Congress, further strengthened Disraeli's case. Henry Collins, on his way home from acting as Julius de Reuter's representative in Persia, via Berlin (where he was to deliver some urgent official despatches to Lord Salisbury, the Foreign Secretary), had an extraordinary experience. On the Caspian steamer he met the Russian Chief of Police, whom he succeeded in putting into a very expansive mood. The Chief of Police showed himself impressed by Disraeli's strong British policy, but was equally anxious to show off Russian resources too: Collins listened with great interest to the convincing account of a plan for a Russian army expedition to Krasnovodsk, to take place in a month. The expedition was to transform large tracts of Turkestan into 'Russian Central Asia' (it was also to come perilously near collision with the British on the India-Afghan frontier). Collins, on reaching Berlin, burst in on Lord Salisbury's Private Secretary. He found that the British Government had known nothing about the subject of his private intelligence. Its reliability was thoroughly supported, not only by general British suspicions, but by the Russian preparations for some move Collins had himself seen along the Volga.

This extraordinary indiscretion by the Czar's Chief of Police came, ironically enough, at a time when the strict Russian censorship was doing its best to block the normal outlets of news. Even *The Times* found a full-time correspondent in the Russian capital, 'dogged by detectives at every turn', not worth his pay and keep, and its occasional correspondent was assured that 'really important events come to us at once through Reuters, either from St. Petersburg direct or indirectly through Berlin'.

In Constantinople, the agent of a free Press had by no means an easier time. The Sultan was no less suspicious than the Czar of public opinion inside and outside his country, and he feared and disliked Engländer – who, of course, had soon become an institution in Constantinople – for his knack of getting inconvenient news out of the country. Twice the Sultan threatened him with expulsion.

In 1883, he began to train a new assistant correspondent, W. H. G. Werndel, to take his place. He trained him well. For twenty-five years Werndel was to be Reuters' chief correspondent in Turkey; by the end of that time he had become one of the best-known British foreign correspondents in the Balkans; and after the First World War he was Reuters' natural choice as permanent correspondent to the League of Nations at Geneva. When Engländer finally left Constantinople for the more congenial buzz of news-agency politics in

Paris, Werndel was joined, at the end of 1888, by another young man whose long career in Reuters was strangely like his own. Fergus Ferguson also stayed mainly in the Balkans until the First World War; both Werndel and he had distinguished records as war correspondents in Macedonia and Palestine, and Ferguson succeeded Werndel as correspondent to the League of Nations in 1932. Both were Reuter correspondents for very nearly fifty years.

For the next twenty-five years, these two, as Reuter correspondents in the Balkans, worked right at the centre of the most fateful events in Europe. They reported the terrors of the Armenian massacres of 1895 and 1896, Germany's growing influence in Turkey, the Kaiser's visit to the Sultan, the movement of the Young Turks, the two Balkan Wars. It was a long and intricate history which led up to 1914. During this uneasy period Reuters' foreign correspondents were first allowed to add political comments (if clearly shown as such) to their political news. It was due to the intelligence, initiative and political tact of such reporters as Werndel and Ferguson that the Press soon accepted, and often relied upon, Reuters' development into a 'vicarious newspaper'.

8

Home Trials

THE FLOURISHES AND SUCCESSES OF REUTERS IN EUROPE
and overseas could not disguise a severe period of testing at
home. The Agency had grown up in an atmosphere of free
Victorian expansion, and reaped the fullest rewards from it;
it now had to contend with equally thriving competition from
other quarters. For almost twenty years it was virtually the
only English news agency. Conscious of its position, and
already very much a part of English life, it would have found
it difficult, by the turn of the century, to be anything other
than what the Head of another great Agency, Kent Cooper of
the Associated Press of America, later called it: 'dignified, conservative, omniscient'. But to certain new newspapers at home,
rather more conscious of change and the passing of time, dignity, conservatism and omniscience were far from being at a
premium. The last quarter of the century saw Reuters em-
broiled in an inevitable series of struggles.

They were not all against external enemies. There were
rivals at home too, and for one short, critical period the comfortable agreement with the European Agencies threatened to
break up. Fits of dissatisfaction within the Press took the form
of schemes by groups of the large newspapers to pool their
foreign news instead of having to rely on an Agency; the
smaller papers used the cruder weapon of piracy. With no
copyright in news, nothing was easier for a newspaper with no
national reputation to lose than to 'lift' Reuter telegrams from

the previous morning or evening papers without acknowledgment and without payment. Then the Agency had to fight its own over-conservatism, in methods, equipment and, above all, outlook. Even the question whether or not there was such a thing as a 'revolution in journalism' was for a long time a vehement internal issue. Finally there was the struggle to organise and support the 'subsidiaries' – the ventures which Herbert de Reuter constantly embarked upon in the eternal hope of paying for the news service.

Julius de Reuter had successfully overcome the early hostility of a part of the Press and of the Cable Companies; he had to fight also a war with Wolff in Germany. He suffered no real competition from rival Agencies in England. From the beginning of its operations in 1870, the Press Association was an ally. It made no attempts to gather news outside the United Kingdom, and with very few complaints accepted its foreign service from Reuters. Reuters, in its turn, was careful not to trespass on the Press Association's home ground. Few monopolies in Victorian England were allowed the peace from competition Reuters enjoyed for so long.

The Press Association's rapid success seems to have been the chief spur to other telegraphic ventures. Within two years of its start, two new English news agencies were founded, both competing in different ways with Reuters: the 'Central News' and the 'Exchange Telegraph Company'. The Central News grew out of a considerably older concern. In 1863, William Saunders, Member of Parliament, social reformer, newspaperman and philanthropist, had, with a friend, established an Agency which they called the Central Press, to supply newspapers in the provinces with home news only. Eight years later, Saunders issued a statement to the Press that he would 'supply telegraphic news personally', and his newly named Central News was soon sending correspondents abroad and supplying world news in direct competition with Reuters.

Particularly active in the Egyptian campaigns and in the Boer War, it soon gained a name for speed. Until World War I, and for a short time afterwards, when it began to lose support from the Press and to fall on bad times, it was one of Reuters' most feared competitors.

The following year, 1872, the Exchange Telegraph Company was incorporated, one of its founders being Sir James Anderson (grandfather of the present head of the Company), Captain of the *Great Eastern* when it laid the Atlantic Cable, and an expert on telegraphic communications. Its primary aim was to report Stock Exchange prices and dividends, and it soon gained the exclusive right to be represented on the floor of the Exchange. Twenty years earlier, Reuters had agreed to supply the Stock Exchange with prices from the Continental Bourses; but the arrangement had come to an end in the 1860's. From now on, the inside of the Exchange was to be alien territory to Reuters. In the sphere of financial news particularly the new Company became in time a rival.

Technically, Reuters gained much from the competition of these two new Agencies. Until the 1880's everything in the Old Jewry head office was written by hand. Typewriters, by 1880 in common use in most newspaper offices, were hardly used in Reuters' Agency before the Boer War; telegrams were copied out on to 'flimsies', thin oil-sheets, with a stylus; and their only distributors to the newspaper offices were the Reuter messenger-boys, smartly conspicuous in their field-grey (rumour had it that their uniforms had been bought up cheaply from the suppliers of the Army of the South after its defeat in the American Civil War), or, for the most urgent despatches, special hansom cabs. Only such conservative methods would, it was thought, ensure Reuters' absolute accuracy.

In the early 1880's, competition forced certain innovations. In 1882, the telephone was first used to send the sudden news of the British Fleet's bombardment of Alexandria to the Press

Association. The following year, Herbert de Reuter told his Directors he had arranged to acquire from the Exchange Telegraph Company a 'new and improved kind of instrument for the simultaneous transmission of the intelligence which is at present manifolded and delivered by messenger'. This 'column printer', as it was called, looking rather like a grandfather-clock from the side, with weights hanging down in front, had messages played on to it as though it were a piano; it transmitted them electrically to the offices of all the London papers, to which Reuters now connected itself by wire. It was the ancestor of the Creed machine and the modern teleprinter. At the same time typewriters gradually made their way into Reuter offices. But respect was still paid to the past: messengers delivered confirmatory copies of all despatches transmitted to the newspapers; electricity was not yet fully respectable. The staff who worked the new column printer was still known under its old name of the 'Manifolders' Department'. On the whole, however, the arrival of the Machine Age had been acknowledged.

More worrying to Reuters than the competition of rival English Agencies were various plans made by its own newspaper subscribers to collect foreign news for themselves. It was invariably the larger and wealthier papers that put these plans forward. The pattern was still that of the original hostility to the Agency showed by the Manager of *The Times*. To *The Times*, conscious of its own unique organisation of foreign correspondents, the Agencies were at best a necessary evil. They were guilty of two unforgivable sins: they levelled up the standard of foreign news-reporting, and they helped the smaller papers. In any discussion of a rival project, however, *The Times* was highly realistic. A first proposal to build up an association of London newspapers to collect foreign news, on the same co-operative principle under which the Press Association gathered home news, did not receive its support. Its

Manager, Mowbray Morris, realised that Reuters was already entrenched too firmly to be touched by such a scheme.

Instead, *The Times* concentrated on perfecting its own telegraphic news system. The 1880's were a period of heavy outlay for both the Agency and the newspapers. 1884 was for the shareholders of Reuters the first year without a dividend; the expenses of reporting the campaigns in Egypt and the Sudan, followed by wars in Bulgaria, Burma and China, had been too heavy. The London papers resisted a proposed increase in subscription rates; but the following year the main morning papers, the *Morning Post, Telegraph, Standard, Chronicle* and *Daily News*, all agreed to a compromise. In future, they would pay extra 'in time of war or prolonged political disturbance'. The principle of a 'special service' was accepted. Only *The Times* remained aloof, leaving itself free to take the service if it wished. Behind the aloofness was hostility still. On four occasions within the next five years, *The Times* showed itself prepared to foster rival concerns in an effort to end its dependence on Reuters. It considered a proposal of Lloyd's, in 1886, to add general news to its service of shipping intelligence; but, after opposition from other quarters as well as from Reuters, the Lloyd's plan was dropped. Instead, Lloyd's agreed to supply *mailed* news only to the newspapers – and to pay an annual indemnity to Reuters for the privilege. A second proposal to encourage Havas to invade England and distribute its news directly to the London papers was soon abandoned. And a third suggestion, in 1890, that *The Times* should syndicate both its London and foreign news with a group of the wealthier provincial papers, was defeated by the Press Association's faithfulness to Reuters.

The Times' final attempt to support a rival Agency was, for a time at least, only too successful; and for nearly two critical years Reuters' whole position in the London Press was menaced. On October 7th, 1890, Moberly Bell, as one of the first acts of his Managership of *The Times*, made an agreement with a news agency quite fresh to the international field. It operated under the name of Dalziel – a highly reputable one in British journalism – and it had a respectable London address: No. 222, The Strand. Its main backing came from America, its methods were American, and it was from America that most of its news came. It skilfully set out to give the London daily Press the sort of news, presented in the sort of way, which was making the new weeklies a success all over the country.

The first of these weeklies, George Newnes's *Tit-Bits*, founded in 1881, had in itself all but effected a revolution in English journalism. It consciously ignored the 'cultivated' reader; its aim was to appeal to 'the million'. The million wanted its reading to be easy, bright and, above all, entertaining. The 'snippet' – the short paragraph or extract, the more 'human' the better – was the obvious answer. Alfred Harmsworth's first venture, *Answers*, brought out in 1888, when its founder was twenty-two years of age, and Arthur Pearson's *Pearson's Weekly* (Pearson was twenty-four) used the same technique. Disconnectedness became a main principle of the 'New Journalism'. So far, this new popular tone had not been accepted by the national morning Press. *The Times*, the *Daily Telegraph*, the *Morning Post*, the *Daily News*, all remained faithful to their old class of readers. There were two notable exceptions. W. T. Stead's editorship of the *Pall Mall Gazette* was one: his 'interviews', campaigns, sensational attacks on national abuses, all presented with a fiercely personal note, were utterly new to the English morning Press. The other was T. P. O'Connor's bringing-out of the evening *Star* in 1888, startlingly arrayed with a full range of American headlines, and blazoning a new 'appeal to the people' learned by the Editor in the London office of Gordon Bennett's *New York Herald*.

The 'Dalziel Agency' now set itself to offer this 'popular' news to the London morning Press. It was not the first to do so. Twenty years before, James McLean, Reuters' Chief Representative in America during the Civil War, and the hero of the early report on Lincoln's death, had tried to do the same. He was no mean expert in sensationalism. A fantastic report that the island of Tortola, in the Virgins, had been overwhelmed by a tidal wave with the loss of several hundred well-known American families holidaying there had earned him dismissal. A rival Agency, specialising in sensations, had been his revenge. But Dalziel did the thing far more systematically. With its main agents in America – already endeared to many of the new class of newspaper readers as the Continent of Sensations – it was in a strong position. Its agreement with *The Times* was a major victory. At one swoop, it had reached the heart of traditional British journalism. Moberly Bell saw in the arrangement a chance for *The Times* to defeat its new popular competitors at their own game, and the exhilarating hope of giving a hard rap to Reuters. On the surface, it was a clever move to set one rival against another. If it marked the beginnings of an ominous concession to the new forces of sensationalism, its final effect on Reuters at any rate was entirely salutary.

But that first autumn of the new Agency's activity was alarmingly successful. In two months *The Times* paid to Dalziel over £700 for his telegrams, nearly double its normal subscription for the same period to Reuters. It received in return an even higher proportion of the new news. A murder in Canada was followed by a series of crimes, cyclones, and ravages of escaped animals, all suffered by obscure townships in the United States. In every case full details were given: and the names and mishaps of unknown citizens of Utah or Ohio suddenly provoked intense interest among the British public. An even greater sensation was the German Emperor's premature announcement to the world of the remarkable powers of Dr. Koch's tuberculin as a cure for certain forms of consumption. The implications of this news, unchecked and quite beyond what Koch himself claimed, were exploited to the full by the new Agency. By Christmas, Dalziel's telegrams were supplanting Reuters' in London papers outside *The Times*. Both the Press Association and Reuters' London subscribers now demanded the same sort of 'human interest' stories themselves. The crisis brought to the fore an issue already gathering within Reuters over the entire constitution of the news service.

The conflict centred in the creation of a 'Reuters' Special Service', supplying news to subscribers outside the general service of telegrams. The idea had come from Engländer two years before, enthusiastically proclaimed in two of the voluminous letters he wrote daily to Herbert de Reuter from Paris. The danger then was from the challenge of the newspapers' special correspondents: they were a 'dark point spreading more and more on the horizon threatening the further development of our Agency'; and, without a special service of its own, Reuters 'would be forestalled and morally ruined by the revolution in journalism', he wrote in January 1889. Herbert's fears that such a service 'would grant one paper a monopoly over its rivals, or be done secretly and thus be treacherous to the other papers' he finally allayed. Havas had sent a circular to all its subscribers announcing terms for a 'special service', open to them all. Reuters should do the same. With John Griffiths, the Secretary, at first sceptical about the whole business, Engländer was much sharper. 'You are still dominated by superstitious, blind, dogmatic adherence to past journalistic traditions,' he wrote, 'and your Editors still shrink from developing any light and colour in the Service.' His own ideas were quite clear. Reuters should not only report political events, but offer comment on them, as the papers' special correspondents did. He wanted a special interpretative service, quite separate from the general Reuter telegrams, open to any paper that wanted it. He knew it would appeal particularly to the provincial Press; and at the same time he had the sense to realise that the papers must not be made to seem too dependent on Reuters. 'We cannot ask the papers to appear tattoed with Reuters' Agency all over their bodies,' he wrote to Herbert.

The Dalziel success decided the issue. In December 1890, two months after Dalziel's agreement with *The Times*, Engländer's idea was adopted in principle, and a joint Reuters–Press Association 'Special Service' inaugurated. The plan Herbert de Reuter worked out with the Press Association went far further than the original idea. The new supplementary service, to be paid for by individual papers per word used, did include political interpretation, but it aimed at providing much non-political excitement as well. The 'General Instructions for the Guidance of Correspondents' later sent out showed that the 'New Journalism' had made its mark. The following 'sudden and unforeseen occurrences' were regarded as particularly meriting the new detailed 'Special Service' – in addition, of course, to the normal telegrams reporting them:

> *The wreck of an ocean liner or steamship.*
> *A calamitous railway accident.*
> *A fire or explosion involving serious loss of life.*
> *A destructive earthquake, cyclone or inundation.*
> *Especially startling crimes and outrages.* ('Mere brutal murders and domestic tragedies, such as occur almost daily in every part of the world, *should not be noticed at all.*')
> *Popular disturbances.*
> *The sudden or tragic demise of any illustrious or famous personage.*
> *An attempt upon the life of a monarch or statesman, or the discovery of some far-reaching plot.*

At the same time, radical measures were taken to increase the supply of news from the United States. From now on Dalziel would at any rate be fought on equal terms.

For the first months of 1891, the Reuter correspondents in the main world news-centres – Engländer in Paris, E. A. Brayley Hodgetts, who had been sent to start the Reuter Special Service in Berlin, after being the St. Petersburg Correspondent of the *Daily Graphic*, and S. L. Lawson, the Agent in New York – were kept extremely busy. While the fight was on, sheer quantity of news had a value of its own. By April, *The Times* had decided to take the Reuter Special Service, and Dalziel was on the wane. For a time, Dalziel tried to make up by a still more lurid colouring of his news, but his reputation was fast falling. By 1892, Dalziel was curtly told by Moberly Bell of *The Times* that his task – 'to infuse a spirit of competition' into the Agencies – 'was now accomplished'. The following year, almost every message from Dalziel was, according to Bell, 'absolutely devoid of foundation – every line is pure invention'. The end came when Reuters was able to show that what had purported to be a Dalziel original New South Wales Budget message from Melbourne was in fact the Reuter despatch of the Budget rehashed. In September 1895, *The Times* paid Dalziel £1 for his telegrams for the month – instead of the £360 of five years before. Reuters had emerged victorious.

The contest had been costly. It had followed hard upon another challenge, successfully dealt with for the moment, and finally to be of the utmost importance to all news agencies: the fight with the pirates. News piracy, the copying of the Agency's telegrams from a subscribing newspaper, or from a Reuter bulletin, without payment or acknowledgments, had been a problem as far back as 1870. It had soon become a regular method of news-gathering among some of the smaller papers in India, South Africa and Egypt. It cost nothing; and, since English law recognised no copyright in news, gave no fear of legal action. But when the habit spread to England itself, and, in the autumn of 1889, to the London edition of the *New York*

Herald, some form of action became imperative. It was taken that year. For a short while Reuters went directly into the newspaper business itself. From Arundel Street, off the Strand, was published, through 1890, *The Epoch or Reuters' Journal*, a bulletin of the day's most important Reuter telegrams. It was on sale through the London streets, the proprietorship of the contents was clear, and copyright in them was claimed. Publication of a Reuter telegram without authority could now be challenged as an infringement of the new right. Threats of legal action proved sufficient; and the same year two of the more successful 'pirates' – the *Western Daily Mercury* and the *Belfast News-Letter* – became respectable again, and renewed their official subscriptions. Piracy only became a major Reuter problem again thirty years later, with the beginnings of regular dissemination of news by wireless.

Meanwhile, Reuters was once more experiencing on the Continent the full impact of nationalist power-politics. This time, however, there was a difference. Twenty years before, it had been a struggle with Wolff supported by the Prussian Government. Now, with the old 'European Agency Treaty' coming to the end of its twenty years in 1890, certain politicians awaited the outcome with interest. Soon after returning to office as Premier of Italy in 1887, Francesco Crispi paid a visit to Friedrichsruh, Bismarck's country home near Hamburg. His main object was to strengthen the Triple Alliance – Italy, Germany and Austria – particularly against increasing French power. An important subject of their discussions was the influence of the news agencies. Crispi realised as well as Bismarck the part their own two national Agencies could play in mobilising public opinion. He left with a plan to organise the Agencies of the Triple Alliance Powers – Stefani of Rome, Wolff of Berlin and the Korrespondenz-Bureau of Vienna – into an association designed to crush Havas's dominant position in Europe. Nothing could be done until the spring of 1889, when the old agreement expired. The Triple Alliance Agencies spent the two years in between hastening on preparations for the rupture.

The initiative soon passed to Wolff in Berlin; and it was Wolff which decided that the new alliance needed Reuters' support at all costs. As partners in the old Treaty, Wolff and Reuters had in 1887 signed what they called an 'offensive-defensive alliance', providing for joint action in case the old agreement should not be renewed. The hope of future 'friendly relations' with Havas was expressly stated. From then on, Wolff brought every pressure to bear on Reuters to persuade it to throw in its lot entire with the Triple Alliance; to have a complete break with Havas, and to fight her with the other three Agencies' aid in Turkey, Roumania, Greece, Italy and Belgium. Wolff's motive was quite clear. 'Bismarck', said its Director to Engländer, 'is getting more and more stubborn and even unreasonable in his hatred against France . . . the charges he brought against our own Agency recently could only be dispelled by our declaration that we would break off relations with Havas.'

Reuters had never attracted this kind of pressure from the British Government. Occasionally, as has been said earlier, the India Office paid for the transmission to London of telegrams containing official news it wanted in full. Apart from this, Government relations with the Agency had remained formal, a reflection of traditional reserve in official dealings with the Press. There had been no Bismarck or Crispi to attempt to create a new policy of intimacy. This fitted in with Reuters' own conception of the political independence of its news.

The approaching rupture between the Agencies on the Continent was alarming to Reuters, not politically, but for its likely commercial effect on the news service. Engländer, who had himself transferred from Constantinople to Paris on the first rumours of the break, tried for a strenuous six months to stop it. Given full powers to negotiate, he spent half his time rushing between Paris, Berlin and Vienna, trying to bring all sides to their senses; and the other half writing frantic letters, at the rate of two a day, to Herbert de Reuter in London, insisting that a break would mean disaster. 'You may believe me that war with Havas would lead to our ruin,' he wrote in April 1889; and letter after letter reiterated that there must be 'complete solidarity between the Agencies'.

By the middle of April it was clear that any hope of solidarity was in vain. Engländer now switched his policy to trying desperately to keep Reuters on terms with both the rival camps. He even went so far as drafting a proposal for an 'offensive-defensive alliance' with Havas. It only served to smooth momentarily a fierce quarrel that had broken out over their joint office in Brussels. The obvious danger now was of falling between two stools. When the crisis came, Reuters was firmly with the Triple Alliance Agencies, Wolff, Stefani and the Korrespondenz-Bureau of Vienna; and in May 1889 the pact of aggression against Havas was concluded.

The result was a fiasco. It gave Reuters very little satisfaction to know that its Agent had gloomily prophesied it. Success depended largely on the proposed offices to be operated jointly by Reuters and Wolff in Rome and Paris. In Rome, Crispi, worried apparently by Francophile demonstrations which were taking place at the time throughout Italy, and above all by Bismarck's capriciousness, let them down. In Paris, the joint office was a failure. Engländer's foresight had been right: Havas was too wealthy and too powerfully entrenched on the Continent to be isolated.

Reuters itself was by now strong enough not to be ruined by being on the wrong side in Europe. Its policy of expansion overseas was completely justified: no European Agency could afford to be without the Reuter service of British imperial news. The real losers were the Triple Alliance Agencies.

Stefani of Rome, and the Korrespondenz-Bureau of Vienna, found their news-frontiers shrunk; they were more and more forced into being mainly domestic Agencies, collecting and distributing news in their own countries only. Wolff was glad to return to the old position of 1870. In the New Year of 1890, the old European agreement was renewed for another ten years; but this time with important additions. Havas's claim to distribute news exclusively in South America was now acknowledged, as was Reuters' similar claim in East Asia. Wolff alone had to be satisfied with purely European territory.

The outcome of the struggle was remarkable evidence of the power of the independent news agencies. Of the two Agencies relying on their professional skill and organisation alone, Havas (backed by its advertisement business) had been entirely successful, and Reuters at any rate kept its head above water. The three Government-backed Agencies had all gone under.

Wolff's real complaint was not against ineffective politicians, but against a weak and decentralised newspaper industry. There was no German national Press to guarantee it continuous support. Behind Reuters, and guaranteeing it its regular subscriptions, stood the English newspapers, the strongest and most independent in Europe. The Agency's resilience in the fight just finished was an indirect tribute to that backing. In the news-agency world the Press was stronger than Governments.

On the other side of the Atlantic, control of news-gathering by the Press had become the centre of an even more bitter struggle. In 1848, the 'Year of Revolutions' in Europe, six New York newspaper-publishers had founded the Associated Press. It was, as its historian Oliver Gramling, in his book *AP: The Story of News*, has said, 'the first real co-operative news-gathering organisation': unlike the great European Agencies formed just before and just after it, it was owned from the beginning by the newspapers it served. Press ownership now became the main issue in a violent competition with the old privately owned United Press (not connected with the present United Press Associations, founded in 1907), controlled by William M. Laffan. In 1893, Reuters suddenly became a stake in the battle and was pitched into it almost overnight. Both American Agencies saw a contract, giving the exclusive right to Reuters' European news, as a trump-card in their struggle for supremacy in America. In February 1893, this contract all but fell to Laffan of the United Press, who himself came to London to get it. That Herbert de Reuter finally gave it to the Associated Press (then newly incorporated in Chicago as The Associated Press of Illinois) was due largely to the recommendations of Reuters' Manager in New York. It was a dramatic beginning to the long and chequered relations between Reuters and the great American Agency.

The new agreement was at the same time the logical outcome of British interest in news from America and the growing interest of Americans in Europe. The official United States policy of isolationism did not kill the demand for European news. From early days, Reuters had been more impressed than the other two European Agencies by the importance of a traffic of news with America. The *casus belli* of the war with Wolff in the 1860's had been Reuters' ambitions for the American cable service. In 1866, when Alexander Wilson, the old New York Associated Press's first European agent, had arrived in London, Reuters had agreed to supply him with a full report of both English and European news. And from the late 1870's Reuters had had a Manager in America, to organise a stream of American news to London. This new agreement gave the Associated Press exclusive American rights to the complete news reports of Reuters, Havas and Wolff and, through them, of their smaller European satellite Agencies.

Melville E. Stone, founder of the Chicago *Daily News* and first General Manager of the newly organised Associated Press, arrived in London, to sign the new agreement, on St. Patrick's Day, 1893. 'I went to Europe and arranged an alliance with Reuters. This was a blow from which the United Press never recovered,' was the later entry in his diary. The terseness emphasised two important things. It showed that Stone knew full well that no major United States Agency could exist without a complete service of European news. How right he was, the United Press's bankruptcy and dissolution proved four years later. It also showed the extraordinary power Reuters had won by the 1890's. Outside the reports of a few correspondents of individual papers, Reuters was by now the only news-viaduct between Europe and America. European news from Havas, Wolff and their satellites went to America through Reuters; American news from the Associated Press came to Europe the same way. British trade, the early enterprise of British cable companies, and the resourcefulness and reputation of Reuters, had combined to make London the centre of the world's news. For nearly thirty years, the United States' isolationism and preoccupation with their own domestic problems let the situation be. Then, with much else British, Reuters' domination was challenged. That challenge, made between the two World Wars, was to be by far the fiercest of Reuters' struggles abroad.

9

The British Empire

ONE WOULD HAVE EXPECTED REUTERS TO DOMINATE
the British Empire. Based upon London it would be logical
for the British Agency to send news after the British flag. And
in the European Agency Treaties it had been agreed that the
British Empire would be exclusive Reuter territory. But in fact
the development of the Reuter service in the Empire was by
no means uniformly successful. There was no Empire pattern for Reuters and each component part of the Empire
presented special problems which were approached with vary-
ing degrees of success.

In India the story was one of early accomplishment and
successful fulfilment. Reuters was quickly accepted as an indispensable link between England and the Anglo-Indian community. No rivals appeared to challenge it.

In Australia and New Zealand Reuter agents were appointed
in the early 1870's. In 1878 Henry Collins, who had successfully established Reuters in India and the Far East, moved on
and became General Manager for Australasia.

In Australia, where a small number of newspapers prospered
in the metropolitan cities and where there was no strong provincial Press, individual newspapers or groups of them soon
sought to create news-gathering organisations of their own.
It was in 1887 that the newspapers started to break away from
Reuters and establish their own offices in London. And, because the few newspapers were concentrated in the great towns

and there was no widespread provincial Press to be catered for, Australia, almost unique among countries, failed to develop a domestic Australian news agency. The newspapers banded themselves together in groups and established the principle of buying the Reuter service in London for selecting and cabling to Australia at the discretion of their London representatives. This deprived Reuters of the advantage of a news-distributing organisation in Australia and prevented the Agency from having that close and intimate relationship with its newspaper customers which is generally so important a feature of the Agency-newspaper relationship.

The New Zealand newspapers, small and financially weak, adopted the course of taking their world news at second hand from the Australian newspaper groups. For many years, although Reuter news went to Australia and New Zealand, the relationship between Reuters and its newspaper clients was remote. It was only to be in the final decade of this story of Reuters' first hundred years that a revolutionary change came about, and the distant and not very friendly relationship was converted to one of such intimacy as might have shocked the two Barons out of their graves.

Despite the attitude of the Australian newspapers, Herbert de Reuter persevered in a series of Australian experiments. He developed a Reuter Australian organisation despite the aloofness of the Australian press. In 1891, a 'Telegraph Remittance business' was founded between London and India, and London and Australia. Through the Reuter Agents it was found possible, by using elaborate codes, to transfer money by telegraph more cheaply than through the banks. This Reuter service became very popular with the public and thoroughly unpopular with the banks. Progress in India was slow. But in Australia the bank crisis of April 1893 (caused largely by over-speculation in land in the prosperous 'eighties) led to a rush to send money home to England. That year, Reuters remitted £1,500,000 from Australia to London; and from then on the service was established.

An 'Advertisements Branch' founded at the same time in Sydney was also a success. Then there was the 'Private Telegram Service', controlled by the Traffic Department – or 'Eastern Room', as it was still called from its beginnings in India and the Far East. This business was expanded throughout Australia in the 1890's. As cable rates went down, and competition from the telegraph companies grew, it kept itself going by elaborating more and more compressed, ingeniously cheap, codes.

The labour involved was worth while. A twenty-word telegram to Australia still cost £10 in 1885; but a three-shillings-a-word press cable rate came into force in 1886. It was in the ten-shillings-a-word period that Reuters was asked by the New South Wales Government to despatch to London its Treasurer's annual budget speech. The result was a series of telegrams costing more than £1,300, from which Reuters exacted its profit.

But the Reuter service was not always reliable. It was a Reuter telegram from Brisbane which gave Mark Twain the only piece of humour he had ever noticed in *The Times*. This was a telegram giving a summary of news from Queensland. First came a short report on the Maryborough-Olympic Railway, then under construction; then came the words 'Governor Queensland twins first son'. To the Reuter sub-editor its meaning was clear and next day this announcement appeared in the London newspapers: 'Lady Kennedy, wife of the Governor of Queensland, has given birth to twins, the elder being a son'. The Governor, as a great many people informed Reuters next day, was unmarried and well past sixty years of age. The explanation was simple. The Governor had been innocently doing his duty to the State: the last words in the telegram should have read 'turns first sod', and they referred to the Queensland railway. A correction had to appear; and the ruffled dignity of *The Times* was too much for the American humorist.

These subsidiary enterprises for the time being saved Reuters' financial position in Australia; they also helped to finance the more important traffic of news from Australia back to England. Every new Reuter office – and these offices soon extended all over Australia and New Zealand – became a small news centre as well. The Agency remained for some time almost the only news link for Australia with the rest of the world. The changing content of that news is a mirror of the Colonies' quick growth into a state and a nation. In the late 1870's, gold robberies in the ports and hold-ups by the notorious Kelly gang filled many of Reuters' telegrams. In the next decade, the Melbourne land-boom and the fantastic speculation accompanying it had become the main theme of the news; and a few years later, the financial crash. But the movement for Australian Federation was already in the air; and detailed Reuter reports helped to create and foster English interest in it. Every conference and meeting of the Federal Council, from 1883 to the Constituent Assembly's final framing of the Federation Act in 1899, was reported back to England by a Reuter special correspondent.

Australian news was at last becoming world news. Correspondents accompanied the Australian troops to the Boer War; the 'Test Match cricket service' became an essential part of the Reuter news report. A special Reuter representative accompanied the Duke and Duchess of York to Melbourne in 1901 to attend the official opening of the Commonwealth Parliament; day-to-day reports of the tour filled the English Press.

The visit of the American fleet to Australia and New Zealand seven years later was a more important landmark in Reuters' history. It was one of the earliest occasions on which the

Agency used wireless. The American fleet left Honolulu for New Zealand waters direct; and the expectant public in New Zealand and Australia resigned themselves to a prolonged silence enforced by the 6,000 miles of sea in between.

The arrival of full reports on the journey from the Reuter correspondent with the fleet created at first intense scepticism in the Australian Press. The fleet was still 1,200 miles away, and Australia had no wireless station. But the reports continued daily and culminated in an exact forecast of the hour of casting anchor in Auckland, New Zealand. To a continent without wireless, this was uncanny. Reuters' secret was simple and well-kept. An American supply-ship, the *Glacier*, had put in at Suva, in the Fiji Isles, and made contact with the American fleet by wireless. It was a quick step to put Reuters' Agent at Suva into wireless communication with Reuters' correspondent with the American fleet. Suva and Melbourne had a normal cable connection and the rest was simple. Thus Reuters' reports 'from the American fleet at sea' appeared daily in the papers of America, Australia, New Zealand and Great Britain.

During the whole of this period Canada remained outside the Reuter picture. It seems that no attempt was made to establish a service there during the nineteenth century. This would have been impossible in any case during the early days of Reuters' expansion in the 1860's and 1870's. Two decades had to follow the Confederation of 1867 before the Canadian Pacific Railway bridged vast spaces between east and west and the growth of telegraphic communication made it possible for Canadian newspapers to receive news from overseas by cable. Easy communications and geographic propinquity – a common frontier of 4,000 miles – led the Canadian newspapers to a quick acceptance of the United States as their main source of news. This fact of geography was acknowledged by Reuters and no attempt seems to have been made to bring Canada into the Reuter orbit on what might be termed Imperial grounds. Soon after the American Associated Press had made its first agreement with the European news agencies in 1893, its claim to treat Canada as coming within its own 'sphere of news interest' was confirmed. In 1894 the Associated Press made its first contract to supply news to Canadian newspapers. It was not until after the First World War that some Canadians began to turn towards Reuters as a source of British news.

Thus there was no general pattern for Reuters' activities in the Empire. Reuters never became a British Empire Agency by concentrating its main strength in the countries under the British flag. It did, however, secure a unique position in India and (as will be seen in the next chapter) in South Africa. In these two special cases an exceptionally intimate relationship grew up between Reuters and its newspaper clients, and in both countries, by entering and dominating the domestic news field, Reuters obtained and held for many years a position of immense strength and influence.

Reuters in India went from strength to strength. At about the turn of the century the career and personality of Edward Buck reflected both the India of those days and the position that Reuters had in it. Buck was appointed Reuters' Political Correspondent in India in 1897 and he came to be one of the best-known Englishmen at Simla. His published memoirs (*Simla Days*) describe the background – now so dead and distant – against which a Reuter correspondent worked in the India of those far-off days. The week-end shooting parties, the entertaining of Viceroys, the personal friendships with Lord Curzon, the Viceroy, and Lord Kitchener, the Commander-in-Chief, each quarrelling bitterly with the other – all these reflect the colourful veneer of Anglo-Indian life.

In those days Reuters was essentially part of the British scheme of things in India. It was only gradually, as the twentieth century drew forward, that the Reuter organisation began to adapt itself to the new India and the growing Indian nationalism.

Despite the calls of his busy social life, Buck found news to report all the time – wars on the North-West Frontier, Legislative Council meetings, visits of crowned heads from Europe, great festivals and durbars, expeditions to the Himalayas and Tibet.

Until World War I the Reuter organisation in India, expanding continuously with the development of a vigorous newspaper Press, kept the same pattern. Indian newspapers and merchants respected and relied upon the Reuter service: news from India flowed into London as an important component of the Reuter news service to the world.

Buck himself had a flair for being first with the news. Amiably easy-going with routine messages, he had the instinct to be at the centre of anything of importance. Reuters gave the first report to the world of the armed British Mission's arrival in Lhasa in 1904 – the first Europeans to reach the mysterious and legendary capital of Tibet. Four years later, Buck rode out himself into the hills to meet the famous Swedish explorer, Sven Hedin, after his two years in the Himalayas, and Reuters was the first to describe this remarkable journey.

But Buck's most memorable feat was his reporting of the attempt on the life of the Viceroy, Lord Hardinge, two days before Christmas 1913. A bomb thrown from a house-top pitched on the howdah of the Viceroy's elephant, as he rode in procession to the durbar to be held in the Fort of Delhi. It killed one attendant, wounded another, and severely injured the Viceroy himself. By a combination of luck and instinct Buck was outside the Delhi Gate, not far up the road, when this happened: he had decided to watch the procession, instead of going by the correspondents' special route to the Fort. For a journalist it was a unique opportunity, and Buck made the most of it. Disregarding the soldiers lining the route, he rushed into the road, obtained the facts from the commander of the Viceroy's bodyguard, and seized a telephone in a nearby shop. Within five minutes the Central Telegraph Office in Delhi was sending Buck's first brief message to London. A local censorship was then clamped down, and not even an official despatch was sent until Hardinge's condition was known. By that time Reuters had given the news in London to the King, the India Office and the Press and to the rest of the world. Inevitably, the Reuter message became the subject of a question in the House of Commons.

Three years earlier, a new Agency had been launched in India. In 1910, in Madras, was founded the Associated Press of India, a domestic news agency, collecting news throughout India for the Indian newspapers, in the same way as the Press Association collects news throughout Great Britain. It was backed by Edward Buck; but the real genius behind it was an Indian journalist who was also one of the most remarkable Indians of his time. K. C. Roy was the son of poor Hindu parents, he had little education and few prospects. But he became the most trusted and distinguished journalist in India, the confidant of every political party. A man of absolute integrity and singular charm, he owed his position among Indians to his burning belief in Indian nationalism; and among Englishmen to the wise moderation with which he forwarded it. In 1919 the Associated Press of India became wholly owned by Reuters. K. C. Roy worked loyally for Reuters until his death in 1931. His dream was to see the Associated Press of India become the great national news agency of India, owned by the Indian Press. This came to pass by agreement with Reuters and the Indian newspapers in 1948, seventeen years after Roy's death.

The First World War found Reuters' links with the Indian newspapers as close as ever. The great bulk of the news to

India from the world, and of the news from India to the world, went through Reuters. The internal news of India was dominated by the Associated Press of India. From 1919 onwards Reuters, through its ownership of the Associated Press of India, was the great domestic news agency of India as well as the great provider of world news to the growing and vigorous Indian Press.

IO

War in South Africa

FROM EARLY DAYS, REUTERS' ACTIVITIES IN SOUTH
Africa were charged with a peculiar tension. Through the
twenty years of storms that broke over South African politics,
Reuters had the task of giving the main day-to-day news to
the world. It was a task made harder by the passions involved;
and through it the Agency suffered the most searching test of
its detachment it had yet had to undergo.

Omens came early. In April 1884, Cape Town was suddenly
startled by news of the German annexation of Namaqualand
and Damaraland. Establishment of a foreign Power on the
coast to its immediate north seemed far more disturbing to the
Cape than to the distant Government in London. The High
Commissioner's representations to the Imperial Government
met with little response; they were soon followed by claims
and demands from the Cape Colony traders themselves.
Reuters' telegrams gave full reports of this agitation to the
English Press and thereby drew public attention in England to
what was happening in Africa. As a result Reuters became an
immediate target for German charges of bias. In Cape Town,
the offices of the tiny German Consul-General and of the
six-foot Reuter Agent adjoined, and soon there were violent
verbal battles each day between the two incongruously
matched men.

1884 was also the year when Reuters made contact with the
two great antagonists whose struggles decided the fate of
South Africa: Cecil Rhodes, creator of the British South Africa

Company, with his headquarters in Cape Town, capital of the British Colony of the Cape, and Paul Kruger, President of the Boer Republic of the Transvaal.

Until then there had been no Reuter correspondent in the Transvaal. As far as the Agency's activities were concerned, South Africa meant the British Cape Colony. The first Reuter reports affecting the Boer Republic were messages describing the Convention of London, settling an early British-Boer quarrel. And Paul Kruger was pleased with their impartiality. From then onwards Reuters became increasingly aware of the fact that South Africa contained two peoples – British and Dutch.

Reuters' first important contact with Cecil Rhodes followed upon the London Convention. Both Rhodes and a Reuter correspondent were with the British expedition which went north from the Cape to deal with Dutch farmers who had broken out of the Transvaal and settled in disputed territory. This expedition set the scene for Rhodes's expansive ambitions in South Africa.

In 1886 a Reuter telegram announced the discovery of gold on the Witwatersrand. The gold rush began; a new town was founded at the centre of the new riches and within six months became one of the largest in South Africa: Johannesburg. From now on Johannesburg vied with Cape Town as a centre of Reuters' South African operations.

The following year, 1887, M. J. M. Bellasyse was appointed Reuters' Chief Agent, later General Manager for South Africa. With the cable-head moved from Durban to Cape Town, and Johannesburg quickly growing in importance, he had to divide his attention between Cape Town, seat of the Cape Government, and Johannesburg, where wealth and friction were rapidly on the increase. It was between Cape Town and Johannesburg, between British and Dutch South Africa, that the tension grew which was to make the business of South African news-reporting more and more difficult.

In his first years, however, Bellasyse's many difficulties were technical, not political. During the gold-share boom of 1889, speed in getting telegrams to and from London became essential. Reuters organised a special despatch-rider service from Johannesburg to Mafeking, in order to avoid the delays invariably caused by the overcrowding of the Johannesburg cable.

In addition, Bellasyse had, in the following year, to organise a news service covering those British campaigns which were finally to lead to the founding of Rhodesia. As no correspondents were allowed to accompany the expeditions, officers in the field had to play the part of reporters. Colonel Baden-Powell, later world-famous as founder of the Boy Scout movement, proved himself an able Reuter correspondent.

Yet the real difficulties for the Agency came when the tension in Johannesburg grew and the alignment of hostile interests became clear. The position in Johannesburg of the Uitlanders – British settlers who, attracted by the new gold mines, had come to live in the Boer Republic – was the point at issue. These settlers had formed the Transvaal National Union to assert what they regarded as their rights in the Transvaal, the country in which they lived and worked. By December 1895 this organisation, through its executive organ, the Reform Committee, had become very outspoken in complaints and demands alike. Johannesburg newspapers took up definite positions in support of either the Uitlanders' Reform Committee or of Paul Kruger's nationalist Transvaal policy. Some were founded or changed ownership for the purpose of taking sides in the dispute. Soon rumours spread of preparations for an armed rising of the Uitlanders against Kruger's government. The British South Africa Company under Cecil Rhodes posted a strong police force at Pitsani, close to the Transvaal frontier. Its commander was Jameson, Administrator of Rhodesia. The tension mounted: and Reuters was besieged by requests for information from all sides, or rather – and this made the situation delicate – from supporters of both sides. Accusations of giving biased reports were inevitable, and they came from the protagonists of both camps.

In December 1895, Bellasyse left Cape Town for Johannesburg to see for himself what was happening. He was distressed by what he found. Reports were circulating that the British police force at Pitsani was on the point of invading the Transvaal in aid of the Uitlanders' Reform Committee. He wired to the Cape, demanding information from Rutherfoord Harris, Secretary of the British South Africa Company. Harris denied the allegation – and then warned the Reform Committee to be more cautious. At the same time he attacked Bellasyse for being biased in favour of the Transvaal. The result was that the Cape Town newspapers accused Reuters of partiality for Kruger.

Ironically enough, it was a Reuter telegram, sent by Bellasyse from Johannesburg, that Jameson chose as the occasion for intervening in the Transvaal with his police force. The Reuter message, dated December 28th, 1895, reported that Johannesburg was agitated by rumours of warlike preparations and that women and children were leaving the Rand. Seizing this as his pretext, on Sunday, December 29th, at 9.5 a.m. Jameson despatched from his outpost on the Transvaal frontier the following words to Harris: 'Shall leave tonight for the Transvaal . . . to prevent loss of lives . . . Reuter [meaning the above Reuter message] only just received . . . compel immediate move to fulfil promise made . . .' He also sent a telegram to Reuters in Cape Town, stating that his troops were moving east, fit for active service. Then the wires were cut.

For four days Cape Town was in suspense. Reuters' Agents waited anxiously for news, staying up until the early hours of the morning. There were many conflicting rumours. On January 2nd, 1896, Harris called a small press conference, including Reuters' Agent, to announce that Jameson had succeeded in reaching Johannesburg. The conference was dramatically disturbed by the Editor of the *South African Telegraph* rushing in with a telegram saying that Jameson had surrendered.

In Pretoria, capital of the Transvaal, Reuters' eighteen-year-old assistant correspondent was the only journalist whom Kruger would allow to see the defeated Jameson. It was this correspondent's account of Jameson, tired and jaded, that gave the first news in England of the fate of the raid. The young correspondent was Roderick Jones, many years later to become Head of Reuters.

The raid was a failure, and it was unequivocally condemned by the London Parliamentary Committee of Enquiry in 1897; but agitation against Kruger by the British population of Johannesburg increased. Many newspapers in England regarded sympathy for the Transvaal's attitude as truck with the enemy. Reuters was accused of Transvaal partiality, and the London *Daily Mail*, recently founded by the Harmsworths, led the attack. The Transvaal Government's subscription, paid, as by all other clients, for the use of Reuters' telegrams – £300 a year – was characterised by the *Daily Mail* as a 'subsidy'. At the end of June 1899, it denounced Reuters in a sensational editorial for 'trading with the enemy'. In the autumn Reuters delivered up a scapegoat, and with obvious satisfaction the *Daily Mail* reported Reuters' decision 'to make certain changes in the staff'. The truth of the matter was that Henry Collins, on his way home from Australia, had been asked by Herbert de Reuter to enquire into the allegations against Bellasyse. At the end of April, Bellasyse had come to London himself for consultations with the Baron. And the Baron was still sufficiently convinced of his impartiality to send him back to South Africa at the end of July. But, with war approaching, Reuters decided to send their much-tried foreign correspondent, H. A. Gwynne, to South Africa. The situation demanded the skill and experience of a special reporter. Gwynne was to serve under Bellasyse's general management. Soon, however, it became obvious that the two could not work together. Gwynne was an all-out enemy of Kruger, and was intolerant of even the slightest symptoms of sympathy with the Boers. Herbert de Reuter yielded to the pressure of the situation and in November dismissed Bellasyse.

Bellasyse certainly had more sympathy with Kruger than the prevalent temper of the English public would allow. He had been shaken by what he saw and heard in Johannesburg before the Jameson raid. The atmosphere among the mine-owners, and his suspicion that many of them wanted neither the British nor the Dutch flag but an independent republic of their own, weighed heavily on him. The charge of personal bribery or betrayal was totally untrue. He had been angered by Harris's furtiveness; and his sympathies and prejudices – at heart he was an Ulster farmer and country gentleman – had perhaps been too keenly involved.

Henry Collins, on his 'special mission' to Bellasyse in Johannesburg and before continuing his journey to England, reported the Bloemfontein Conference between Kruger and Milner, the new British High Commissioner in Cape Town, held in May 1899. It was the last attempt to avert war. Collins was invited to come to the Cape on the High Commissioner's special train, the moment the Conference was over. An embargo on all news had been placed for forty-eight hours. During the journey from Johannesburg the long final report of twenty-seven typewritten foolscap pages was given to Collins. His report for Reuters, written overnight in a swaying railway carriage, was despatched at the stop before the Cape. But ill luck overtook it. At Cape Town Collins was told that Kruger's representative at Brussels had already given the world the Boer version of the Conference through Reuters' Brussels correspondent, who apparently had not been told of the forty-eight-hours embargo. Moreover, a faulty cable held up Collins's report for a further two days.

With the Conference ending in a deadlock and no agreement reached on the status and political rights of the British settlers in the Transvaal, war seemed inevitable – and indeed soon broke out. Reuters prepared itself for the new situation. Gwynne wanted to get to the front. Collins, back in South Africa from London, could take charge of the Cape Town office. Gwynne, at the special request of Lord Roberts, the Commander-in-Chief, accompanied the British in their advance to Bloemfontein, Johannesburg and Pretoria. He enjoyed Roberts's complete trust and he had an old friend in Kitchener, who had been appointed Roberts's chief of staff. There could be little doubt that this big test of Reuters' Special Service to the British Press would be passed with success. Collins directed the extensive news operations from Cape Town. Practically the whole British Press relied on Reuters for the day-to-day news of sieges, relief marches and Boer commando raids. On the Boer side, Reuter correspondents had no choice but to go as fighting men. The chief Reuter correspondent in the field was J. de Villiers Roos, who later became Auditor-General of the South African Union Government. One of the most successful Reuter correspondents in the British camp was a woman, Miss Maguire, daughter of a friend of Cecil Rhodes. Three of the Agency's correspondents were killed in action.

Reuters' most spectacular exploits during the Boer War are connected with the name of Mafeking. Here, for several months, Colonel Baden-Powell and his soldiers were cut off and besieged by the Boers. A Reuter correspondent, keeping a complete record of the siege, lived with the British troops in Mafeking. Yet England, for a whole month, waited in vain for news of her soldiers. Reuters was determined to break the silence. A 'bushman', named Anderson, was engaged; he knew the country well and, despite the pervasive presence of the

Boer patrols, he managed on his bicycle to reach the neighbourhood of Mafeking. He remained undetected and, under cover of night, got into the besieged town and out again. On the following day Reuters was able to telegraph a complete record of the siege to London.

When Mafeking was finally relieved, not long afterwards, Reuters was first with the news. This was due to the enterprise of Reuters' Pretoria correspondent, W. H. Mackay, who was sufficiently trusted by the Boers to be allowed to remain in the Republican capital. The British column marching to the relief of Mafeking was far from its base and out of telegraphic touch with the rest of the world and with Roberts's headquarters; and the Boers, who had the news and gave it to Mackay, were confident that their censorship would prevent any information from getting through to England. But Mackay defeated the censorship. He rushed with his news to the frontier with Portuguese East Africa and bribed the engine driver of a train destined for Lorenzo Marques. There his telegram was delivered to the Eastern Telegraph Company's office. It is said that Mackay had given the engine driver £5 to put the message inside one of his luncheon sandwiches. It reached Reuters in London at 9.15 p.m. on Friday, May 18th, 1900. Within a few minutes copies had been sent to the Queen, the Prime Minister and the Lord Mayor, who read it from the steps of the Mansion House. Special editions of the evening papers soon spread the news and almost immediately London was in the throes of the jubilant and boisterous demonstrations which resulted in adding the word 'mafficking' to the English vocabulary. That same night, Joseph Chamberlain, the Colonial Secretary, said in reply to questions in the House of Commons, that confirmation had not reached the Government, but that 'he had no reason to doubt the accuracy of Reuters' information'. The news had already been sent round the world by Reuters and in this way came back from London to Cape

Town. Thus Lord Roberts himself, Commander-in-Chief in the field, received the news: he trusted Reuters and read the message to his troops at Bloemfontein on Sunday church parade. It was only the next day that the official despatch reached the British headquarters overland from Mafeking. The Queen requested that the original Reuter telegram should be sent to her. For two days both the British and Cape Governments, and the Army headquarters, had had to rely solely upon Mackay's telegram.

The difficulties of a news agency in periods of international crisis were demonstrated first by the *Daily Mail*'s anger at Reuters' alleged bias for Kruger between the Jameson raid and the outbreak of war, and later, during the war itself, by German attacks on the Agency's British partiality. Wolff, under the contractual news-exchange arrangements, used Reuters' South African reports; and he thus found himself exposed to the criticism of the German Press. British resentment of the Kaiser's famous telegram of sympathy to Kruger increased Anglo-German tension, and this made Wolff's position in Germany by no means easy. The result was the springing into existence of a number of 'independent' German news agencies with a marked Anglophobe flavour. Some of their reports went so far as to invent news of Boer victories with Pretoria, Johannesburg or Cape Town shown as datelines of fabricated telegrams. One of these Agencies, the 'Kabel-Korrespondenz', was, until its methods were exposed in Germany by the London correspondent of the *Hamburger Zeitung*, selling its news concoctions to about fifty German newspapers. Modern nationalism was beginning to find its methods of counterfeiting truth under the guise of news.

The Boer War affected Reuters in two ways. The prestige of the Agency was increased: its profits were reduced. The expense of maintaining war correspondents had been enormous and many South African newspapers whose subscriptions would have helped to meet Reuters' costs had ceased to appear.

In South Africa the British newspapers closed their ranks and demanded a voice in the selection of the news sent to them from London. Herbert de Reuter decided to inaugurate a South African Department in London under an editor with a full knowledge of South African affairs. Roderick Jones, who had become Reuters' chief correspondent in Cape Town, was transferred to London in 1902 as Reuters' first South African editor. This was the first recognition by Reuters that the newspaper users of the service had a right to be consulted: the first move towards a greater flexibility and a system of devolution in the handling of news. This policy of a closer association between newspaper buyer and Agency provider of news has become one of the most significant and important features of Reuters' modern development.

But this early experiment had soon to face a major crisis, and it had to be remoulded before complete harmony between Reuters and the South African newspapers was achieved. In 1908, a group of South African newspapers formed a syndicate with the intention of supplying a service of cabled news from London for the South African Press. The newspaper group offered Reuters a partnership in its syndicate; but the joint organisation was to have the right to withhold its service from any newspaper it pleased. Roderick Jones, whom the Baron had sent back to South Africa as General Manager, was summoned by the group at a few hours' notice to a conference to accept or reject this offer. His rejection of it was endorsed by London; and he now had to run the Reuter sevice in competition with the new 'South African Amalgamated Press Agency', which the group now established with the intention of driving Reuters out of South Africa. But a South African newspaper group could not succeed against the world news resources of Reuters; and after a year the struggle was abandoned. Roderick Jones, as Herbert de Reuter's representative, negotiated with the newspaper group the formation of a jointly owned Reuter South African Press Agency – 60 per cent owned by Reuters and 40 per cent by the group. The interests of the smaller newspapers were protected and, by calling this agreement a 'co-operative covenant', Reuters expressed its feeling that it had answered the demand for partnership voiced by the South African newspapers without damaging the position which Reuters had built up for itself as the basic distributor both of domestic and overseas news in South Africa.

Meanwhile, political reporting had become centred on the movement for a South African union. Reuters' telegrams kept the English public informed about the proceedings, in so far as the news was released for publication, of the National Convention which sat in secret between October 1908 and February 1909. By the time of the proclamation of the Union on May 31st, 1910, Roderick Jones could declare with justice that under Reuters' leadership the South African Press was stronger and more united than it had ever been before. Reuters was to remain in fact the national news agency of South Africa for nearly thirty years – and it is still today the principal provider of world news to all the newspapers of South Africa, Afrikaans and English alike.

Death of the Founder

ON FEBRUARY 25TH, 1899, JULIUS DE REUTER DIED AT his villa on the Promenade des Anglais at Nice. The world Press printed this terse announcement: 'Baron de Reuter, the founder of Reuters' Agency, died at Nice this morning in his eighty-third year. – REUTER.' The source of the message itself was his most appropriate epitaph. *The Times* referred to him as 'one of the most intelligent men of his day'. 'No daily newspaper', wrote the *Sun*, 'could afford to dispense with Reuters' service of foreign intelligence.' The *Daily News* called him 'one of the pioneers of modern journalism'. The Press expressed its gratitude to a 'pioneer of telegraphic intelligence'. The *Daily Telegraph* obituary notice would probably have pleased Julius de Reuter most of all: 'This important telegraphic agency has been conducted in the face of great temptations with an impartiality and integrity that are beyond praise.'

His body was brought back from France and buried in South London. His funeral, in the presence of only his family, a few friends and the representatives of the Agency, was in accordance with his personal modesty and complete lack of ostentation. His monument was Reuters itself, which continued to be guided by the tradition he had created.

Julius de Reuter had seen his Agency's fortunes righted again after a period of financial anxiety. The costly competition from Dalziel had led Herbert de Reuter to venture upon several purely commercial subsidiaries. Imitation of Havas in using the Agency's ramifications for advertising had been suggested by Engländer as early as 1876. Herbert had then expressed his dislike of the idea, confirmed in it by the Manager of the *Daily News* who said that 'such business would tend to lower the Telegraphic Service in the eyes of the Press'. Unfortunately, in the crisis of 1890, such susceptibilities were brushed aside. An agreement was made with a firm of advertising agents in London, £30,000 extra capital was raised, and Reuters' Advertisements Branch launched in 1891. The ubiquitous Engländer was its greatest protagonist, but he totally lacked both the necessary specialised knowledge and commercial experience. All the advertising experiments ended in failure, the most typical and financially the most disastrous being concerned with the Chicago Exhibition of 1892. Reuters believed that it had acquired the European monopoly for the sale of the Exhibition's guide book, and told its advertisers so. Unfortunately no such monopoly existed. Instead of a hundred thousand copies, as originally proposed, only two thousand could be distributed by the Agency. A host of actions from the angry advertisers followed. Not surprisingly, the Advertisement Department closed down in 1894 with a loss of over £27,000. It was salutary to the Agency and to its whole position within British journalism that this enterprise came to nothing. But the lesson was expensive for Reuters. No dividends were paid for 1893 or 1894; and in the latter year Reuters' £8 shares went down to £3, their lowest point.

Fortunately, two other subsidiary enterprises flourished and made up for what the advertisements had lost—the Private Telegrams service and a new Telegraph Remittance business. The financial crisis in Australia of 1893, and the heavy speculation in gold-mining shares in Western Australia and South Africa, ensured the success of the Remittance business by increasing the public's zest for cabling money. By the year before Baron Julius's death, the advertisement losses had been more than made good.

In spite of these financial difficulties and the energy diverted into subsidiary activities, the real Reuter tradition – the tradition of the news service – remained intact. It had its centre in the friendship and trust that prevailed between Herbert de Reuter and his Chief Editor, G. D. Williams, who had been responsible for Herbert's own training in the office. The two main tenets of this tradition were expressly stated for the first time in the contract of May 1878 which made Herbert Managing Director. After giving him the 'sole and entire management of telegraphic intelligence', it went on: 'and it shall be his duty to communicate such telegraphic intelligence equally and impartially to all subscribers for the same fees without giving priority to any one over another'. The other principle, that of impartiality in the news service, rested on the provision that there should be no outside interference, at any time, with editorial direction. Throughout his forty years with the Agency, Herbert de Reuter regarded both principles as equally inviolable.

Abroad, despite new demands made by ever-changing situations, the pattern of Reuters' offices remained much the same. They reflected the organisation of the Head Office in London, and still corresponded in many points with 'the large and varied establishments which Mr. Reuter has on the Continent', described in charming detail by James Grant in *The Newspaper Press* in 1871:

I will furnish some idea of how the matter is managed, by describing the organisation which existed in Paris some years ago, under Mr. Reuter's superintendence. He has an office there in a prominent place, and connected with it, as described to me by one, of all others, best fitted to give a faithful description, there were then five parties, each of whom had his own special department in the working of the telegraphic machinery. The highest in Mr. Reuter's service in Paris is a gentleman alike in manners and education. His duty is to call, on stated occasions, on one of the leading officials holding a position which enables him to acquire such information as Mr. Reuter requires. During Louis Napoleon's reign, the party whom Mr. Reuter's principal agent in Paris most frequently saw, was the Emperor's secretary; but whether Louis Napoleon's secretary or not, there was always some reliable party from whom correct and exclusive information was to be had. His salary was a few years ago £10.10.0 per week and I have reason to believe it is higher now because of the great increase which has taken place in the telegraphic business in the French capital since then. There was another party under him who rendered services which required a man who at once possessed capacity to do a certain kind of work, and so high a character for integrity, that every confidence might be placed in him. His salary is, or lately was, £7.7.0 per week. He is the chief in the office which, if I remember rightly, was in the Palais Royal. The duty of a third is to examine all the Continental papers, and prepare for telegraphic purposes anything of importance which he meets with. His salary is £5.5.0 per week. There is a fourth in the establishment whose duty it is to prepare the information which it is intended to send to the metropolitan daily papers. For his services he receives £3.3.0 per week. And lastly there is a fifth, whose sole duty consists in carrying the messages to the Government telegraph station, and to see that they are properly despatched. For this inferior work he receives £80 per annum, or about that amount.

Grant's hopeful belief that the salaries had increased was true to a point; but to a point only. The other side to the family-business atmosphere was that many of its staff were expected to work as much for love of the institution as for their salaries – salaries which remained in many cases extraordinarily low, considering the high responsibilities involved.

The decade following the end of the South African War favoured the news service in every respect. It was a reflection of England's buoyancy at the beginning of the new century. Success in war, expansion of trade, technical advance in communications, and the drawing together of imperial ties, were all reflected in the Agency. At the Board Meeting in October 1901, the Jubilee of its foundation, the Chairman was able to announce that the celebration 'coincided with a period of unprecedented prosperity in the business of the Company'.

The competition of the early 'nineties had, in the event, done only good. From its very beginning, the Special Service, Reuters' answer to Dalziel, had been a great success. Backed by the Press Association, it gave the provincial papers what the London papers could afford to get for themselves. Soon the London papers became subscribers as well. The new service began, as we have seen, candidly sensationalist, with the main intent of defeating Dalziel's competition. Its appeal would be to the new class of newspaper-readers catered for by Harmsworth and Pearson. The first correspondent sent to the Continent under the new scheme was told that he should model his reports on, and compete with, Dalziel's service for *The Times*. He was E. A. Brayley Hodgetts, who had been the St. Petersburg correspondent of the *Daily Graphic*. He was sent to Berlin, and within three months *The Times* took the new Reuter service in place of Dalziel's.

It was not so much the substance as the new tone of Hodgetts's reports that counted. The thing was to add a more personal emphasis to the stereotyped and official bulletins issued by Wolff. The eye-witness accounts of von Moltke's funeral, and of the unveiling of the Holy Coat at Trier (a ceremony that takes place only once in forty years) pleased Herbert de Reuter – and pleased the English public. A personal interview with the leader of the new German Social Democratic Party, August Bebel, some of which he denied dramatically in the German Press, was in the best tradition of W. T. Stead's sensational interviews for the *Pall Mall Gazette*.

With Dalziel conquered, the service could evolve more freely. What started as a special weapon became a new attitude. It followed the new readers, trained by Harmsworth and Pearson, into their new political interests and prejudices, as presented in the *Daily Mail* and the *Daily Express*. Pride in the

Empire demanded expression. Reuters gave British communities all over the world a new series of identical news messages, 'dropped off' on the way at each destination; called the 'Omnibus Service', it flourished during the Imperial Conferences initiated by Joseph Chamberlain.

A new interest in politics had arisen among a broader public, which demanded more information about the mounting diplomatic tension throughout Europe. To the old official communiqués and diplomatic despatches Reuters now added political comments and the 'opinions of informed circles'. The Special Service was not used as a pretext for a departure from Reuters' principle of accuracy. It remained, as it still is today, an absolute rule of the Agency that all sources must be shown. Views can be reported; but the correspondent is never allowed to mix his own interpretation with the facts.

With growing political excitement in Europe, Reuters' best correspondents were soon being sent to supplement the service of the Continental Agencies. Special missions, interviews and calls on Government representatives made the Agency's work more and more like that of a newspaper. A circular sent out in 1902 to all Reuter Agents requested information on the latest movements of 'explorers to and from expeditions, statesmen, naval and military officers, missionaries'. 'Persons of public interest' had to be interviewed 'before the other newspaper representatives have an opportunity of doing so'.

These projects increased under the new Chief Editor appointed on G. D. Williams's retirement in the spring of 1902. F. W. Dickinson, an exact contemporary of Herbert de Reuter (he had been at preparatory school with him), joined Reuters' editorial staff in 1874. An excellent linguist and a serious student of international affairs all his life, he was a good choice as successor to Williams. With regard to the Agency's tradition, he kept a balanced sense of perspective through his twenty years' editorship. He fully favoured the Special Service and the new

143

methods it called for; but, trained in the 'seventies, he also stood for adherence to more established Reuter principles. Under his editorship, special missions and interviews became a normal part of the Reuter service, and he obtained a privilege for Reuters' diplomatic correspondent in London which until then had been reserved for *The Times*: daily calls at Government offices. From now on, Reuters was able to join *The Times* in its encroachments upon Foreign Office aloofness.

In this new sphere of Reuters' activity, H. A. Gwynne, in particular, distinguished himself. In 1904, after more war-reporting in the Balkans and after accompanying Joseph Chamberlain on his visit to South Africa, he was appointed Reuters' Foreign Director. But his political interests were too deep for him to remain for long the politically detached observer: the same year he became Editor of the *Standard*, and seven years later he began the work that really satisfied him – his long editorship of the *Morning Post*.

The public concern for politics had a deeper reason than merely the growing-up of a new reading public. By the turn of the century it was clear that the age of English 'splendid isolation' from the affairs of Europe had passed. The new commitments on the Continent were inevitably reflected in the Press. The years that saw the stage set for the First World War – the break-down of hopes of an Anglo-German alliance, the Anglo-French Entente, the Anglo-Russian Convention, and the inevitable crises caused by the growing antagonism of Germany – were naturally years of extreme journalistic activity. The more serious-minded newspapers accepted it as their duty to inform their readers as accurately as possible of the state of affairs in Europe. Reuters' duty became the increasingly harder one of maintaining objectivity. The main danger-spot was Berlin: and the Press, wittingly or unwittingly, could make things worse by accentuating the strains already obvious enough in Anglo-German relations. The judgment of one of the most searching critics of the Press during this period is anything but friendly. 'From the outbreak of the Russo-Japanese War to Algeciras', writes Professor Oron James Hale in *Germany and the Diplomatic Revolution* (Philadelphia, 1931), 'Anglo-German relations formed an unbroken chain of misunderstandings, false statements, malicious suppositions, invidious mistrust and acrimonious polemics. While official relations were correct, if not cordial, the Press seemed bent on maintaining such an atmosphere of suspicion and hostility in the public mind that an incident might have precipitated an armed conflict.' But this criticism was mitigated by his acknowledgment that Reuters' correspondents in Berlin confined themselves to straight factual reporting of spot-news and its background, with the emphasis on completeness and accuracy.

The situation in Berlin was complicated by the position of Wolff. To gain influence over the Berlin Agency was one of the main aims of Otto Hammann, chief of the Press Department of the German Foreign Office. It was a policy as congenial to his new masters, Caprivi and Holstein, as it had been to Bismarck. The results to Reuters were twofold. Wolff, from the Boer War onwards, was constantly criticised by the German Government for its dependence on Reuters and Havas for foreign news; and one of the healthier results of this criticism was the appointment of a regular Wolff correspondent in London.

The chief embarrassment to Wolff, as to many German Ministers, was the Kaiser. His flair for publicity was alternately a terror and a delight to the professional correspondent. To the German Agency it was a source of keen anxiety. Its editors found themselves constantly obliged to take off the rough edges of some of the Kaiser's speeches before publication to the world.

Austin Harrison, Reuters' chief correspondent in Berlin, had to deal with the repercussions of such an imperial pronouncement during his first year. In July 1900, the Kaiser made an extraordinary speech to his Marines before they embarked on the international expedition to China to take revenge on the Boxer rebels for killing Baron von Ketteler, the German Minister in Peking. He exhorted them to behave like, 'a thousand years ago, the Huns under their King Attila, who made such a name for themselves as still resounds in terror through legend and fable'. 'Give no quarter,' he told his Marines, 'take no prisoner, kill him when he falls into your hands.' The German Government successfully induced Wolff to play down the words of its Kaiser. Harrison sent the right version to London, and evoked deep resentment in Berlin. Herbert de Reuter gave him his full support. 'I am greatly indebted to you for your statement concerning the action of Wolff in partly withholding and garbling the Emperor's speeches in reference to the German expedition to China,' he wrote to him. 'We shall . . . trust to your good offices to watch such incidents in the future so as to be able to remedy these Bowdlerising methods on the part of the Wolff Bureau.' In a private letter, four days later, he referred to the speech as 'an outburst that might have suited Ajax, but is simply astounding in the mouth of a European Potentate'.

By the time that Valentine Williams succeeded Harrison in Berlin in 1904, the situation had become still more precarious and individual crises more disturbing; and the Agency had, on many occasions, to make it its business to soothe both French and German feelings.

In 1907 Lord Haldane, the British Minister for War, staying as a guest of the Kaiser, attended a parade of the Prussian Guards, which, following close on Sedan Day, was regarded by the French as part of the German celebrations of their national defeat. It was hard to calm French susceptibilities. Haldane had to point out, first, that the official Sedan celebrations were over at the time of the parade, and, secondly, that he was a spectator in civilian dress; and thirdly, he asked

Reuters to publish to the world the fact that the same day he had called officially on the French Ambassador.

The next year a blustering speech by the Kaiser at a military review at Dobritz called forth intense activity from both Wolff and Reuters to calm European panic, as alarmed reports quoted the Kaiser as saying: 'Yes, it now appears as if they wanted to encircle us. We will know how to bear that. Just let them come and we are ready.' Five days later, an article in the *Norddeutsche Zeitung*, inspired by Prince Bülow, maintained that the speech had been incorrectly reported and denied the use of the word 'encircle'. Reuters circulated this as a semi-official pronouncement.

Many times, during the uneasy years that led up to the First World War, the Agency had to play this new and unaccustomed role of a European agent for peace.

12

The End of the Family Business

THE END OF THE FIRST DECADE OF THE TWENTIETH century saw Reuters' prosperity at its height. The increase in revenue and reserves from 1898 to 1908 is striking. The annual revenue from all sources went up from £140,000 to close on £200,000. Reserves at the turn of the century were less than £30,000: by 1910 they had become £100,000. The cautious policy of not paying more than 5 per cent dividends during the last fifteen years had borne fruit.

Much of this profit came from the Telegraph Remittance business; but the increasing sums involved were causing anxiety. In practical terms it was a logical decision in 1910 to found a Banking Department. The principles of this policy were not closely examined. The banking business was to be kept entirely separate from the news agency itself, and the possibility of any collision between the two interests was never considered. Although the venture turned out far from well for Reuters, it did not affect the news service, except to shake its financial basis.

The Bank came into existence in the spring of 1912, after an appeal for more share-capital. The public were invited to subscribe for £10 shares, and a bonus of 25 per cent was allotted to the existing shareholders on their fully paid shares of £8. The result was a large influx of capital, and a dispersal of Reuter shares among a much increased public. Two years later 'Reuter's Bank' changed its name to 'The British Commercial Bank', the new Company's paid-up capital of £500,000 being

148

held by Reuters itself. Its head office was at 43, Coleman Street – a discreet distance from 24, Old Jewry – and Herbert de Reuter was Managing Director.

With new capital to support him, Herbert de Reuter once more tried to retrieve the previous disasters of the Advertisements Branch. In the autumn of 1913, 'Reuters' Financial Publicity Department' was founded. Circulars were sent out to business houses setting forth the advantages they would gain by giving their advertising business to Reuters. Attention was drawn to the Agency's size, its influence and its cordial relations with City editors. But no scheme was likely to provoke more hostility from the Press and from regular advertising agents; and, after strong attacks from both, the new Department was abruptly closed down. It was Reuters' last attempt to imitate Havas's success with advertising. Criticism of this final venture made it quite clear that the Agency owed its alliance and its chief responsibility to the Press.

It was a foretaste of worse anxieties to come. The First World War was the greatest crisis Reuters had yet had to face. Other wars had brought their local expenses; a total European war could only be crippling. At one blow went all Reuters' revenue from every enemy country; communications were disrupted; the whole future was uncertain. There were two further and more acute anxieties: suspicion over Reuters' relations with Wolff, growing as anti-German hysteria mounted in London – and the precariousness of Reuter's Bank.

In September 1914, the despatches of Sir Edward Goschen, British Ambassador in Berlin, on German plans to establish a secret semi-official Company to spread official news of Germany abroad, were published as a White Paper. It stated that the new German Company, substantially financed from the German Foreign Office secret service funds, 'has entered into an agreement with Agence Havas that the latter will in future only publish news concerning Germany if supplied through

Wolff's Telegraph Bureau. The latter will receive its German news exclusively from the new Company. The Company intends to make a similar arrangement with Reuters for those foreign countries in which Reuters controls telegraph communications.' The White Paper created a hubbub in the news-agency world. The plan was a brilliant stroke by Hammann, the Head of the German Press Bureau, not only to spread German propaganda, but to embarrass the other news agencies. The scheme, hatched at a secret meeting between the German Foreign Office and a group of powerful German industrialists, led by Krupp, was virtually an immense plan to bribe the foreign Press. The chief German industrialists would in future only advertise in foreign papers which confined their German news to despatches from the new German Company. Wolff was to be an intermediary, and the despatches delivered free or at a nominal price.

The new Company's cleverest move was to spread abroad that its agreement with Havas had already been made and that it was intending to make a similar one with Reuters. Both the English and French news agencies immediately became targets for suspicion. Wolff had in fact approached Havas, but had been rebutted, while its 'intentions to make a similar arrangement with Reuters' had not yet come into the open. Élie Mercadier, the London correspondent of Havas and a prominent member of the French colony in London, at once denied any such agreement in a letter to The Times, and three days later this denial was issued by the Press Bureau in London and published in the Press. The White Paper was revised to read that 'the agreement, whilst apparently intended by the German Company, was not in fact entered into, or indeed ever contemplated by the Agence Havas'.

Herbert de Reuter was questioned by Sir Edmund Robbins, Manager of the Press Association, about any German approaches to him. Herbert then invited The Times to send a representative to investigate the position, and, in a subsequent letter to the paper, wrote: 'Our relations with Wolff were confined to the mutual exchange of news as obtained between all principal agencies. Neither Wolff nor we ever exercised or sought to exercise the least influence over the other, being perfectly free to publish or suppress news so received at our sole discretion.' In any case, Reuters' relations with Wolff had ceased at the outbreak of war.

In the prevalent atmosphere of suspicion, directed particularly against any international concern with a past alliance with Germany, it was inevitable that Reuters should be a target. In fact, the old international news Treaties between the three chief Agencies had few provisions against the rabid nationalism of 1914. The real answer to Reuters' critics was that, ever since Hammann's policy of exerting Government control over the German Press, Reuters had been subject to calumny all over Germany. In the last news Treaty of 1900, Reuters had been finally ousted from Hamburg by Wolff's threat to break off all relations. During the war German abuse of Reuters constantly increased in violence.

The Bank gave further acute anxieties. Its Manager, a Hungarian national, was spending a holiday in Austria in the summer of 1914, was caught there when war was declared, and conscripted into the Austro-Hungarian army. Several German and Austrian members of the staff in London were interned. For a time the Bank was closed altogether; and by the beginning of 1915 Reuters' £10 shares, which before the war reached £12.10.0, dropped to £6, and were still steadily decreasing. No dividends were declared after the outbreak of war, and any profits made were written off for contingencies. Herbert de Reuter began the new year extremely depressed and anxious.

On Thursday, April 15th, 1915, Herbert was working late at Old Jewry when a telephone message came that his wife had died suddenly. She had been at the house near Reigate which the Reuters rented for the summer. For many years she had been an invalid, and he had given his devoted care to her. He went there immediately, in an utterly stricken state. He hardly spoke to a soul. Three days later, on the afternoon of Sunday, April 18th, he was found shot by his own hand in the summer-house in the grounds. A letter by his side addressed to the 'Spirit of my dear wife' ended with the two lines in Greek from Sophocles' *Œdipus Coloneus*: 'to go as quickly as possible thither whence one has come is much the second-best thing'. His whole outlook on life had been that of a Stoic. It is hard to think that his death was not the final consummation of resigned fatalism.

He was just sixty-three. For close on forty years he had devoted himself to the Agency. A few weeks earlier, the London staff had shown their acknowledgement of that devotion, in an address presented to him on the Company's Jubilee. His father had the excitements and pains of Reuters' creation, but from 1872 onwards was mainly preoccupied with his Persian Concession. Herbert had to carry on the immense responsibilities of the Agency through its most difficult period. He never gave up his many intellectual interests, nor his passion for music; but his main working life was given to Reuters. Something of the great influence which the quality of his mind had on the Agency is reflected in a tribute that Melville E. Stone, the great General Manager of the Associated Press of America, once paid to him: 'During twelve years of intimate intercourse he has shown at all times journalistic qualities of a very high order. A man of brilliant intellect, scholarly, modest and having a keen sense of the immense responsibility of his office, but of nervous temperament and tireless energy, he has shared every impulse to reach a higher level of excellence in the service.'

A year and a half later the last male descendant in the direct line of the Reuter family fell in action, fighting with the Black

Watch on the Somme. Hubert de Reuter, Herbert's only son, had joined the Essex Regiment as a Second Lieutenant at the beginning of 1915 at the age of nearly forty. The same year he resigned his commission and enlisted as a private in the Black Watch. He was killed carrying in wounded men under heavy machine-gun fire, and, his Colonel wrote, 'would have gained a very high decoration had he lived'.

Hubert's personality had drifted away from the sober rational efficiency of the founder. It had taken Herbert himself some time to overcome this tendency; but his rebellion against joining the Agency had lasted for only a year. In his turn, he wanted his son to work by his side. But here he faced temperamental opposition far stronger than his own had been. Hubert had many of his father's eccentricities; but with him they were more deeply ingrained and more decisive. His real interests were German romantic poetry, German philosophy, and music. Whatever the weather or the temperature, he was to be seen walking around in an overcoat, with an umbrella and a small leather bag containing French translations of the works of Kant and Schopenhauer. He began – under protest – to work for the Agency, first in Constantinople under Werndel, then in Australia. Later, he tried his hand on the editorial desk in London. Everything proved uncongenial. Finally, his father gave up, and Hubert became a schoolmaster.

Hubert was the last near-link of the family with the Agency. But if the family's own dynasty within Reuters had ended, the name went on; and, traditionally ending every despatch of the Agency, it is still essentially that of Julius Reuter, Telegraphic Agent, of Royal Exchange Buildings, London.

Herbert de Reuter's death marks, in more than one sense, the end of the first part of the Reuter story. Under his directorship, a Victorian family business had gradually changed with a changing world. The numerous failures of subsidiary enterprises which Herbert launched are symptoms of the difficulties of adaptation. The new difficulties facing the Agency during the period between the two World Wars, extending into the Second, follow a different pattern. With power politics becoming more and more intricate, and national and social self-consciousness growing in all parts of the world, freedom from Government interference, and indeed the necessity to demonstrate this in the news service, became the major issue. American competition, and the New Continent's sensitivity to any signs of 'British propaganda', gave rise to problems and conflicts. Slowly the concept gained ground that a news agency should be owned by the Press it served and that there should be a far greater degree of freedom in international news exchange than the old exclusive European news Treaties allowed. The second part of the story of Reuters is largely that of these new developments.

PART II

FIGHT FOR LIFE

1915-1941

Mightier and more dangerous than fleet or army is Reuter.

BERLINER TAGEBLATT
(SEPTEMBER 1918)

News makes all of us inhabitants of a world community, subject to world changes and world ideas. Day and night, every second of each day, news travels from everywhere to the wires of the great world press associations. Within a fraction of a second it is available to the people wherever there is a newspaper or a radio receptive and free. The world is indeed not only like a small town, but the smallest town is an inescapable part of the world. International news is the most far-reaching and powerful force in modern civilisation. News as an international force may extend or curtail nationalism, strengthen or destroy democracies, and bring peace or war.

ANNUAL REPORT OF
CARL W. ACKERMAN,
DEAN OF THE SCHOOL OF JOURNALISM,
COLUMBIA UNIVERSITY, NEW YORK
SEPTEMBER 24, 1934

13

The New Company

THE SIX MONTHS FOLLOWING HERBERT DE REUTER'S death were the blackest in Reuters' history. The spirit behind the news service seemed gone; the majority of the Board were more anxious about the state of the Reuter Bank. Rumours about the Agency's critical financial position were widespread. The great European news-exchange contracts – the life of the Agency for half a century – were in abeyance: Wolff of Berlin, the Korrespondenz-Bureau of Vienna were enemies. The Bank, with its foreign investments frozen, was in as precarious a situation as the news service. The prohibition applying to all private cabling codes under the Defence of the Realm Act killed the Traffic Department: in 1915 that meant a loss in revenue of £34,000. On the Stock Exchange Reuters' £10 shares were being quoted at £3.0.9.

This was more than a domestic crisis in a great firm. Political events had accelerated a process already obvious in the European Agencies. After a year of war, Wolff and Havas were acting avowedly and aggressively as national Agencies. Mounting patriotism in Britain demanded a reply. If Reuters failed now, there would certainly be pressure on the Government to act.

There was no obvious successor to Herbert de Reuter as working Head of the Agency. The Chairman, Mark F. Napier, now in his twenty-seventh year on the Reuter Board, saw the responsibilities involved. Likeable and respected – 'one of the most lovable men I've known', as his lifelong friend Herbert Asquith, Britain's Prime Minister, said of him in *Memories and*

Reflections – he carried in himself something of the atmosphere of Reuters' past. The present crisis clearly called for the help of a a younger man.

In July 1915, Roderick Jones, still in charge of Reuters at Cape Town, sailed from South Africa to advance his claims for succession. He was thirty-seven and almost unknown outside South Africa. But he had much to favour him. He had served the Agency for twenty years, the last ten in charge of its considerable interests in South Africa. He had won there a considerable reputation as a journalist and administrator. And he came to London with a strong personal recommendation to Mark Napier from Lord Gladstone, who had been the first Governor-General of South Africa.

For the rest of the summer W. F. Bradshaw, who for so many years had been Secretary of the Company, acted as Manager. But this was only an *interregnum* and he retired in the autumn. In September the Board appointed Roderick Jones to take over Herbert de Reuter's duties, and S. Carey Clements Secretary of the Company.

By now there was a division on the Reuter Board. Mark Napier was concerned about the news agency; the rest of the Board about the future of the Bank. Convinced about the urgency of improving the news service, Napier and Roderick Jones were thrown increasingly together. They were certain that only a drastic reorganisation could save Reuters – a change not only of structure, but of policy.

They now decided in effect that Reuters' only hope lay in adopting a new and explicitly patriotic role: in placing its resources and experience at the disposal of the Allied cause. In Reuters' critical situation this appeared the only realistic decision. The dangers, as both men well knew, were great. For the rest of the war, Reuters must serve the State without succumbing to Government control: it had also to persuade the world that its freedom remained intact.

In this policy the first essential was to give the organisation an absolutely British complexion. With little capital between them, Mark Napier and Roderick Jones decided on the ambitious plan of forming a small group to buy up the entire Reuter shareholding and to create a new private company. By the autumn of 1916, they had found friends to back them. Lord Glenconner, Chairman of the Union Bank of Scotland, Lord Peel, a Director of the London and Provincial Bank, Sir Starr Jameson, of Jameson raid fame and now President of the British South Africa Company, offered the project their support. With their backing, on the security of the Bank's assets and the Old Jewry property, the Union Bank of Scotland was prepared to advance a loan of £550,000. In November 1916, the 1,200 holders of Reuters' 50,000 shares accepted the offer of £550,000 for their entire shareholding, and shortly afterwards 'Reuter's Telegram Company' ceased to exist.

A private company – to be called 'Reuters Limited' – was then incorporated. There were no changes in the staff; nor in editorial policy. F. W. Dickinson retained his control as Chief Editor. Mark Napier remained Chairman. The three Directors associated with the interests of Reuter's Bank stayed on the Board, so long as Reuters kept the Bank. John Buchan, a friend of Roderick Jones, became a Director. He had already made a name as a *Times* war correspondent in France. With two years' gap, when he was Director of the Department of Information and later in the Ministry formed from it, Buchan remained a Director of Reuters until his appointment as Governor-General of Canada in 1935. It soon became clear that Roderick Jones, appointed Managing Director 'with enlarged powers', was to be the dominating spirit on the new Board.

There was a new feeling of confidence. £11 had been paid for shares which had sunk during the first year of the war to just over £3. The Press looked upon the reorganisation with favour. *The Times* expressed its satisfaction; the *Observer* supported it as a 'patriotic undertaking' in a time of national crisis. Reuter's Bank, a valuable potential asset, but an embarrassing burden to the Agency during the war, was then sold for nearly £500,000 to a financial group. This group wanted the Bank in order to be able to issue the unissued capital of 50,000 £10 shares, which was half of the authorised capital of £1,000,000. By the end of 1917, the Reuter loan from the Union Bank of Scotland had been reduced to £50,000.

Roderick Jones now applied himself to cementing Reuters' new relations with the Government. The danger was that Reuters would be laid open to the charge abroad of using its position as an independent world Agency to disseminate British propaganda. But arrangements were made for Reuters to send out a service of Allied communiqués and official news to neutral countries, the British Empire and to Allied troops, as a special service entirely separated from the general Reuter service. This service was given the special prefix 'Agency' – or 'Agence Reuter' – instead of just 'Reuter'. The Government financed this service by paying the transmission costs of the telegrams – a total of £120,000 per annum.

Reuters had to persuade the outside world that the news transmitted at Government cost was free of Government influence. It would not have been reasonable to expect the Germans to be convinced; but there was now a striking change from the emotional hatred of Reuters in Germany at the beginning of the war to a reasoned analysis, sometimes even approaching admiration.

During the first years of the war Germany had no doubts about Reuters' villainy. Hysterical charges in the Press were echoed more scientifically in a pamphlet published in 1915 called *Los von Reuter und Havas!* ('Be rid of Reuter and Havas!'), alleging the persistent anti-German policy of the English and French news agencies.

In March 1917, *Kladderadatsch*, the German comic news-paper, devoted a whole issue to Reuters, called 'Reuter (Lies) Number'. On its front and back sheets were full-page cartoons depicting Reuters. The first presented a strange human creature clad in a long-tailed black coat, white waistcoat and breeches and spurred boots, striding along the top of telegraph wires. From his gaping mouth issued forked tongues which resolved themselves into more telegraph wires, while from a huge cornucopia he scattered a shower of miniature alligators, cray-fish and other creatures, representing Reuters' news. The back-page cartoon showed a monstrous globe upon which perched a sort of Caliban with huge claws from which issued cable lines stretching over the universe. Beneath was the legend '*Die Lüge ist der Welt Gesetz – dies lehrt das Reuter-Kabelnetz*' ('The lie is the law of the world – so teaches the Reuter cable network').

By the end of the summer this tone was beginning to change to a mixture of annoyance at Reuters' success and reluctant admiration. On August 15th, 1917, the *Vossische Zeitung* corre-spondent in Holland used Reuters as a stick with which to beat Wolff. 'When the Entente achieves successes', he wrote, 'the Amsterdam newsboys run about shouting with extra editions, and vivacious groups form in the streets. We might march into Petrograd or Paris tomorrow, but if Reuter shows the honest neutral that this is of no importance, he is believed. Reuter rules the market, not Wolff; London makes foreign opinion, not Berlin. We Germans have remained, despite all our exer-tions as regards impressing foreign opinion, the same bunglers we always were ... Where concise and journalistically apposite attacks or rebuttals are required, we give long and profound leading articles ... an interesting Reuter report of fifty lines is always preferred to a long-winded leading article.'

As the war neared its close in the autumn of the following year, the *Berliner Tageblatt* raised a bitter cry: 'mightier and more dangerous than fleet or army is Reuter'.

In London the Reuter editorial staff was still directed by F. W. Dickinson. At the war fronts the corps of correspondents appointed jointly by Reuters and the Press Association under 'Special Service' arrangements was steadily strengthened. The new revenue from the services financed by the Government gave Reuters an opportunity in other directions. The volume of words sent overseas was soon greatly increased, and new countries were served.

At first the censorship had proved a major restriction. The veil over military news had been thickly spread. The first blow, from the journalistic point of view, had been the suppression of a Reuter telegram from St. Petersburg, sent by the Russian official Agency, announcing the shattering by von Hindenburg of the Russian army at Tannenberg. Then the news of the fall of Maubeuge, French fortified town near the Belgian frontier, was withheld. On this occasion Reuters lodged a complaint immediately with F. E. Smith, then Chief of the British Press Bureau. After a hurried conference, one of the censors admitted that the telegram to Reuters, although the first to arrive, had been held back 'because if Reuter published the news, it would be believed, and the public is already discouraged enough'. From then on F. E. Smith did his best for the Agency; and, as the censorship was gradually lifted, the work of the war correspondents began to bear fruit.

By 1915, the majority of the British newspapers were beginning to rely on the Reuter–Press Association special correspondents for their main day-to-day reports of the fighting.

Chief Reuter correspondent with British Army Headquarters in France for that year was Douglas Williams, the former Chief Editor's younger son. His despatches were an immediate success. From him the public heard the first news of the German use of gas, of the battle of Ypres and the Guards' baptism of fire at the battle of Loos.

Fergus Ferguson went to Egypt in 1916 and later was attached to General Allenby in the march on Jerusalem and Damascus. For most of this march censorship enforced complete silence; it was suddenly broken by Ferguson's vivid despatch of Allenby's entry into Jerusalem.

There was an odd development in neutral Holland. The son of Abraham Delamar, who had sold the original Dutch Agency to Julius Reuter in the 1860's, was embarrassing Reuters by insisting on his rights as a neutral to continue to publish Reuter and Wolff telegrams together. And he was printing Wolff's telegrams from Germany in the Dutch Press under Reuters' name, under the old news-exchange agreement. William Moloney, until now Reuters' correspondent in Persia, was sent to Holland to establish a Reuter Agency, with the principal object of getting German news for the United Kingdom from German papers and from telegrams sent by Dutch correspondents in Berlin. Amsterdam, as well as Berne and Copenhagen, was one of the chief neutral centres for the dissemination of news. For the rest of the war, two Agency offices in Amsterdam, both owned by Reuters, but the one publishing English telegrams and the other German telegrams from Wolff and English telegrams from Reuters, faced each other in the same street.

The most important neutral ground both for the Allies and Germany was the United States. Reuters' interests were there in good hands. Manager in New York was still S. L. Lawson, who had held the post since his appointment after the Associated Press–United Press crisis in 1892. More important, during the two and a half years of American neutrality, was the representation in Washington. Here Reuters enjoyed the services of Edwin Milton Hood of the Associated Press. The doyen of the corps of correspondents in Washington, he held an unequalled position in American journalism. He was never more valuable to Reuters than during these war years. Time and again the Agency, through Hood's reports, was able to give the rest of Europe and Germany the first news of America's policy and attitude to the war. Hood had the confidence of the American President, Theodore Roosevelt, and of the State Department. Bethmann Hollweg, the German Chancellor, said in a Reichstag speech that Reuters' representative in the United States possessed a 'golden key' to the door of the White House. Climax to the various moves and counter-moves, as both sides tried to win the United States to their cause, came with the American reaction to the German Government's Note of January 31st, 1917. This Note informed the United States Government of Germany's decision to wage 'unrestricted submarine warfare'. The reaction was imme-diate. The German Ambassador was given his passport; and on February 3rd a Reuter message announced that diplomatic relations between the United States and Germany had been severed.

For the rest of that month feeling throughout the United States hardened and was reflected in intense diplomatic activity in Washington. Then, on March 1st, the American newspapers carried the extraordinary news of the Zimmermann Note. It came from the Associated Press, and the amazing story of Hood's part in it is told in the Associated Press's History.* The British Intelligence Service had intercepted a copy of a coded note from Dr. Arthur Zimmermann, German Foreign Secre-tary, to Count von Bernstorff, German Ambassador at Wash-ington, for relay to von Eckhardt, the German Minister in Mexico City. It directed von Eckhardt to make a secret pro-posal to Mexico that she should ally herself with Germany and declare war on the United States, if the United States failed to remain neutral. Mexico's reward would be the States of Texas, New Mexico and Arizona, the provinces lost sixty years before. It also proposed that Japan should be persuaded to abandon

* *AP: The Story of News*, by Oliver Gramling. New York, 1940.

The First and Second Barons. In their one surviving photograph together, 'Herbert looks the artist, Julius the man of affairs'.

Editors of the
Bloemfontein *Friend*,
a paper run in 1900 by
war correspondents with
Lord Roberts's army.
Left: H. A. Gwynne,
Reuters' chief
correspondent. In the
background: Julian Ralph
(*Daily Mail*), Perceval
Landon (*The Times*).
Right: Rudyard Kipling.

A junior Reuter
correspondent in the
Boer War.
His name: Edgar Wallace.

the Allies and join with Mexico in attacking the United States. This astonishing document, decoded in London, was given to the American Ambassador, who immediately cabled it to the State Department. Edwin Hood was allowed to act as the medium for its release by the Associated Press a day before President Wilson confirmed it.

The end of American neutrality was now certain; but it took a further month for the final decision to be proclaimed. On April 2nd President Wilson addressed a joint session of Congress. He was scheduled to begin to speak just after 6 p.m. Washington time. He actually began just after 8 p.m. – one hour after midnight in London. Delays on the cable were notorious. Reuters was emphatic that America's momentous decision must be in the London newspapers next morning. Arrangements were made for a clear wire to London; Hood arranged for the speech to be transmitted immediately the President began speaking; and the plan was successful. At 8.38 p.m. (1.38 a.m., April 3rd, London time) the first message was flashed to London: 'President Wilson tonight asked Congress to declare that a state of war exists between the United States and Germany'. It appeared in the London morning editions, and was accepted throughout the world as an official announcement. The full text of the President's speech was published the following day in almost every newspaper of the world, as a Reuter despatch.

The scene changes to Russia. The Bolshevik Revolution broke out in May 1917: the Czar was deposed, and the Russian troops at the front were soon demoralised. There was chaos and bloodshed in St. Petersburg. Reuters became involved. In December the official Russian Agency, Vestnik, was seized by the revolutionaries, the service of Russian news supplied to Reuters suspended and then resumed under Bolshevik control. The position of Guy Beringer, still Reuters' correspondent, was reported as 'delicate'. He escaped with his wife into

Finland; but his zeal as a journalist overcame his discretion, and he decided to return. The Peace of Brest-Litovsk had been made with Germany, and Russian hostility to the Allies was at its height. Soon after reaching Moscow, he was arrested and thrown into prison. For six months he was in imminent expectation of joining his many fellow-prisoners who were taken out night after night for summary execution. Finally Reuters' representations prevailed, and one night he was taken in a motor-car to join a train of refugees destined for Sweden. He arrived home in England visibly marked by his experiences.

Meanwhile, the unrestricted submarine warfare of 1917 was playing havoc with communications. By the middle of that year the main submarine cables were in a chaotic state and all traffic except official Government messages was subject to the heaviest delays. Press messages across the Atlantic were taking up to forty-eight hours. The German submarines sometimes extended their warfare directly against communications by cutting the sea-cables. On one occasion that summer an Admiralty repair ship found attached to one of the ends of a severed cable a bottle in which was a slip of paper saying: 'This is the work of U-Boat No. 26 and puts a stop to Reuters' damned anti-German lies.'

On September 15th, 1918, Werndel, who had stayed with the Serbian army until its crushing by typhus and the combined armies of Austria and Bulgaria, and J. W. Calvert of *The Times* were the only British correspondents left in distant Macedonia to witness the beginning of the final Allied offensive from Salonika. Werndel's reports described the break-through of the Serbians, the frantic Bulgarian retreat to their frontier, and finally the arrival of Bulgarian emissaries bearing a white flag. On September 29th, almost three years to the day since he had reported Ferdinand's secret pact with Germany, Werndel sent a message telling of Bulgaria's unconditional surrender to the Allied Commander-in-Chief, Marshal Franchet d'Esperey. It reached London three hours ahead of any other source. Within a very short time the world knew that the turning-point of the war had come. The story of the despair of Ludendorff, now beginning to retreat before the relentless blows of the Allies on the Western Front, when he heard the news from the East, is well known. The same day he made his decision to sue for peace.

The first German Peace Note from Max, Prince of Baden, the Imperial Chancellor, was sent to Wilson on October 3rd. Reuters issued this message on the 6th: 'The German Government requests the President of the United States of America to take in hand the restoration of peace. . . . It accepts the programme set forth by the President of the United States in his message to Congress of January 8th, 1918, as a basis for peace negotiations. With a view to avoiding further bloodshed the German Government requests the immediate conclusion of an armistice on land and water and in the air.' By the 10th Wilson's reply was known; but the official despatch containing it had not yet reached the German Government from Switzerland. That evening at 6 p.m. the German Imperial Chancellor assembled his Secretaries of State to discuss Wilson's terms – and, as recorded, 'The Reuter announcement of the speech was taken as a basis of discussion, no official despatch having reached the Government by diplomatic channels'.

The end of the war in the Middle East followed quickly. Ferguson's account of Allenby's destruction of the Turkish army in Palestine and the Turkish signing of an armistice reached London on October 30th, 1918. By then the Austrian army had been routed by the Italians, and on the 28th a Reuter message announced the Austrian Foreign Minister's request for an immediate armistice. In the first days of November Foch's armies reached Lorraine; the Americans supported by a stream of reserves were storming the Franco-German frontier; the British had pushed round the Hindenburg Line and were now racing forward in northern France. By the 8th the German plenipotentiaries were on their way to Foch's headquarters in the Forest of Compiègne. At 7.45 a.m. on November 11th the news that the Armistice had been signed at 5 a.m., and that the war would end at 11 a.m. that day, started round the world. The official despatch went from Compiègne to Paris, and Paris to London. It was given to Reuters at once, and almost simultaneously Reuter telegrams were on their way to the Empire and the Far East. The difference in time of nearly eleven hours meant that Reuters' office in Melbourne received the news at about 6.45 p.m. that evening. The *Melbourne Herald*, one of Reuters' oldest Australian subscribers, had kept open waiting for the news long after normal hours. Within a few minutes it had a 'special' on the streets, and before midnight a quarter of a million copies had been sold. As in the case of Mafeking eighteen years earlier, the celebrations that night for many people rested entirely on the Reuter despatch.

With the war over, the Agency could momentarily take stock of its situation. It had passed, in 1915, through the severest crisis of its history and, reorganised anew, adapted itself with success to a war-time role. Its prestige with both Government and public was high. For 'services in connection with the war', Roderick Jones was honoured in the New Year List of 1918 by being made a Knight Commander of the British Empire.

Reuters' peace-time tradition of anonymity had been modified sufficiently to make some of its special war correspondents household names in the British Press. Many of the despatches of Douglas Williams from Flanders, H. F. Prevost Battersby from American headquarters in France, Lester Lawrence from the French armies, and E. Lacon Watson from the British army in Italy, were published under their own names. For many people, especially in the provinces, where few of the newspapers had special correspondents, these were the main day-to-day links with the war. The knighthood given to Herbert Russell in March 1920 was a tribute to his graphic and truthful reporting of every phase of the British Army's fighting and endurance during his three years on the Western Front.

Almost miraculously, Reuters lost none of its special correspondents, although many had near escapes. Of the staff who served in the armed forces, 15 of the 115 on active service were killed and several were missing. In London the building at 24-25, Old Jewry, with its flimsiness and ancient dilapidation, went unscathed through the Zeppelin and aeroplane raids.

The Headquarters staff had stood up well to a vast increase of work. For the first time, women were employed on the editorial staff and were an immediate success. The skill that had gone into the old private-telegram services was given to the new problems of the 'Agence' service sent throughout the Empire and to all neutrals. By the end of the war, daily handling of news had increased by many millions of words a year. The supplementary services for the Government during the war had themselves totalled ten million words over and above Reuters' normal services.

Nevertheless, there were some who questioned the propriety of Reuters' new relations with the Government. At the annual meeting of the Press Association in May 1918, reassurance on this important question was asked for. Members wanted to be certain that sufficient safeguards had been taken to preserve Reuters' independence, and to prevent what had happened in many Continental countries being experienced in England. H. C. Robbins, who had succeeded his father as General Manager of the Press Association, gave the meeting the reassurance it requested.

But what worried the House of Commons and, soon afterwards, the Press was the personal position of the Managing Director. When the Department of Information was formed at the beginning of 1917, Roderick Jones was invited to exercise some supervision over its cable and wireless services. He accepted this offer and devoted some hours each day to the Department, while remaining Managing Director of Reuters. When the Department of Information was made into a separate Ministry, at the beginning of 1918, John Buchan became its Director of Intelligence under the first Minister, Lord Beaverbrook, and Sir Roderick Jones, as he had now become, was asked to become full-time Director of Propaganda. He accepted, but made it a condition that he would receive no remuneration from the Ministry and that he could in no circumstances consent to the formal resignation of his position as Managing Director of Reuters; at the same time he arranged to have his work as Managing Director temporarily placed in commission.

The first allusion to Sir Roderick Jones's relations with the Government was contained in the 'Sixth report of the Select Committee on National Expenditure' presented to the House of Commons on July 31st, 1918. 'During the last financial year', it stated, 'about £126,000 was paid for cables, mainly to Reuters' Telegram Company Limited . . . The position of Sir Roderick Jones, who is both Managing Director of Reuters and also a high official of the Ministry of Information, is on principle open to objection.'

The objection was echoed in the Press, and the question of Sir Roderick Jones's dual position was raised in the debate on the Ministry of Information on August 5th, 1918. His position was defended by Stanley Baldwin, then Joint Financial Secretary to the Treasury, who explained that his services to the Ministry had nothing to do with policy or finance. The payment of Government funds to the Agency was defended by C. A. McCurdy, Member of Parliament for Northampton. He disclosed the Government's decision to employ Reuters as a counter to Wolff's propaganda, by 'disseminating accurate news to all parts of the neutral world'. He stressed that the service supplied by Reuters 'was not altered or interfered with, but that there should be gratuitously added and cabled at the expense of this Government such news as the British Government officially desired to be communicated and to be at the disposal of newspaper proprietors and editors in all parts of the world'. He said that, from the point of view of publicity, the value obtained by the Government had been very high.

Sir Roderick Jones's position was also defended by Mark Napier in a letter to *The Times* the next day, August 6th. Napier said that both in his capacity as Director of Propaganda, and as Managing Director of Reuters, he had 'scrupulously refrained from having anything to do with the Ministry of Information payments from the moment his services were requisitioned by the Government'.

The controversy was in any case settled at the end of September by Sir Roderick Jones's resigning from the Ministry owing to ill health, the following announcement appearing in *The Times* of October 1st:

The Secretary of the Ministry of Information announces that, acting under urgent medical advice, Sir Roderick Jones has resigned his position as Director of Propaganda at the Ministry of Information, and his resignation has been accepted with regret by the Minister.

A few weeks later, with the end of hostilities, the Ministry of Information was itself wound up.

This controversy drew attention to the delicate situation of an international news agency in time of war and to its difficulty in resisting the claims of its government. Except from Germany, there had been no charges of Government interference with Reuters' editorial policy. But the report of the Select Committee on National Expenditure showed that both the large payments to the Agency and the dual position of Sir Roderick Jones were open to misinterpretation. It also showed that the public were concerned about the position of the Head of a news agency: more so in the United States and Great Britain than on the Continent, where links between the Press and the State have been traditionally closer. It is true that the call on Sir Roderick Jones's patriotism to give his technical ability to the Government was a strong one. But many people felt that he ought to have severed his connection with either Reuters or the Government for the duration of the war.

The end of the Ministry of Information in the late autumn of 1918 meant the end of Reuters' special war commitments. The 'Agence Reuter' services had availed the country well and they were brought to a close the following March.

Two months later, the Agency was presented with a task which called for as much technical skill as any during the war. At the request of the Government it was asked to exercise for a short but important time the functions of the recently dissolved Press Bureau, by taking over the official reporting of the delivery of the Peace Terms and the signing of the Peace itself. The Government wanted these distributed to every British official abroad. The Press Association, and the Newspaper Proprietors Association of London, agreed that Reuters should be the medium for communicating them to the Press of Great Britain. William Turner, who had started his Reuter career under Roderick Jones in South Africa, was put in charge of the team in Paris. To assist him he had Lester Lawrence, Douglas Williams (now returned from the expeditionary force to North Russia), Vernon Bartlett, and Mary Coules, one of the most successful of the women recruits to Reuters' editorial staff during the war.

The results justified this concentration. Winston Churchill *
has given a picture of the extraordinary difficulty the Press were confronted with during the plenary sessions of the Conference. It was the first, and many hoped the last, experience of peace-time censorship, with the 'Council of Ten' holding

* *The World Crisis: The Aftermath*, pp. 137 *et seq.*

its important meetings in secret. An enormous task fell to the staff in London. On the night of May 6th, 1919, they were requested to distribute a summary of the Peace Terms submitted to Germany to every daily newspaper, every Government, every embassy and every consulate in the world outside of North America. It was tantamount to publishing a book by telegraph simultaneously throughout the world. A special courier brought the first batch of printed copies of the Terms from Paris to Old Jewry a little after eleven o'clock that night. Soon after arrived the inevitable corrections. By six o'clock the next morning a summary of more than 12,000 words, despatched in 66 sections, had been sent round the world.

The next day came the similar distribution of the official summary of the ceremony of handing over the Treaty to the German delegates at Versailles. Here the main burden lay upon the staff in Paris. The official verbatim report was rushed to Paris by car in three batches, Turner of Reuters taking the first, Sir George Riddell, Vice-Chairman of the Newspaper Proprietors Association and the official representative of the British Press, the second, and the British official shorthand writer bringing up the rear. The whole operation was done at great speed; while Lester Lawrence, inside the Chamber in the Palace of Versailles, sent vivid descriptions of the ceremony hour by hour to London. At 3.31 p.m. in the afternoon of June 28th six large flags which had hung folded along their staves all day outside 24, Old Jewry, suddenly fluttered into the breeze of the City. Nineteen minutes earlier in the Galerie des Glaces of the Palace of Versailles the two German delegates, Müller and Bell, the one bowed, the other proud and erect, had signed the Treaty. Turner had telephoned this news on a line laid for the occasion from the Palace to Reuters' Paris office in the Place de la Bourse; telephoned from there to the Hotel Astoria, it had taken a further four minutes to reach London. By 3.33 p.m. the message had been given to the Press

Association and to the London newspapers and was on its way round the world.

That January, while the Peace Conference was going on in Paris, Reuters and Havas had signed a new Treaty and discussed their plans for the peace. The Treaty cemented the bond between the Agencies of the two victorious Powers and, *inter alia*, gave Reuters more 'territory' in Southern Europe. During the year talks had gone on between the French and English Agencies as to their new relationship with Wolff and the Austrian Korrespondenz-Bureau. The result left no doubt as to who were the conquerors and who the conquered. It was agreed 'that the alteration in international conditions resulting from the war should be reflected in the relations between the Agencies, and that the new Treaty made should limit the sphere of operation of the German Agency to Germany itself'. This new position was accepted by Melville E. Stone, General Manager of the Associated Press, then in Paris, on behalf of the American Agency.

Reuters and Havas then made a succession of 'joint Treaties' with the national Agencies springing up in the countries whose news had been previously monopolised by the German and Austrian Agencies. These agreements were made with the Agencies of Hungary, Bulgaria, Roumania and the new Yugoslavia and Czechoslovakia. Similar joint Treaties were concluded with the Agencies of every other European country except Russia. By the end of 1921, the 'National Agencies' Alliance', as it was now called, was complete. Reuters and Havas were its acknowledged leaders.

14

The Development of Wireless:
and a New Ownership

THE END OF THE WAR BROUGHT A VAST INCREASE IN BOTH
the volume and importance of international news. One immediate expression of the new spirit of nationalism abroad was
the setting-up of national news agencies by the States created
or given independence by the Peace Treaties. Political news
became a more intricate part of national life than ever before:
it was also liable to be charged with far more emotion, quickly
stirring up national resentments whenever its tone could be
identified with a particular Government's point of view. The
news agencies were made growingly aware of national temptations and international responsibilities.

For the Agencies of the victorious European Powers, the
future held unique chances of expansion. The crumbling-away
of the old Europe removed the balance of power carefully preserved by the first European news Treaties. The Agencies of
the two fallen Empires, Wolff of Berlin and the Korrespondenz-
Bureau of Vienna, lay discredited: the new European States
looked to Reuters and Havas for world news.

For the first years after the war Reuters was in buoyant
mood. The impetus of the 1915 reorganisation carried it on.
In Europe it shared the throne with Havas as '*une agence
doyenne*'; overseas, its enlargement in the war gave larger possibilities for peace. Most important of all, new communications-

systems, essential for expansion, could draw upon the advances of war-time experiments.

The lease in 1923 of the Port of London Authority's building on the Thames Embankment, to house the growing Reuter news departments, seemed to reflect the Agency's new prosperity. But it was soon clear that this was not altogether a true reflection. Shadows were already on the horizon. The ending of the Government war services in 1919 meant a considerable loss of revenue; the trade depression of two years later took its own toll. Before the war, the Traffic Department had been the panacea for hard times. Now, with a far cheaper public telegram service in operation, its life was ending: the Remittance Section lingered on in some parts of the British Empire; but the Private Telegram service showed continuing losses and was finally abolished in 1926.

Meanwhile, the news service was justifying itself. From Reuters' Paris office came the first news of the French Government's sudden recognition of General Wrangel, leader of the White Russians: a message which led to an immediate informal Cabinet meeting in London. From W. J. Moloney, Reuters' correspondent in Berlin, came the earliest news of the German Socialist Revolution of 1920.

The 1920's saw, too, the full effects of Lord Northcliffe's impact on British journalism. Newspapers of every complexion had a public anxious to read about every conceivable human activity, and as much about sport as about politics: a public which demanded ringside reporting of its boxing, and in which *The Times* headed a newspaper syndicate prepared to pay £20,000 to the archæologists in Egypt excavating King Tutankhamen's four-thousand-year-old tomb, in return for first rights to the news of the discoveries. In this fever for news, competition between the Agencies reached a new intensity. Speed counted for everything, and fantastic sums were spent to ensure it. Reuters here too had its successes: in the suddenly important sphere of boxing championships Douglas Williams telegraphed Dempsey's knock-out of Carpentier from Jersey City to London in less than two seconds; while, in Egypt, his brother Valentine defeated *The Times'* syndicate to make the first news of the Tutankhamen discoveries a Reuter despatch.

But the cost of satisfying the public's thirst for such news was enormous. It was soon apparent to Sir Roderick Jones – as it had been to the two Barons – that it was all but impossible to make the news service pay for itself. In September 1922, Reuters lost its Chief Editor. F. W. Dickinson was working at the desk that he had occupied with conspicuous success and great devotion for twenty years, until the day before he died. The newspapers paid tribute to a great Editor. With him went something of the patriarchal atmosphere which had clung to one of the few surviving members of the first Baron's staff. Intensely English himself, he was a last link with those more cosmopolitan days, when the Wolff and Havas correspondents were important denizens of the London office, and German and French were spoken in it as freely as English. One of his colleagues had been Reuters' first Parliamentary correspondent, James Hecksher, known to his fellow-correspondents as 'the Bismarck of the Gallery'; and there had been another Bismarck, also a well-known Reuter figure – the cat brought daily into the London office by Dr. Petri, one of the German editors. Every year Dr. Petri, a good patriot, celebrated the battle of Sedan by parading his cat and beating on a kettledrum; and every year one at least of the Frenchmen on the staff – equally good patriots – threatened to resign.

Dickinson's sudden death raised the problem of his successorship. Temporarily, Roderick Jones vested the Chief Editorship in himself. Douglas Williams, now head of the New York office, was offered it; but he preferred to remain in America. The following August, the post went to Herbert Jeans, for many years Reuters' chief parliamentary correspondent. When Roderick Jones went on a tour of Reuters' overseas territories the same month, an Editorial Council was left to assist the new Chief Editor. Its Chairman was John Buchan, who had rejoined the Reuter Board at the end of the war, and now became Deputy Chairman of the Company.

The Reuter news service held its own, and Roderick Jones's world-tour brought it increased subscriptions. But its real financial salvation came from elsewhere: from a re-animation of the business which had made Julius de Reuter's fortune – the reporting of commercial intelligence. In the wake of this development came technical experiments which kept London the centre of world communications for another generation.

It was soon after the war that Cecil Fleetwood-May, then a junior Reuter sub-editor – now European Manager – saw the chances that Reuters was missing in this field. Intense conservatism still confined the commercial service to stereotyped market reports and stock-exchange quotations. The immense amount of information of commercial interest that passed daily through the normal news services was wasted. His proposal was to extract this, and to offer it to trade newspapers and business firms as 'Reuters' Trade Service'. Roderick Jones adopted the plan; Fleetwood-May was given a few clerks to help him; and the new Trade Department began operations on January 1st, 1920.

From this humble origin sprang a service that was soon almost indispensable to business-men, brokers and bankers all over the world. Within ten years, a staff of ninety was handling messages received from special correspondents at all the world markets. As one example of the new department's activities, the prices of wheat from Winnipeg and cotton from New York reached London within fourteen seconds of being called and were almost instantaneously re-transmitted to the world's commercial centres – to Bremen, Alexandria, Bombay, Shanghai.

Repeating Julius Reuter's pattern of expansion, the new service produced offshoots in India, in Australia, in South Africa, and in Egypt. And despite civil wars and banditry, China and the Far East continued to flourish as its chief market. In his report for 1934, Carl Ackerman, Dean of the School of Journalism, Columbia University, New York, treated Reuters' Commercial Service – as it was by now called – as one of the main developments in world journalism.

Even more important were the advances in communications directly brought about by the new service. Speed and the simultaneous reception of messages by centres throughout the world were the chief essentials for the Commercial Service. Fleetwood-May quickly realised the possibilities of wireless – and particularly of broadcast wireless telegraphy – for achieving both.

In retrospect, it seems strange that the news agencies did not explore the advantages of wireless earlier. It was twenty years since Marconi, on a December day in 1901, received his first message across the Atlantic. But, apart from services to ships at sea by the Associated Press, the Agencies for some time made no serious experiments in international wireless communications. Then came the war, and the use of Morse broadcasting by every Government for propaganda purposes.

Wireless emerged, immensely developed and crowned with technical successes. And it had new ambitions: the Wireless Telegraph Companies, like the first Electric Telegraph Cable Companies in the 1840's, were anxious to provide news themselves, as well as to carry it for others. To the news agencies, dependent on cables, the prospect of wireless agencies, selling news picked up in the air to the Press, was disquieting. But in Great Britain this never materialised. Headed by Reuters, strong representations were made to the Marconi Company, which had a Government monopoly of wireless for the war. In 1919, Marconi announced that henceforth they would limit their activities to carrying messages: wireless would assist the news agencies, not compete with them.

In one other sphere both Reuters and the Press watched the advance of wireless with some trepidation. In 1922 the British Broadcasting Corporation was formed. In the United States and Canada the first wireless-broadcasting of news precipitated a bitter conflict with the newspapers: it was seen as a dangerous competitor. In this country, thanks largely to J. C. W. (now Lord) Reith's policy of ensuring the BBC an adequate income from its semi-public status and of keeping it absolutely free from all commercial and advertising interests, there were, after the first panic, few repercussions in the Press. Moreover, the newspapers came to see that the BBC's news reports did not kill interest in their own news, but stimulated it. From the first, the BBC relied on the news agencies for its main news broadcasts; and Reuters began by editing this news on the Agencies' behalf. At the beginning of the news bulletins, it was announced that the news came from Reuters, the Press Association, the Exchange Telegraph, and the Central News. Although the BBC soon took over the editing itself, it remained one of Reuters' most important customers and continued to draw largely on Reuters' news for its home and overseas services.

Reuters now began to make its own experiments with wireless. In 1922, Fleetwood-May, intent on using broadcast telegraphy to speed up the Commercial Service, asked the Reuter Management to grant him £30 to establish Reuters' first private wireless listening post in his own house in London. Scepticism from some of the older members of the staff was overruled by the Chairman, and the scheme went ahead. The next year brought a new realism to the experiments. The Germans, after their radio successes in the war, were also conducting experiments with broadcast telegraphy. They too had seen how wireless might transform commercial news-reporting,

Lutyens's building in Fleet Street,
designed to house Reuters and the Press Association.

and two Agencies were already broadcasting exchange rates to subscribers in Germany and neighbouring countries. Fleetwood-May suddenly found his plans for a Reuter broadcast wireless service fully endorsed by the Reuter Management.

The Post Office alone had the right to transmit such a service. That autumn began an association – Reuters as customer and the Post Office as purveyor – which laid a pattern in news-agency radio communications for the next twenty years.

Reuters at first leased transmission facilities for a purely European Commercial Service: price quotations and exchange rates were sent in Morse from the Post Office wireless station at Northolt seven times a day. A new technique had to be mastered: once that was done the success of 'Reuterian', as the new circular broadcast service was called, was rapid; in time it became the chief Commercial Service in Europe. Soon Reuters needed a transmitter capable of reaching its Commercial Service subscribers in more distant parts of the world. At Rugby the powerful long-wave station built by the Post Office for the Admiralty during the war was idle for much of its time. Use of it was offered to Reuters at a high tariff rate. The minimum charge for starting up this huge transmitter 'from cold' was £5 a time, and this was the cost of some of the Reuter two-word messages carrying price changes to distant parts of the world.

Reuters thus extended still further the range of its Commercial Services. Meanwhile, the Post Office research teams were making new experiments. In November 1929 they offered Reuters a smaller but very powerful transmitter at Leafield near Oxford. The result was a jump forward in the Commercial Service and, before long, an extension of the use of broadcast telegraphy to the general news service as well. The cost of using the Leafield transmitter was reasonably low; Reuters found that it could use the transmitter continuously for sending general news as well as Commercial Services to Europe – 'and,

Sir Roderick Jones was Managing Director 1916-41, and Chairman 1919-41. Christopher Chancellor is Head of Reuters today.

an important development, it succeeded in persuading the Post Office to operate the transmitter direct from Reuters' office in London.

In December 1929 Reuters' first continuous service of general news was broadcast by radio to Europe. Far-reaching developments followed. Within twelve years this broadcast radio system, now using a group of short-wave transmitters, carried more than 90 per cent of the news sent by Reuters from London to the world. The system was adopted in other countries, and every Agency in due course followed the example of Reuters and the British Post Office. The result was the establishment all over the world of multi-address radio news services.

The use of wireless by Reuters in Europe resulted also in a complete change in the European Agency system for transmitting news. It was no longer necessary for Austria and Hungary to take the Reuter service only through the medium of Wolff in Berlin, or for Spain and Portugal to receive it second-hand through Havas. London now had a direct link with the Agencies on the Continent.

But, the European Agencies soon felt, why not give this new intimacy a more permanent form? From common interest in the new Commercial Services and in the immense possibilities of radio telegraphy sprang, in 1924, the first articulate 'alliance' of all the European news agencies. That summer, in Berne, grouped together round Havas and Reuters, *les agences doyennes*, the representatives of the Agencies of twenty-one other European countries presented an impressive spectacle of solidarity. It was the first of a series of Conferences held every year until 1938.

Seventy-five years before, the three founders of Europe's first telegraphic Agencies had realised the power of commercial reporting to override the barriers put up against political news. In a new way, the old pattern now repeated itself. Soon the

Conferences passed from commercial and technical discussions to a concern with all aspects of news-agency activity, and on this more delicate ground a surprising harmony still prevailed.

The political situation caused occasional embarrassments; but successive Conference Presidents showed tact in handling national susceptibilities. Even the flat refusal of the German and Italian delegates to go to Moscow, where the biennial 'Plenary Assembly' was to be held in 1939, was smoothed over. This problem was, as the minutes put it, 'resolved in a very elegant manner', thanks to the Russian Agency's 'finding it possible to refrain from insisting upon its invitation'. These discussions undoubtedly showed the possibility and the value of such practical European co-operation. They led to an increase in the interchange of news throughout the Continent; they wrestled with such worrying problems as the international piracy of wireless news; and they brought all the European Agencies into closer touch with each other.

Meanwhile, a most important decision for Reuters' own future was being taken. In May 1925, Sir Roderick Jones offered the ownership of a majority interest in the Agency to the British newspapers: half to the Newspaper Proprietors Association, representing the London papers, half to the Press Association, representing the provincial papers. He had been principal proprietor of Reuters since Mark Napier's death in 1919, when, under a partnership arrangement made between them in 1916, he purchased a further 10 per cent of the shares to bring his holding to 60 per cent. Under Napier's will, he was also a trustee for the remainder of the shareholding. After his retirement, he described his motives in making this offer to the newspapers in a letter which he wrote to *The Times* sixteen years later, just before the ownership of Reuters passed finally to the entire British Press:

'I felt strongly', he wrote, 'that the future of so important a national and international organisation should not be dependent upon the life of one man, myself, and be open at my death to the danger that threatened it during the last War. I could have allowed the Agency, with its solid corpus and its world-wide reputation, to be floated very advantageously as a public company. But that would have revived the danger: a free market in the shares would have exposed Reuters to the menace of undesirable influence and perhaps control.

'No such risk could spring from ownership by the news-papers as a body, representative as they are of every shade of political, social, and economic thought, and penetrated as they always have been, whatever their internal business rivalries, often acute, by a healthy patriotism and robust independence.'

But the 1925 offer evoked disagreement between the London newspapers and, to Sir Roderick Jones's disappointment, nego-tiations with the Newspaper Proprietors Association broke down. The Press Association went ahead; and on the last day of 1925 the provincial newspapers became owners of a majority interest in Reuters. Four years later they became the sole owners of Reuters, and – except for a small minority holding which Roderick Jones retained – remained so until October 1941.

The Reuter Board was reconstituted with seven members, four of whom the Press Association elected as representatives from its own Directorate. In April 1926, Arthur Pickering (*North Eastern Daily Gazette*, Middlesbrough), Sir Charles Hyde (*Birmingham Post*), Sir James Owen (*Western Times*), and H. D. Robertson (*Glasgow Herald*) became the first provincial newspaper Directors of Reuters. Apart from this, the change in ownership meant little difference to the Agency's practical control. Sir Roderick Jones remained Chairman and Managing Director. There were no changes in the staff. Business relations with the Press Association remained the same: each Agency continued to sell its news service to the other at the best price it could obtain.

Reuters had now, for the first time, the direct backing of a large section of its home subscribers. But from the first operations of the Press Association in 1870, and earlier still, the provincial newspapers – most of them with no foreign correspondents of their own – had been Reuters' chief supporters. The new owners were old allies. The events of the next fifteen years made heavy calls on their support. At home, the General Strike of 1926 was a foretaste of the general economic unrest to come. Abroad, the American Agencies were gathering themselves for an all-out attack on what they saw as Reuters' domination of world news. And, in both America and the British Empire, new and strong forces were accusing the Agency of being a voice of the 'Old World': of standing for a monopoly in international news, of reflecting an ultra-British point of view, of being too intimate with Government. They were charges that aroused strong emotions on both sides. With the 1930's, Reuters entered upon the tensest and most critical decade of its history.

15

Enter the New World

BETWEEN THE TWO WORLD WARS THE GROWING DETER-
mination of the great newspaper-owned American Agency,
the Associated Press, to exchange news with the rest of the
world direct had an explosive effect upon the old-established
Agency system in Europe. The Associated Press's attitude was
readily understandable. Despite America's new power in the
world, and her part in the War and the Peace, her oldest and
largest news agency was unable to give news of America direct
to the world's newspapers. Under the European Agency
Treaty, the Associated Press's news had to pass through
Reuters. American isolationism in the nineteenth century had
left its mark. While Reuters, Havas and Wolff were building
up their intricate pattern of Agency Treaties, and dividing up
the world for 'news-exploitation', the co-operative American
Agency was fully occupied at home, organising the supply of
news through its own States.

The origins and early domestic struggles of the Associated
Press have already been described. Its predecessor, the New
York Associated Press, made its first agreement for an exchange of news with the European triumvirate – Reuters,
Havas and Wolff – in the early 1870's; twenty years later, in
1893, a quadrilateral Treaty made the new Associated Press a
member of the alliance itself. The new Treaty did not greatly
disturb the *status quo*. The three European Agencies kept their
rights intact in most of their old domains. But 'exclusive rights

to issue news in the United States and its possessions' passed from Reuters to the Associated Press; and the Associated Press was given a free hand (but not exclusive rights) first in Canada, later in Mexico, Central America and the West Indies. In general, the principle of exclusivity, on which the whole fabric of European news-gathering rested, remained as sacred as ever. Under the new Treaty, the European Agencies were barred from selling their news direct to any newspaper, or Agency other than the Associated Press, in the United States, just as the Associated Press was similarly barred throughout the territories exclusive to Reuters, Havas and Wolff. It was the price paid for membership of the alliance; and until the First World War, the Associated Press found the alliance worth that price.

With the end of the war, a very different mood was apparent. Like many American organisations, the Associated Press began to look outwards: to South America, Europe, the Far East. Wherever it hoped to expand, to sell its news direct to a newspaper or to a national Agency, the European Agency alliance stood in its way. There was, moreover, now strong competition at home. In 1907, a new Agency had been founded in America – the United Press Associations. Privately owned, and controlled mainly by the Scripps-Howard chain of newspapers, it was soon a powerful rival to the Associated Press. Under its active President, Roy Howard, it was forging ahead with plans to extend its service throughout the world. Outside the European alliance from the start, it had neither its advantages nor its restrictions.

In some quarters of the Associated Press the Agency alliance became increasingly unpopular. This was not a universal feeling: to Melville Stone, General Manager of the Associated Press for thirty years, the support of the European Agencies seemed still a fundamental necessity; and his voice commanded great respect. But the newer view gained ground and intensity. Its chief protagonist was Kent Cooper, a man of exceptional

energy, devoted to the Associated Press, head of its communications department during the 1914 War and soon to succeed
Stone as its General Manager. Kent Cooper had no doubts
about the European alliance. To him it was not only the chief
obstacle to the Associated Press's plans to expand abroad: it
was also a bad thing in itself. He saw the alliance as the worst
kind of international monopoly, the ghost of an outworn
European system ruling from the grave and in the process
deliberately using its power to give an untrue picture of
American life. Americans still complained that their country-
men's chief activities, as seen in the English and Continental
papers, were gangsterism, lynchings, crooked politics and
fighting Red Indians. Kent Cooper, moreover, was convinced
that all the European Agencies were either controlled by, or
responsive to, their Governments and, under the name of news,
dealing in propaganda – open or disguised.

It is impossible to read *Barriers Down*,* Kent Cooper's
dramatically told record of his twenty years' struggle to destroy
the old exclusive news-agency Treaties, without being impressed by its author's sincerity and without feeling his ethical
fervour. Kent Cooper regarded his struggle as a crusade; and
he was convinced that he was fighting something that everywhere threatened the freedom of international news.

Barriers Down explains how that conviction was born. Soon
after the outbreak of the First World War Kent Cooper acci-
dentally learnt about Havas's refusal ('*Nous sommes Français*')
to include the German war communiqués in its world service
to its newspaper customers in the neutral countries of South
America. Under the Agency Treaties, Havas had exclusive
rights to send news to South America: if news was suppressed,
a newspaper depending for its world news on the Havas service
could not give its readers a complete service of information.
The three European Agencies – Reuters, Havas and Wolff –

* New York: Farrar and Rinehart, 1942.

were all known to be receiving facilities to transmit war publicity services for their respective Governments: all three were
quickly identified in Kent Cooper's mind. The German and
French Governments undoubtedly had a voice in the policies
of Wolff and Havas: it followed that the British Government
must have a similar influence over Reuters. Roderick Jones's
acceptance of the post of Director of Propaganda in the British
Ministry of Information, while at the same time remaining at
the head of Reuters, added colour to Kent Cooper's belief.

In fact all the records show that no direct financial subsidy
was ever paid to Reuters. The publicity services conducted for
the Government ended immediately after the war. There is no
trace of evidence that at any time the Government interfered
with the Agency's editorial policy. But, although Reuters
gained greatly in prestige in Great Britain as a result of its war-
time work for the British Government, it had to pay heavily
for that gain elsewhere. None of the European Agencies could
afford to throw stones – they were too deeply involved themselves. But in America, the Associated Press had the wisdom to
regard an invitation to join the United States Government's war
publicity scheme as jeopardising its independence – and it had
firmly refused. In the campaign against the European Agencies
that lay ahead this refusal was given immense significance.

Kent Cooper saw Reuters as the leader of a monopoly of
Government-influenced Agencies, deliberately obstructing the
free flow of international news and misrepresenting America
to the world. Roderick Jones saw the Associated Press campaign against Reuters as stemming largely from American ex-
pansionism. To him, the Associated Press was responding to
pressure from public opinion and commercial interests to send
American news into South America and the Far East. It was a
pattern with which he was familiar. 'The Associated Press was
acting under force of circumstances,' he told the Reuter Board
in March 1930, 'driven by the American population in the Far

East.' He told Frank Noyes, the President of the Associated Press, that Reuters would certainly take a like course in a similar situation. He saw clearly the American Agency's ambitions to expand; but he missed the fervour behind Kent Cooper's crusade, the objective force of his belief in the free exchange of news.

The result was a struggle much more embittered than normal commercial rivalry. The conflict was really between the Associated Press and the three chief European Agencies. But, with Germany's defeat in the war, Wolff had lost its old position: its head, Dr. Heinrich Mantler, became, during the period of the German Republic, rather a pathetic figure, an emblem of vanished power. Apart from South America and the French colonies, Havas sent its news mainly to Europe. Reuters, with exclusive news rights in China, Japan and most of the British Empire, soon became for Kent Cooper the real power behind the system he had set himself to destroy. 'Reuters Rex', as he put it in *Barriers Down*, 'sat at the crossroads of the world of news and controlled traffic.'

Kent Cooper's attitude to the European Agency alliance has been stated. Roderick Jones regarded the alliance as an essential pillar of Reuters' whole news-gathering position. With the basic European news sources secure to him, he could pursue the traditional Reuter policy of commercial expansion in the British Empire and the Far East. He had been brought up under the old system: his ambition was to maintain the *status quo*. It was not apparent to him that the Associated Press had a superiority in resources that was bound in the end to be decisive. Its more than a thousand newspaper members gave Kent Cooper a domestic backing nearly ten times the size of Reuters' home subscribers. As a Press co-operative from its foundation, owned entirely by the newspapers it served, it had an obvious appeal to other co-operative Agencies. Never having been profit-making itself, it could (and did) point to the fact that Reuters,

Havas and Wolff were all managed for profit and subject to commercial considerations.

The motives and attitude of the Associated Press, advanced by the masterful personality of its General Manager, have been described at some length because the initiative in this struggle was American, not European. The drive to change the order of things in the news-agency world came from the Associated Press, not from the Agencies in Europe. But no Agency was untouched by the result of a conflict which affected the exchange of international news throughout the world.

In November 1918, just before the signing of the Armistice, the Associated Press gained its first concession from the European alliance. With certain reservations, Havas granted it a free hand in South America. But the Treaty terms with Reuters stood between the Associated Press and its hope of expansion into the Far East. For a further fifteen years relations remained cordial on the surface: there was still a formal alliance between the two Agencies; meetings between their Heads took place on both sides of the Atlantic. After each meeting, however, the Associated Press edged a little nearer to the complete freedom of movement it desired. Naturally enough the two men most closely involved saw this process in a different light. To Roderick Jones, each change was a new concession to the Associated Press's territorial demands, for which Reuters obtained no apparent compensation. To Kent Cooper, each delay was part of Reuters' ingenious tactics to prevent the barriers of the 'European news-monopoly' being lowered.

The real issue between Reuters and the Associated Press was finally joined in the Far East. This was Reuters' oldest and traditionally strongest overseas territory. It consistently provided the Agency with important revenues. But it was also the area which America increasingly regarded as an outlet for overseas trade. The battle for the right to supply news here was part of a larger rivalry.

The crisis came in the end over Japan. Japan provides a good example of how the Agency Treaties worked and of the basis of the American objection to them. Since the early 1870's, when Tokyo, still suspicious of the outside world, received its first regular news of the West from a Reuter Agent, Japan had been 'Reuter territory'. Reuters kept virtual control of all the news coming into Japan from the rest of the world and of most of the news going out. Until 1913 the position was practically unchanged. Then, with Reuters' support, a group of Japanese business-men set up the first Japanese news agency, Kokusai, which was soon distributing domestic and foreign news to newspapers in Japan and Japanese possessions. But the foreign news still came almost entirely from Reuters, and Reuters had exclusive rights in the rest of the world to Kokusai's own domestic news of Japan.

The first incentive to the Associated Press to change this order of things was not so much hostility to Reuters' control; it was a belief among prominent American newspaper publishers that Kokusai was giving both the news it supplied to Reuters, and the news it distributed itself in Japan and Japanese possessions, a deliberately anti-American flavour.

Determination to establish a direct interchange of news between the Associated Press and the Japanese newspapers soon followed. It was helped by the replacement of Kokusai in 1926 by a co-operative, newspaper-owned Agency, Rengo. Its full English title, 'Associated Press of Japan', showed the new Agency's orientation; its distinguished Managing Director, Yukichi Iwanaga, although friendly to Britain, desired a direct contact with America. Here was the material for a crisis. To Reuters, Japan was still 'Reuter territory'; to Kent Cooper, that claim was one of the barriers to the free interchange of international news, and he was determined to break it down. The Japanese Agency itself was moving towards the Associated Press and beginning to chafe under its exclusive contract with Reuters.

In response to pressure, Sir Roderick Jones released the Associated Press in 1932 from the restrictive clauses of the Treaty barring the Associated Press from entering China and Japan. In 1933 the crisis came. Kent Cooper went to Japan and made a contract with Iwanaga under which Rengo would take a news service from the Associated Press and would make its own domestic service available to America through the Associated Press. They did not attempt to evict Reuters from Japan: what the Associated Press obtained from Rengo was equality of status *vis-à-vis* the British Agency. This contract was allowable under the arrangement of 1932; but the negotiations were carried out without Reuters being informed first. This Sir Roderick Jones regarded as an unfriendly act from an Agency still in alliance with Reuters. After a special meeting of the Reuter Board he formally denounced the Treaty between Reuters and the Associated Press. A traditional alliance seemed to have ended.

But in London facts had to be faced. More than a relationship between two news agencies was at stake: this was a matter of concern to the newspapers on both sides of the Atlantic. It was clear that the old order was gone and that the new ideas represented by the Associated Press had come to stay. Reuters decided to accept them; and on February 12th, 1934, Sir Roderick Jones was in New York to sign a new agreement with the Associated Press which for the first time gave both Agencies a free hand to issue news everywhere in the world. Each Agency could now serve any newspaper or news agency in any country, without the other's consent. This was the fulfilment of Kent Cooper's ambition. The Associated Press now had what he had fought for since the First World War: the right to the free exchange of news throughout the world and the right to sell Associated Press news in all countries without restriction.

It was also the end of a news-agency era. With the crumbling of the old Four-Power alliance went the central idea upon which news-gathering by the great world Agencies had been based for nearly eighty years: the division of the world into territories for the 'exclusive exploitation' of news. The old system, founded on the commercial liberalism of mid-nineteenth-century Europe, had produced an intricate organisation: its strength was shown by the many years it had held fast and resisted the pressure to change it. Twentieth-century nationalism had replaced that liberal spirit. It was becoming clear that free interchange of news between countries and equal access to all news sources were essential safeguards against the dangers of Government control and nationalistic monopoly. To Kent Cooper's conviction of the truth of this fact must go much of the credit for its general acceptance.

In Europe the ancient alliance, pivoted upon *les agences doyennes*, Havas and Reuters, remained in being; but it was shorn of much of its power. Neither Havas nor the other Allied Agencies in Europe readily accepted the new régime. To Charles Houssaye, Director of Havas, son of one of its first Heads, conservative by nature and upbringing and intensely devoted to the Four-Power Treaties and the elaborate organisation they supported, the passing-away of the old system was a very real blow. But he realised what the outcome of the Reuter–Associated Press crisis meant: that the old Treaties could never be revived; and his acceptance of this carried the rest of the European Agencies with him. Gathered at Riga in conference in 1934, the Allied Agencies were plainly worried by the new and unexpected activities of the Associated Press in their midst: it took all the efforts of the Reuter and Havas representatives to calm them down and coax them into acquiescence.

From a wider point of view, the new system had great significance. News could now circulate freely over most of the world. There was nothing to prevent the newspapers of any country receiving world news from more than one source. It was certainly a move towards greater internationalism in news-gathering.

16

Battles on Many Fronts

IT WAS A HARSH STROKE OF IRONY THAT THE NEW AGENCY
agreements, made to ensure world news freedom, were being
used within a year in a very different cause. The year of crisis
and reconciliation between Reuters and the Associated Press
saw the beginnings of a vast propaganda campaign by the
totalitarian Powers. The Italian Agency, Stefani, controlled by
a close friend of Mussolini, was already heavily subsidised
by the Italian Government. In Germany, one of Hitler's first
acts was to transform Wolff into the official German Agency,
Deutsches Nachrichtenbüro (DNB), a medium for German
propaganda. The Japanese news agency, renamed Domei, became increasingly an instrument of militarised and militant
Japan. The opponents of the Axis were also active. Tass had
been the official, State-controlled Soviet Agency since its
inception; the French Government now began to subsidise
Havas on an ever-increasing scale. In the Far East, Reuters had to
operate in a battlefield of competing nationalist news services.

Nearer home, a darker shadow settled over the face of the
Press itself. During the first year of Hitler's Chancellorship, one
thousand German newspapers were destroyed or suppressed
for Communist or Jewish or democratic sympathies. Ten years
before, in *Mein Kampf*, Hitler had declared his belief in the
power of propaganda and in the necessity of control over the
Press. He now made ruthless attempts to discredit the news
agencies, as the instruments and allies of the Press. In the winter
of 1933, secret instructions given to certain agents of DNB

abroad were found in Paris. They gave an extraordinary list of ways 'to damage as much as possible relations between the hostile news agencies and important foreign newspapers'. These 'hostile Agencies' were Havas, Reuters and the Associated Press: all 'lacked comprehension', as the instructions put it, of the German régime.

The new Agency alignments were becoming clear. The Italian Agency, Stefani, broke off close relations with Havas early in 1934. Stefani and DNB remained official members of the Allied Agencies; but the position was anomalous, and State control was pulling them violently in the opposite direction. In his annual report to Columbia University for 1934, Carl Ackerman painted a depressing picture of the way international news was being twisted and distorted in order to deceive the public in Germany and Italy.

Outward news from the totalitarian Powers was as closely controlled. Government pressure on the foreign Agency and newspaper correspondents was being tightened; behind it lay the final sanction of expulsion. As political passions grew, the reprisals taken against correspondents became hysterical. Five English daily newspapers had their Berlin correspondents expelled. H. D. Harrison, Reuters' correspondent in the Balkans, had to leave Yugoslavia for reporting, with some slight suggestion of irony, the banning by the censor of a Mickey Mouse cartoon objected to by Prince Paul; the laughter of the world failed to change this decision.

On these basic issues Reuters and the American news agencies, the Associated Press, United Press Associations and International News Service, were united against the State-controlled Agencies of the Axis.

In other spheres Reuters had to face problems of a different sort. The attitude of the Dominions towards Great Britain had changed radically since the war; and there was a marked reflection of the change in their new reactions to Reuters.

Emphasis in the Dominions was on full recognition of their independence and on building up their own institutions. Foremost in the movement was the Press; and, in Australia particularly, the Press began to criticise Reuters' news. The emphasis in the Reuter service had, throughout its history, been frankly British. It was not a case of deliberately projecting British policy, but of carrying a particular tone. Sir Roderick Jones's public speeches made his own views clear. 'The Agency, in the ordinary pursuit of its activities, probably has done more than any other single institution abroad to create British atmosphere and to spread British ideas,' he said in 1925. This claim implied that Reuters, under his control, would continue to maintain British prestige abroad. It provoked a mixed response in the Dominions. Traditional sentiment towards Britain as the mother-country was still strong, and with it, in some sections of the Press, went something of the old acceptance of Reuters as a link of Empire. But in many Dominion newspapers a new spirit was growing up, robust, nationalist and independent. Its more aggressive adherents regarded Reuters with hostility as an ultra-British institution.

In South Africa, Dutch nationalist attacks on Reuters as being anti-Afrikaans began soon after the war. Reuters was identified with British imperialism, accused of accepting subsidies from the British Government. In South Africa hostility was the direct result of political prejudice: but in other cases, notably in Australia and Canada, it sprang from suspicions engendered within the Press itself in its relations with Reuters.

A joint British and Canadian Government scheme in 1919 to bring the first Reuter service to Canada precipitated a crisis within the co-operative newspaper-owned news agency of Canada, the Canadian Press. This scheme was to meet strong Canadian demands for direct news of the Empire and a desire for Reuters to supply it. But payment for the service was made dependent upon joint subsidies to the Canadian Press by the two Governments; and it led to a battle over the whole question of Government subsidies. Reuters suggested modifications and proposed alternatives to the British subsidy. But the Canadian newspapers were still hostile, and in 1923 all subsidies to the Canadian Press were abolished. A provisional Reuter service, maintained while the conflict continued, had proved in fact entirely satisfactory to the majority of the newspapers; but its association with the scheme for a subsidy did Reuters much harm in Canada. The aftermath of the quarrel was resentment against their own Government by several influential Canadian newspaper publishers; and much of this resentment they projected onto Reuters. It was an unhappy story.

The toughness of the Australian newspaper Press was, in Reuters' experience, proverbial. Mobilised against the Agency it could be overwhelming. Mobilised – as often – by groups of Australian newspapers against one another, it had been one of the few guarantees of Reuters' continued existence in Australia. Even then, the Australians had a disconcerting habit of sinking their differences in a night in order to oust Reuters and set up a cable service of their own. They had done this in 1890, and kept Reuters at arm's length until 1915, when the Agency's news distribution direct to Australian newspapers was at last resumed.

It lasted until the mid-1920's. But Reuters was constantly under fire in Australia, and the battle came to a head in 1925. Once more, the Australian newspaper groups came together. Reuters' news service to Australia was called ultra-British and too official; its news from Australia to London was considered too sparse. The Australian newspapers once more demanded control over the selection of their international news in London. A year later, 1926, they once again had their way. Under a new agreement the Reuter service was henceforth supplied to an Australian Bureau in London, no longer through the Reuter office in Melbourne. Reuters remained the source of

Australia's basic world news; but the selection of what was cabled to Australia was made by Australian editors in London.

In South Africa the stage seemed set for a stormy repetition of Reuters' recent experience in Australia. Nationalism was mounting; there was a strong desire within the Union for everything to be South African. Reuters' position was unique as the supplier of internal, as well as external, news. The distributing organisation, the Reuter South African Press Agency, was in fact a partnership between Reuters and the principal British South African newspapers, in which Reuters had a three-quarters majority vote. The Afrikaans Press now demanded a voice in the control of their national news service.

Things might have been serious for Reuters. But here the Agency rode the storm. Of the factors in Reuters' favour, the most important was the personal position won by two men, Roderick Jones and James Dunn, who in turn were in charge of Reuters' South African interests. James Dunn, who succeeded Roderick Jones in 1915, had joined the Reuter Cape Town staff in 1902. He inherited from his predecessor the personal affection for Reuters which was felt by General Botha, the Afrikaans Prime Minister, and by Lord Buxton, the British Governor-General. Dunn retained this goodwill in high quarters, and this was of great assistance in steering Reuters through the tensions of the inter-war years.

In a peculiar way, Reuters under Roderick Jones had become a part of the web of South African life, and so it continued under Dunn. Both the British and Dutch in South Africa made use of the Agency on special occasions. When the two South African parties finally agreed to a fusion, it was Reuters which carried the notes between General Hertzog, the Prime Minister, and General Smuts, Leader of the Opposition.

But the feeling that the internal news service should be an exclusively South African affair was growing. Luckily Reuters saw the dangers in time. Some concessions to the newspapers were made in the early 1930's. Evolution to a wholly South African national Agency took a further eight years; but it was a peaceful evolution and beneficial to both sides. In February 1938, delegates from the South African newspapers came to Cape Town to frame a constitution for the new Agency. The Chairman of the Argus group of newspapers, John Martin, was the leader; Sir Roderick Jones was invited to come from London to preside at the conference. The South African Press Association came into being that April as a co-operative news agency owned by the newspapers of South Africa and open to every paper, British and Afrikaans, that wished to join. The new Association took over from Reuters the collection and distribution of all internal news in South Africa; for world news it made a long-term agreement with Reuters, and its South African news was to be Reuters' property outside South Africa. James Dunn became General Manager of the new Association and remained at the same time Reuters' chief representative in South Africa.

This was the most satisfactory Dominion arrangement Reuters made between the two wars. Significant in a wider sphere, it brought the British and Dutch in South Africa together in a national institution of first importance which had to work harmoniously in order to work at all. General Smuts called it a symbol of the new spirit of nationhood in the Union.

The real strain of being a British institution, in a period of persistent attempts to undermine British influence abroad, was borne by Reuters in its traditional stronghold and source of greatest power and revenue, India and the Far East. It is not realised in England how consistently and often violently during the inter-war years Reuters was charged out there with being a mouthpiece of the British Government. That the Agency throughout this period kept its position as the basic world news service in the East, despite these attacks and despite mounting financial difficulties at home, was due largely to the three able men who managed Reuters' affairs in these territories and, in India, to one remarkable Indian journalist.

The three Reuter officials were William Moloney, who was General Manager in India from 1923 to 1937; William Turner, General Manager for the Far East from 1920 to 1931; and Christopher Chancellor, who stayed in Shanghai as Turner's successor in the Far East until 1939. All in turn became high executives of Reuters in London; and in 1944 Christopher Chancellor became executive Head of the Agency. The Indian journalist was K. C. Roy, one of the founders of the Associated Press of India and its guiding spirit under Reuter ownership until his untimely death in 1931.

Few men were better suited to take control of a Reuters in India facing the impact of Indian nationalism than William Moloney. An Irishman, friend and protégé of the passionate home-ruler Wilfrid Scawen Blunt, he had a quick and instinctive sympathy with Indian aspirations. The policy laid down by London was unequivocally clear: Reuters must retain its predominance in India over any other world Agency at all costs. That meant remaining as the basic world news service to India in Reuters' own name, and controlling the distribution of domestic news throughout India in the name of Reuters' subsidiary, the Associated Press of India. For most Indian nationalists Reuters' control over the internal news-channels was a source of resentment. Reuters, through Moloney and his chief assistants in India, sensed and understood this, and the organisation was moulded accordingly. The Associated Press became staffed entirely by Indian journalists, carefully chosen and well trained. A real confidence grew up inside Reuters' Indian organisation which became increasingly, except in ownership, an Indian concern. This was true of the whole Reuter organisation in India, as well as of the domestic Agency, the Associated Press.

Moloney was greatly helped in his task by the attitude and

extraordinary influence of K. C. Roy. Roy's status as the lead-ing Indian political journalist was mentioned in an earlier chapter. His identification with the Associated Press of India brought a prestige which meant much to Reuters. His death in 1931, in the middle of intensive work on the Government's sub-committee on the Press, was mourned as a national loss.

Moloney owed much to Roy. Also, as the years progressed, he became increasingly indebted to John Turner, his chief assistant, who later succeeded him in charge of the Reuter organisation in India. Turner in his turn was aided by an out-standing Indian collaborator, A. S. Bharatan, who today is in charge of the great national news agency of India which, early in 1949, as a result of arrangements made with Reuters, became the property of the Indian Press.

One of Reuters' achievements in India was to make the news service available at a cost which the new Indian vernacular newspapers could afford: by 1925 fifteen had become Reuter subscribers, and the number steadily grew. The next task was to give a new Indian tone to a traditionally Anglo-Indian news service. Indian susceptibilities were keen: omission from the Reuter report from London of matters considered of major importance in India brought quick reactions from the Indian newspapers. The London office had to be convinced of the change in emphasis: there were heartburnings on both sides before a genuinely new Indian service evolved. But the new policy brought its reward. Within twenty years of Reuters' first vernacular newspaper subscription, one hundred and fifty were taking the service; and, despite the mounting demands for Indian independence of the late 1930's and their reverbera-tions in the Indian Press, Reuters was still the basic supplier of foreign and domestic news in India when war came.

It was an even harder struggle to preserve Reuters' supremacy in the Far East. For some years the old Agency Treaties had served as a barrier against competition. But resentment against the British Agency's monopoly was growing, particularly, as has been seen, in the Associated Press of America. And in its Far Eastern operations Reuters had to struggle to prevent itself from being crushed between rival forces in the evolution of what the Japanese called 'the New Order in East Asia'. Japanese expansionists seized every chance to brand the Agency as pro-Chinese; Chinese nationalists attacked it as pro-Japanese; the Chinese Communists identified it with the British 'imperialist' Government.

As in India, Sir Roderick Jones put the right man in charge. William Turner, who was appointed General Manager for the Far East in 1920, came fresh from control of the successful Reuter reporting of the Peace Conference in Paris. He soon saw how formidable was his new task. Reuters' 'Far Eastern territories' stretched from Vladivostok to Singapore; included Japan, China, Hongkong, the Philippines, the Netherlands Indies and Indo-China. In all these territories Turner found that Reuters was widely suspected of connections with the British Government. He faced the problem realistically in a memorandum which he wrote to London in June 1921. In it he diagnosed the dangers and forecast the method of meeting them that remained consistently successful for the next two decades. 'The service should', he wrote, 'be in our opinion international, neutral, and British only in efficiency. . . . China is international territory so far as the importation of news is concerned. . . . The only satisfactory service for China and Japan is an impartial news service. . . . The Reuter service stands charged with being a British propaganda organ and is condemned as guilty unless its innocence is proved. This innocence can only be proved by confining the service to a cold, dispassionate chronicling of events.'

In China, from now onwards, civil war was almost continuous and Japan at regular intervals intervened. To understand the position of Reuters it is necessary to know that the

Agency was not only the chief provider of world news in the Far East: it had also, to fill an existing vacuum, built up a regional news service supplied by local correspondents and known as 'Reuters' Pacific Service'. This meant that during a situation of almost constant civil war, and of tension and fitful armed conflict between China and Japan, Reuters supplied the local news, maintained correspondents on both sides and held the balance between contending propaganda services. It was an extraordinary position. Reuters was for a long time almost the sole independent service giving news of China to Japan and news of Japan to China. It could never please both sides: yet in a peculiar way it kept the respect of both. Through the long campaigns and chaos of the Chinese Civil War, the Reuter organisation remained intact, and its reputation grew. When Turner returned to London in 1931, to become one of Roderick Jones's chief assistants, the first phase of the Agency's struggle to retain its position in the Far East had been won.

Christopher Chancellor was twenty-seven when he succeeded Turner in the Far East. He had taken a First Class in History at Cambridge, and after eighteen months on Reuters' London staff he now became responsible for the Agency's most difficult territory overseas. That autumn Japanese forces invaded Manchuria. In February 1932 a Japanese army invaded Shanghai, and Chancellor, as Reuters' Chief Correspondent in the Far East, covered what the American Press described as 'the biggest news story since the World War'. From now onwards China and Japan were virtually at war. As the infiltration of Chinese territory by the Japanese army changed to open war in 1937, the personal safety of British subjects in China grew increasingly precarious. There were insults and even attacks on members of the Reuter staff by Japanese soldiers. All the time there were accusations from both sides against the integrity of the Reuter service. Based on headquarters at Shanghai, Chancellor and his staff had to operate an organisation and run a news service in a country divided between the administration of the Chinese Government, moving west from Nanking to Hankow and then from Hankow to Chungking, and the Japanese military administration in the coastal provinces. The continued functioning of the Reuter offices in Shanghai, Peking and Tientsin was menaced by the Japanese army, in complete control of the surrounding country.

News service competition became intensified. Cheap subsidised services from the Russian, German and French Agencies tried to shake Reuters' position. Havas, in particular, used its new freedom and its funds from the French Government to build a strong organisation in China.

Reuters held its own in this atmosphere of nationalist rivalries. Chancellor's final task before coming back to London in 1939 was to organise correspondents to cover the developing war between Japan and Kuomintang China. Reuters' success in reporting this war finally proved its resilience and strength in the Far East. Eye-witness accounts of the bombing of Canton and Hankow and of the occupation of Nanking, where Reuters' correspondent was the last English resident to leave the city, told England and the world about the horrors of the war in China.

The Japanese Army Intelligence, however, credited Chancellor himself with wider interests. A report on his activities, dated July 31st, 1940, and found at Japanese Army Headquarters in Shanghai, had no doubts as to what he was doing in China:

'It was said in foreign circles that Chancellor's wife had connections close to the British Court, while he himself had made a career as a news agency man only because he was in close contact with British Secret Service circles and had offered his fortune and his wife's to Britain . . .

'The activities of this young and precocious head of Reuters were extraordinary. Closely connected with the Vickers Company, Chancellor was the chief commission agent in the arms and aircraft transactions with the Chinese Government. The Chinese "National Government" always held at his disposal a special aeroplane, while the British authorities often sent naval airmen from Singapore to Hongkong to fetch him, or placed at his disposal an aeroplane for trips to London. When foreign arms were without avail and the Chinese were defeated, Chancellor set up the organisation of a special intelligence service focused on Japan itself. There is information that colossal activities were carried on in Japan for the purpose of causing a Japanese upheaval from the inside . . .'

There is much more in the same strain – details of Chancellor's journeys and the names of his Chinese friends. On such factual points, the document is surprisingly accurate and shows how closely he must have been watched by the Japanese Intelligence Service. It is in the deductions from these facts that the story develops into a fairy-tale.

The newspapers of the Far East were more interested in the news service that Reuters was giving them: while the war was still at its height, the Reuter service was praised in leading newspapers from Shanghai to Singapore for its accuracy and its fair presentation of the complicated Far Eastern picture. That it remained strong, despite all attacks upon it, owed much to the fact that Chancellor succeeded in keeping on friendly terms with leading figures both in China and Japan. In Japan his task was made immeasurably easier by his close friendship with the Head of the Japanese Agency, Yukichi Iwanaga, a man of integrity and courage who did all he could, against forces which in the end were too strong for him, to resist the pressure of the nationalist forces in Japan, and who admired Reuters' tradition and its work in the Far East. Yukichi Iwanaga died in 1939: his son is now an official in the newly constituted Japanese Agency, Kyodo, a newspaper-owned co-operative which today issues the Reuter world service to the Japanese Press.

17

The Struggle for Independence

SUCCESS IN THE EAST WAS A BRIGHT SPOT ON A DARKEN-
ing horizon. American competition, especially from the United
Press Associations, mounting rivalry from the heavily subsidised European services operating all over the world, suspicions – encouraged by opponents – of Reuters' own independence, had all taken their toll. The ability to fight back
depended more and more on finance. The only hope lay in
new and larger subscriptions to the news service at home and
abroad and in the full support of the home Press. But the home
newspapers looked to Reuters for improvement in the news
service, and for increased representation by Reuter staff correspondents in foreign capitals. All this necessitated new
revenue.

With critical days ahead, a number of emergency measures
had been tried out: economy campaigns launched and certain
assets sold. During the 1920's much-needed savings were made,
and these went in fighting the competition of the next decade.
But such 'crisis measures' themselves tended to detract from
the quality of the news service. A new move to change the old
order of things had already affected two of the service's traditional news-gathering centres in Europe. Soon after the war,
Belgian business interests had bought the Bureau in Brussels
owned jointly by Reuters and Havas, and set up their own
Agency, Belga; and in 1935 Reuters' Bureau in Amsterdam
was replaced by the Dutch co-operative Agency ANP. More
dependent now for its news on the services of its allied

Agencies, the Reuter service began to lack something of its old individuality. Other economies had the same effect. While Reuters watched every penny, the American Agencies filled the world with their correspondents. The Reuter service had to face criticisms of being too narrow, too full of official British news, too reliant on the national European Agencies for its reports from Europe. In the competitive conditions of the 1930's, these charges undoubtedly had some truth in them. Editorially, the new Chief Editor, Bernard Rickatson-Hatt, who was appointed when Herbert Jeans died in 1931, did what he could to check the process. From New York, where he had been trained, he brought some of the ideas of the American Agencies. 'Human interest' stories were encouraged; 'special services' undertaken. Reuters began to employ more local part-time correspondents to fill gaps abroad.

But the news service still did not pay for itself, and had to rely more and more on profits from the commercial services. Moreover, Reuters' position in the British newspapers no longer lay unchallenged. Some years after the war, a new Agency had appeared in the field: called the British United Press, it was financed from Canada and managed by a Canadian; it acted as the Agent for the United Press Associations' service in Britain and the British Empire. It was soon sending out a fast and colourful service, tempting in its individual quality to London and provincial newspapers alike. The British United Press gained its first British newspaper client in 1927; ten years later it had seventy. This disturbing competition reached a climax at a period when Reuters had few resources with which to fight it.

Four correspondents to report the Abyssinian War (two with each side) cost Reuters £24,000 a year. Equally expensive was the Spanish Civil War. Both the Press Association and the London newspapers had to be asked for special subscriptions.

By 1938, the problem facing Reuters for a decade past was clear. The news service could no longer be run commercially as it stood. Economy campaigns were at best only makeshifts. The 'growing monthly losses' reported by Sir Roderick Jones in 1936 could only be ended by a change of policy.

It was becoming apparent that in the search for more revenue – the sole hope for survival as a world Agency – Reuters had only two courses open to it. Either the British Press as a whole must be convinced of the necessity of paying more money for the Reuter service; or facilities to expand the service without extra cost be accepted from the Government. Meanwhile pressure to enlarge its service, and to spread more British news abroad, was growing. It came from powerful quarters. In 1931, the Prince of Wales declared publicly his distress at the meagre amount of British news he had found during his tour of South America. Reuters responded by experimenting with a small daily South American wireless service for two years. It was a costly failure, not a single newspaper in South America becoming a regular subscriber. Ironically enough, outside the large French and American services, one of Reuters' rivals was the wireless service distributed free by the British Foreign Office.

The cry for more Reuter news abroad assumed a more definite note a few years later. In 1937, *The Empire in the World* (by Sir Arthur Willert, B. K. Long and H. V. Hodson) was published. It demanded a more realistic attitude to the whole question of British prestige in the world and called for a stock-taking of the British Empire. In a chapter on Foreign Policy, Sir Arthur Willert devoted a section to Reuters and the other news agencies. He stressed Reuters' difficulties in competing with the subsidised Agencies, but deprecated any question of the Agency's receiving a Government 'subsidy' to join in the propaganda-war for Britain. Then he made this suggestion: 'that the Governments of the Empire, and especially the

London Government, should consider whether they could not aid Reuters and any other British Agency which could qualify for assistance, by at least extending to them equal facilities for cheap transmission of that copious stream of wireless messages which is more than ever becoming the recognised means of long-distance and large-scale Press work'. Sir Arthur Willert had been Chief of the Press Department of the Foreign Office from 1925 to 1935. It was natural for him to see Reuters as a medium for spreading British prestige abroad. Articles in the *Spectator* and the *Round Table* (of which H. V. Hodson was Editor) echoed the same sentiments. Reuters was reminded of its great days of expansion during the 1914–18 War; told how beneficial it could be as a national advertisement to help Britain's trade recovery. Overseas British Chambers of Commerce went further. Irritated by Italian propaganda, in the Levant and other trade-centres, that the British Empire 'would shortly break up', they urged the need for more British news abroad. 'For years', as the Secretary of the British Chamber at São Paulo, Brazil, wrote in the *Daily Telegraph* in May 1937, 'the British Chambers of Commerce have urged the need for British news services, inaugurated if necessary with official backing in their early stages.'

From the national and commercial points of view such arguments were understandable. It was true that Reuters had served the national interest faithfully during the First World War. Crises, and perhaps war, lay ahead. Reuters had no available revenue to meet the growing demands for more British news abroad. Sir Roderick Jones saw the situation in the same light. 'At a time when the national Agencies of practically every country of the world are operating internationally as part of the political system of their Governments', he told the Reuter Annual General Meeting in July 1938, 'Reuters, as the national Agency of the British Empire, cannot escape the obligations of that status. The problem to be solved is how to discharge the obligations and yet retain, as must be done, independence and freedom from official dictation.'

The decision had in fact been made. Towards the end of 1937 Sir Roderick Jones had had an interview with the Prime Minister, Mr. Neville Chamberlain. They discussed a plan to increase the Reuter wireless service both to the Continent and overseas, with the help of 'certain facilities' from the Foreign Office. Meetings followed with a Cabinet Committee formed under Sir Kingsley Wood to consider British news services abroad.

In September 1938, as the storm gathered over the Sudetenland, matters came to a head. Propaganda for the German case was flooding the world. On October 4th, Roderick Jones announced to the Reuter Board that, under pressure of the international crisis, the Government had granted him facilities to start an enlarged Reuter wireless service overseas at once. Within twenty-four hours the powerful Rugby transmitters had begun their new task. Reuters' version of the Munich crisis was now added to the outpourings of the German and Italian Agencies. Demands by the neutral Press on the Continent for Reuters' reports showed the new service's success. Every available Reuter correspondent was rushed to the Sudeten frontier, Berchtesgaden and Munich. Three of Reuters' men met in Berchtesgaden; two others were arrested and searched at revolver-point by the German Gestapo in the Sudetenland. The new wireless service meant that their hour-to-hour reports could now travel to the far ends of the earth without imposing an additional strain on the Reuter budget.

The Government's facilities were simple – merely the provision free of transmission facilities for messages sent over and above the normal Reuter wireless services for which payment was made. There was certainly no editorial interference; no attempts to insert or suppress messages. But it was understood that Reuters would from now onwards disseminate an increased volume of British news.

The outbreak of the Second World War in September 1939 forced the issue for both the Government and Reuters. To have more British news sent abroad, as a counterblast to Axis propaganda, became a national problem of first importance.

In September, a few days after war began, Roderick Jones's long negotiations reached a formal Agreement signed between His Majesty's Government and Reuters. The Agreement granted Reuters expanded transmission facilities for its new war services, but at the same time affirmed the Agency's complete editorial independence. The Leafield and Rugby Reuter wireless services became the main channel of British news to Europe and overseas; the Government bore the cost of transmitting the additional news.

Some members of the Reuter Board were uneasy. Soon after the outbreak of war, the Government's foreign publicity arrangements, including the Reuter Agreement of September 1939, were handed over to the Ministry of Information. The Ministry confirmed the Agreement's terms and reiterated that it had no desire to interfere with Reuters' freedom. But it became apparent that certain quarters of the Government were pressing for rights of consultation in Reuters' general policy. As the war situation deteriorated, the demand grew.

In June 1940, the capitulation of France brought with it the extinction of Havas. Within a few weeks it had been turned into a Vichy propaganda organ; its name was changed, and the Agency founded by Charles Havas in 1835 – the oldest of its kind in the world – was transformed into the official Agency of Vichy France – 'Office Français d'Information'. In Latin America Havas's vast ramifications remained. To Reuters they offered a prize in a continent in which they had in the past experienced a dismal run of failures. In July 1940, Reuters made a lightning invasion of South America, set up an organisation

and took over some of the former Havas staff and newspaper contracts. This meant a considerable outlay: further
transmission facilities from the Government helped to ease the
burden.

This new development gave additional impetus to the movement within the Government to exert a definite influence over
the Agency's policy. Soon there were inevitable clashes. The
Ministry of Information felt itself committed to supporting
the Free French news service to South America. The leading
South American newspapers did not want this service. Reuters
was determined to make the main service its own. The
Ministry objected to Reuters' inclusion of enemy communiqués in its world service: the Agency was determined to
include them as one of its basic obligations to newspapers in
neutral countries. The year 1940 ended on a note of tension.

The strain was reflected within Reuters itself. The Board
were growing increasingly uneasy. They were concerned about
the Government pressure and they felt that the Agency might
be drifting into a position from which it might only with difficulty be extricated. By the New Year a crisis in Reuters was
certain. It came in the first week of February. On resisting the
Government's immediate demands for a voice in Reuters'
policy, there was agreement. But Sir Roderick Jones felt that
he could repeat his success of the previous war and accept
Government facilities with no loss to Reuters' freedom.
Governments, however, had grown more demanding since
1915. The American Agencies' suspicion of Government aid
had spread wide and deep; provincial newspaper proprietors
on the Reuter Board – men like W. J. Haley (now Sir William
Haley, Director-General of the BBC) of the *Manchester Guardian*, who had inherited the mantle of Scott's keen Liberalism
when he succeeded him as a Director of Reuters in 1938, felt
its full force. They were convinced that, however stern
Reuters' resistance and notwithstanding Roderick Jones's

confidence in his power to maintain the Agency's independence, Government facilities of any kind would jeopardise that independence in the end. And this they rightly saw as a vital principle in the freedom of the British Press. On February 4th, 1941, Sir Roderick Jones resigned his position as Chairman and Managing Director of Reuters.

It is perhaps too close to events to give a proper estimate of Sir Roderick Jones's achievement. Managing Director from the birth of the new Company at the end of 1916, and Chairman from 1919, he was as closely identified with Reuters' fortunes for nearly twenty-five years as any one man could be. His success in pulling the Agency together during the critical years of the First World War was remarkable. So also were the early expansion and continuous technical progress achieved in the face of the formidable economic difficulties of the inter-war years. The impressive new building in Fleet Street, designed by Sir Edwin Lutyens for Reuters and the Press Association, and financed by the provincial newspapers, owes much to Roderick Jones's inspiration. Since July 1939 it has housed both the Press Association and Reuters, and this has been a factor in achieving a closer working relationship between the two Agencies. These were positive and lasting achievements.

The problem which had led to Sir Roderick Jones's resignation remained. How was Reuters to hold its own, with its vastly increased war commitments, without continued facilities from the Government? There were to be further crises before it was solved.

The Press Association, represented by its six Directors on the Reuter Board, were now left with the running of Reuters themselves. They had purchased Sir Roderick Jones's small holding of a thousand shares and now owned all the shares. Samuel Storey, a member of the Board since 1935, Chairman of the Portsmouth & Sunderland Newspapers, and Conservative Member of Parliament for Sunderland, was appointed

Chairman. The Board were agreed that the only way for Reuters to hold its own without Government facilities was for its basis to be 'broadened'; but there were serious differences of view as to how this should be done. Largely inspired by Lord Kemsley and Lord Rothermere, an approach from the Newspaper Proprietors Association, soon after Sir Roderick Jones's resignation, brought matters to a head. The London newspapers felt that the time had come to enter the ownership of Reuters and they offered to purchase from the Press Association a 50 per cent share. Negotiations were conducted by a Reuter delegation of three led by the doyen of the Board, Alexander McLean Ewing of the *Glasgow Herald*; his two colleagues were W. J. Haley of the *Manchester Guardian* and Raymond Derwent of the Westminster Provincial Press. They continued all that summer, under the shadow of the war situation, while the Agency wrestled with reorganising its overseas staff and changing its wireless service to directional beams. The successful completion of the sale – an equal partnership between the Press Association and the Newspaper Proprietors Association in the ownership of Reuters – was announced on October 29th, 1941.

It was not achieved without some heartburnings. Suspicion of the London newspapers' ambitions was an ancient and deepseated force among many elements of the provincial Press. It had been one of the motives that had led to the founding of the Press Association in 1868. Now a strong minority in the Press Association membership painted the proposed partnership as a surrender of Reuters to the London Press.

The issue was settled at an Extraordinary General Meeting of the Press Association on October 17th, twelve days before the partnership was announced. All the arguments were heard: a clear majority decided that the partnership should go forward in the best interests of Reuters.

But opposition to the sale did not end there. Five days later the future of Reuters was raised in the House of Commons. It was characterised as 'a matter of extreme public importance and urgency', and the proposed partnership became the subject of an excited debate. The sale to the Newspaper Proprietors Association was described as a method of concentrating still more power in the hands of the London newspapers. It seemed to be overlooked that Reuters' gain from the full support of the London Press would be enormous. As Brendan Bracken, the Minister of Information, put it: 'the debate has been to a certain extent one-sided, because nobody has spoken for the bad, bold Barons of Fleet Street . . .' No one referred to the concern of the Press in the strength and independence of Reuters. The Government and the national interest were the predominant themes. Samuel Storey, still Chairman of Reuters but hostile to the partnership with the Newspaper Proprietors Association in the form proposed, wanted the Government to take the lead and 'bring about the creation of a Reuter Trust', representative of national interests and of Reuters' 'spheres of action'. Confronted by further proposals from members of the House which he regarded as tantamount to a suggestion for nationalising Reuters, Brendan Bracken leapt into the fray. Speaking as Minister of Information, he declined any invitation to the Government to take control of Reuters: this would be signing the death-warrant of the Agency's position as a world service. As a former newspaperman himself, he defended the London Press; strongly deprecated any suggestion that, under the new partnership, Reuters would be used against the national interest. He made the real issue quite clear: the future of Reuters was the concern of the Press, not of the Government. It was for the Press, through Reuters, to put its house in order.

It had in fact already taken a step in this direction. At the beginning of the negotiations the Press Association had suggested the creation of a 'Reuter Trust'. This should reassert and guarantee Reuters' independence under the ownership of the whole British Press; preserve absolute equality between the Press Association and the Newspaper Proprietors Association; and record the principle that the interest of both partners in Reuters should be in the nature of a trust, not an investment. With this the leaders of the Newspaper Proprietors Association were in full agreement from the first. It went far to win support for the partnership; and it influenced the Press Association at the decisive General Meeting on October 17th.

Another debate, promised by Brendan Bracken if the negotiations broke down, did not have to take place. Instead, on the morning of October 29th, Reuters made the following announcement:

THE REUTER TRUST

The following arrangements are announced:

The Press Association, who were the sole holders of the shares of Reuters Limited, have decided in co-operation with the Newspaper Proprietors Association to enter into common and equal partnership in Reuters and to set up a Reuter Trust.

To this end the Newspaper Proprietors Association has purchased from the Press Association one-half of the capital of Reuters. The effect of this is that Reuters is now owned by the British Press as a whole. A declaration of trust has been signed by both parties setting forth the principles which will be maintained under the new ownership, which is regarded as in the nature of a trust rather than as an investment. In particular the parties have undertaken to use their best endeavours to ensure:

A that Reuters shall at no time pass into the hands of any one interest, group or faction;

B that its integrity, independence and freedom from bias shall at all times be fully preserved;

C that its business shall be so administered that it shall supply an unbiased and reliable news service to British, Dominion, Colonial, foreign and other overseas newspapers and agencies with which it has or may hereafter have contracts;

D that it shall pay due regard to the many interests which it serves in addition to those of the Press, and

E that no effort shall be spared to expand, develop and adapt the business of Reuters in order to maintain in every event its position as the leading world news agency.

An equal number of trustees are being appointed by the Press Association and the Newspaper Proprietors Association to carry out the above undertakings. An independent Chairman of the Trustees is to be appointed by the Lord Chief Justice.

Provision has been made that the Trust shall be irrevocable for a minimum period of 21 years and that thereafter it shall not be amended or dissolved unless the matter has been submitted to the Lord Chief Justice, and shall not be dissolved unless he is satisfied that by reason of the circumstances then existing it is impracticable to secure the objects of the Trust as set out above by continuing its operation in its present or any amended form.

A man from outside the newspaper industry, Sir Lynden Macassey, a lawyer, was appointed as the neutral Chairman of the Reuter Trust by the Lord Chief Justice of England, the highest independent authority in the land.

Under the new arrangements Samuel Storey ceased to be Chairman of Reuters. There was now to be no Chairman of the Company, nor of the Reuter Board. This was a necessary corollary to the principle of absolute equality of control as between the London and provincial Press. Three Directors were appointed by the London newspapers and three by the Press Association to represent the provincial interest. There was no casting vote, and Directors took the chair turn by turn at Board meetings. The new Board confirmed William Moloney and Christopher Chancellor as Joint General Managers of the Company.

As a co-operative newspaper-owned organisation, paying no dividends, Reuters could now look to the British Press for full support. It was not long before the new Board was able to obtain substantially higher subscriptions from the newspaper owners. This was the essential first step in order to make practicable a logical and essential development arising from the new ownership and the guarantees laid down by the Reuter Trust. No time must be lost in bringing Reuters' arrangements with the Government into harmony with the undertakings of the newspaper owners of Reuters that the Agency's independence would be fully safeguarded.

When the war was over, Christopher Chancellor, who had been made Head of Reuters in 1944, chose Washington as the appropriate place to disclose publicly these government associations of the past and to describe the manner in which Reuters had brought them to an end. In a speech before the Overseas Writers at Washington, on January 28th, 1946, he made this statement:

'At the beginning of World War II Reuters was offered and accepted special transmission facilities provided through the British Ministry of Information which enabled it without extra cost to expand its newscasts through the British Post Office to certain foreign countries with a view to matching in volume the subsidised services of Havas, Stefani, Tass, Domei and DNB. It was stated that this war-time arrangement did not affect Reuters' editorial independence and integrity. This formula was accepted by some; but to others it was clear that the expansion of the news wordage through Government-financed channels was in fact nothing less than a disguised subsidy.'

Chancellor told the story two years later to the Royal Commission on the Press in London:

'After the reorganisation of Reuters in 1941 the Board decided that all such arrangements should be cancelled, and this was done. At the same time Reuters went on record as opposing any policy of discrimination in the matter of international transmission rates and facilities. Regarding the transmission of news overseas from London through the "multi-address" system operated by the General Post Office, the Reuter Board communicated its view to the British Government as follows:

'"As a matter of policy and principle similar facilities should be granted to all news agencies: Reuters' policy is equal transmission facilities for all."'

The 'new Reuters', as it was soon widely called, had in its ownership and constitution indeed travelled far from the 'old'. But its ideals and standards remained the same – reaffirmed in the declaration of the Trust. The new support and backing of the British Press was a guarantee that Reuters would always be able to live up to them. *The Times*, in a leading article on the day of the announcement of the Reuter Trust, had welcomed this development as a triumph for a Free Press. Most hopeful of all, as coming from the American who had fought his long campaign against 'Reuters Rex', was Kent Cooper's comment on the new partnership in *Barriers Down*: 'Nothing in the long history of the British Press can be as satisfying.'

PART III

THE NEW REUTERS

1941–1951

I am glad that Reuters, along with the American news agencies, has firmly announced its opposition to any post-war subsidising of international news services. It is most desirable that the same policy should be followed by the news agencies which may in the future be established in other countries and that there should be general international agreement by Governments not to subsidise such agencies or endeavour to use them in any way as instruments of propaganda. Europe and the world needs, as one of the foremost instruments of its revival, independent and untainted international news.

I hope therefore that the great British newspapers which own Reuters and whose combined financial resources are immense if they are prepared to act co-operatively will, whatever their own domestic battles, accept the full implication of their joint responsibility and see that Reuters is provided with the financial resources likely to be required during the next few years.

FRANCIS WILLIAMS:
PRESS, PARLIAMENT AND PEOPLE (1946)

18

The Second World War

IT IS IMPOSSIBLE IN THIS CHAPTER TO GIVE MORE THAN
a slight sketch of the tremendous expansion and quickening of
Reuters' activities in the Second World War. More than in any
previous war, the Agency's continued existence depended upon
the national situation. It was fortunate that the move to 85,
Fleet Street, had been completed two months before war
started. Emergency quarters were set up at Barnet on the out-
skirts of London: Reuters had purchased a private house on
the fringe of London's telephone network and on the route
of the land cables from central London to the radio station at
Leafield. This was to be an alternative editorial and distributing
centre, if Fleet Street were put out of action. It was brought
into use, as soon as war was declared, as a listening-post for
the reception of foreign wireless broadcasts, and it has continued in this role into the years of peace and the 'cold war'.

The successful German invasions of 1940 meant the fall, one
by one, of Reuters' European offices, and the almost total loss
of Reuters' European revenue. In each country Reuter correspondents stayed until the last moment and they all succeeded
in making last-minute escapes. Gordon Young, Reuters' correspondent in Holland – the traditional outpost for news from
Germany – sent the first detailed account to reach the outside
world of the German invasion that began at 2.45 a.m. on
Friday, May 10th. For a few hours the next day he was able
to send the last direct news of Holland's resistance, over a telephone line from Amsterdam to 85, Fleet Street, before the line

was broken. He then managed just in time to embark for England on a cargo ship at The Hague.

In Paris, Martin Herlihy, chief of the Reuter office, packed his staff and a few records into two cars, had the rest of the files burnt, and followed the French Government from Tours to Bordeaux and thence back to London by ship.

Reuters' correspondents in the Far East were less fortunate. Kenneth Selby-Walker, chief correspondent, was overtaken by the Japanese in Java. His last despatch, of March 6th, 1942, widely published in the British Press, ended: 'I am afraid it is too late now. Good luck!' He was never seen again. A dozen more members of Reuters' Far Eastern staff were caught by the Japanese advance, including William O'Neill, the Manager in Hongkong, and Alan Hammond, the Manager in Manila. Both were interned in Japanese camps until the end of the war. James Henry, the Singapore Manager, fortunately escaped to Australia.

Apart from the sufferings of Reuters' men in the Far East, the loss of this territory left a huge gap in the Agency's revenue. This added to the problems which had to be faced in 1942. They were formidable indeed – but behind Reuters now stood the newspapers, pledged under the Trust Agreement 'that no effort shall be spared to expand, develop and adapt the business of Reuters in order to maintain in every event its position as the leading world news Agency'.

The British Press endorsed a forward policy for Reuters and financed this policy by raising their annual subscriptions year by year from 1942 onwards. The news service was expanded and improved and the newspapers met the extra cost. The new Management's energy and effort satisfied the Press that the added costs were justified.

At the end of March 1942, the new Board gave Christopher Chancellor, who had served Reuters abroad almost continuously from the summer of 1931 until the autumn of 1940,

responsibility for 'the entire editorial services'. As his chief
lieutenant he brought into Reuters Walton Cole, a young
journalist who had begun his career in Edinburgh and had then
become Night Editor of the Press Association. With the Press
Association's approval, Cole was appointed first Joint Editor
and later Editor of Reuters. Chancellor and Cole then set to
work together to reorganise Reuters' editorial system. Cole
ran the central news desk himself for months, working a fifteen-
hour day, and sleeping in the Reuter building. New life
transformed the services and there was a general feeling of
confidence. The home and overseas news desks were fully
co-ordinated. Chancellor and Cole brought new men into the
service: at home, they recruited reporters trained in the provinces; abroad, newspapermen replaced local dignitaries. By
1943 the British Press was widely commenting on Reuters'
editorial transformation.

It was essential to increase the number of war correspondents.
Reuters' men were outnumbered, sometimes by three or four
to one, by the American Agencies. Administrative costs in
London were cut down to a minimum and all available funds
were spent on strengthening the reporting staff.

All Agency men suffer from two disabilities as against the
newspapers' own correspondents: from their anonymity,
strictly preserved as a rule, and from the fact that their despatches are never exclusive to one newspaper, but go to all.
But the war saw a change in the rule of anonymity; the names
of Reuter war correspondents began to appear regularly over
their despatches.

In an article in the *Newspaper World* of January 9th, 1943,
the foreign news sub-editor of one of the great London daily
newspapers gave a careful analysis of the war correspondents'
achievements in 1942. He singled out for praise three Reuter
correspondents – Harold King, for his despatches from Russia,
Alan Humphries, for his reports on the first British commando

raids, and Arthur Oakeshott for his account of the sailing of the Arctic Convoy to Russia in 1942 through prolonged and concentrated attacks by German torpedo bombers. The article concluded: 'Possibly the outstanding feature in the opinion of foreign sub-editors has been the remarkable transformation of Reuters which, from the showing of their own tape alone, has become progressively more enterprising, competent and effective as a purveyor of news. . . . So probably the best bit of work of 1942 from the point of view of British journalism has been the re-emergence of Reuters.'

The most searching test of Reuters' new strength came with the Normandy invasion. For D Day itself twelve Reuter correspondents were briefed, and as the operation developed the number in the war theatre rose to fifteen. The first British correspondent into Normandy was Reuters' Doon Campbell, who went in with the Lovat Scouts: his first message was written in a ditch near the shore. Carrier-pigeons flew across the Channel with messages from Reuter reporters with the air-borne troops and the R.A.F. In 1850 Julius Reuter had made his name by using pigeons: they served Reuters once again in June 1944.

The work of the Agency men was in many respects harder than that of the newspapers' own correspondents. They had to provide a full and consecutive account of the campaign: they could not choose the most exciting incidents to report. With a newspaper 'dead-line' in some country or other every minute of the day, speed was of far greater importance than for a newspaper correspondent, who had to watch only the edition-times of his own newspaper.

Reuters' report of the war was not achieved without casualties. Three correspondents were killed in action. Alexander Massey Anderson, Reuters' special correspondent with the British Mediterranean Fleet, was drowned in December 1941, when H.M.S. *Galatea* was torpedoed and sunk off Alexandria by a German submarine. In the Italian campaign, Stewart Sale, who had earlier risked his life in the nose of a Lancaster bomber to report the first air raids on Berlin, was killed by a shell-burst while covering the British Fifth Army near Naples. And in August 1944, William Stringer, correspondent with the United States First Army in France, was fatally wounded in the forward zone.

Two others were missing, and for many months it was not known whether they were alive or dead. John Talbot, Reuters' special correspondent who had arrived by parachute in Yugoslavia, was taken prisoner in a German raid on Tito's headquarters. Another parachutist, Jack Smyth, was missing, after having jumped with the air-borne force at Arnhem in September 1944. Talbot suffered at the hands of the Gestapo. But he and Smyth turned up from German prison camps safe and sound in April 1945. Patrick Crosse, now chief of Reuters' Rome office, was captured in Cyrenaica in 1942 as a Reuter war correspondent in the North African campaign: he too was released from a German prison camp in April 1945.

But Fleet Street was in the front line too, and the Press Association-Reuter building survived the long aerial bombardments by a miracle. In the great Central London fire of December 29th, 1940, the Reuter look-outs on the nine-storey-high roof saw incendiaries rain down and set on fire St. Bride's Church, only eleven feet away from the east wall of the Reuter building. Only once – for three and a half hours in the early morning of April 17th, 1941 – did Reuters have to stop its twenty-four-hour service. That was when a land-mine weighing twenty-five hundredweight landed in Fleet Street exactly opposite Reuters' front door, miraculously checked from exploding by one of the lamp-lines running across the street. The Reuter garrison carried on, until ordered to evacuate the building – bombs falling still on all sides – while the naval commander of the demolition squad gallantly disposed of the mine.

The underground shelter system of 85, Fleet Street, was used during the air raids; and in the worst raids, when the Central Telegraph Office in London was isolated from Fleet Street and finally destroyed, the emergency lines from Reuters' Barnet house came into action, and much to the surprise of the Germans the Reuter service continued without interruption. In the worst period of all, when the City of London was in flames and almost every telegraph line damaged or destroyed, the whole of the Reuter staff responsible for the overseas service moved over as a body to Barnet and many of them slept where they worked.

As in the First World War, the Germans showed their appreciation of Reuters' power by much abuse and propaganda. Pamphlets were devoted to Reuters; but now there was a note of surprise that Reuters continued to function at all. Many times the German radio announced the total destruction of the Reuter *'Lügenbureau'*. Sir Roderick Jones's resignation in February 1941 was seized upon as a prelude to the imminent collapse of Reuters, if not of Great Britain itself. Rome Radio announced that Sir Roderick Jones clearly realised that 'Great Britain is a sinking ship', and fully sympathised with his wish – as the broadcaster put it – 'not to remain on board much longer'. Berlin saw him as a 'scapegoat for Reuters' unreliable news service'. His successor likewise was singled out for comment. To him William Joyce, broadcasting in English from Germany, devoted a special postscript on Christmas Eve, 1944: 'It would be impossible for me to leave the subject of propaganda without referring to the supremely cynical utterances of C. J. Chancellor who has the dishonour of directing Reuters' news policy.'

In this history it has been shown that twice in twenty-five years, with England at war, the British Government turned in stinctively to Reuters to assist it in spreading the British point of view and in supporting the war effort of the British

Empire and Commonwealth. On each occasion almost precisely the same thing happened – ways and means were found of utilising the Reuter organisation, its world network and its great technical experience, in the interest of the nation at war. In each case a genuine effort was made to maintain the Reuter service as an honest news service and to safeguard the independence of Reuters' editorial policy. But by the time of the Second World War new ideas had crystallised, and a Reuter Board composed of newspapermen from the provinces – from Manchester and Belfast, from Glasgow and Birmingham – saw clearly that the two things were incompatible, that a news service at all costs must avoid financial contact with Government, however hedged around with safeguards. The price of this decision was a heavy one. It required courage in war-time, and during a war which was going desperately badly for England, to refuse to co-operate in a manner which to some members of the Government seemed a natural and patriotic duty in time of grave emergency. And it meant sacrificing revenue and facilities which could have been precious to Reuters at a time when the Agency's fortunes stood low.

It was a unique decision, reflecting credit upon the men who made it and upon the motives of the British Press, both of London and the provinces, which stepped into the breach and provided the funds enabling Reuters to shake itself totally free of all Government associations.

It soon became clear that the newspaper backing now behind Reuters, and the improved technical efficiency of the news service, had made a considerable impression in Government circles. In the nature of things, some friction was inevitable between Reuters on the one hand and the War Cabinet, the Foreign Office, British Embassies abroad and the Ministry of Information on the other. The first allegiance of all the latter was naturally to their country at war; they found it hard to concern themselves with a world news agency's insistence that its first duty was to the public all over the world, and to the principle of truth in news. But in Reuters the conviction was equally strong that a vital principle was at stake and that no compromise was possible. It was not always easy, and 'lack of patriotism' was a charge to which the men running Reuters had to harden themselves.

With effort and pains Reuter succeeded in explaining its point of view. The Ministry of Information, most closely concerned with the problem, showed a remarkable tolerance and understanding. It was constantly under pressure from Service Chiefs or members of the War Cabinet, furious at the Minister of Information's failure to deal with a refusal by Reuters to suppress news unfavourable to the national cause. The Director-General of the Ministry from 1941 to 1945 was Cyril Radcliffe (now Lord Radcliffe, a Law Lord). In retrospect he sums up the Ministry's attitude in these words: 'Reuters was a headache – but a worthwhile headache.'

A meeting between the Foreign Secretary, Anthony Eden, and Christopher Chancellor in June 1943 led to a new understanding in the Foreign Office of the aims and principles of the Reuter Trust. It resulted in a memorandum being sent to all British Embassies abroad, in Eden's words 'setting out the principles of the Trust, emphasising Reuters' independence, and insisting upon understanding of the Agency's position and problems'. Controversies between Reuters and individual Embassies and Press Attachés occasionally flared up over minor incidents; but the Foreign Office from now onwards understood where the duties and responsibilities of Reuters lay.

Reuters' new status, and the public declaration of its independence, had a remarkable effect upon the Agency's goodwill abroad. In April 1942 a special mission to the United States was undertaken by William Haley on behalf of Reuters. Christopher Chancellor accompanied Haley on a second mission to the United States at the end of 1942, and

Haley went on in 1943 to Australia. The purpose of these missions was to lay the foundation for a new relationship of mutual confidence, trust and respect between Reuters and the Associated Press of America and, through the Australian Associated Press, between Reuters and the newspapers of Australia.

The new Reuter Board realised at once that the first task was to establish a fresh relationship with the Associated Press. Although formally allied under the contract of 1934, relations were cold and distant. There was no friendship between the two organisations. The spirit behind the 1934 contract, obtained by Roderick Jones after the old agreement had been denounced, was far from good. Reuters felt that the time had come for a new agreement, and that there should be a far more genuine collaboration between the two great English-speaking Agencies.

It was primarily to create, if this could be done, a new spirit that Haley set off on his first mission in April 1942. In New York he told Kent Cooper, with whom he spent a week discussing the world Agency situation from beginning to end, that he came to find for Reuters 'a comrade not a customer'; and in this he succeeded.

'I do with all my heart', wrote Kent Cooper, 'wish that since Reuters now has proclaimed its ownership by the entire English Press, a sponsorship that approximates with that of the Associated Press, the avenue will be found on which the Associated Press and Reuters, dominant and representative of the Press of their two countries, can march down arm-in-arm toward a greater Press freedom . . .'

Haley, in his reply, emphasised the British tradition of freedom of the Press and reassured Kent Cooper that Reuters stood squarely behind its ideals.

'Reuters is now', Haley wrote, 'owned by the British Press and I do not think that in the matter of freedom of expression, liberty of printing, and what C. P. Scott once called "the sacredness of news", the British Press has ever been anywhere but in the forefront of the fight. By its striving came many of the rights which are now our common heritage. It realises its great responsibilities and, so far as Reuters is concerned, it has clearly expressed them in a Trust Deed.'

There could be no doubt about Kent Cooper's views on the ethics of news-gathering. Haley and Chancellor were made vividly aware of them when they arrived in New York on their joint mission in the December of 1942. *Barriers Down*, Kent Cooper's story of his fight to break down what he saw as the 'barriers' of the old European Agency alliance, was published a few days before their arrival. The target of the book was Reuters, and a sensation was created in the American newspaper world. But the 'new Reuters' had already made such progress that the book did Reuters good rather than harm. Arthur Robb, reviewing *Barriers Down* in the influential *Editor and Publisher* of New York, stressed a new note in the American attitude to Reuters. 'At the time of writing', he said, 'relations between the new management of Reuters and the Associated Press are closer and more cordial than at any time since 1914'; and the American newspaper world listened to him.

The year 1943 saw the first beginnings of a new relationship with the Australian Press. Haley went on to Australia from New York to arrange a new contract between Reuters and the leading newspapers in Australia through their co-operatively owned association, the Australian Associated Press. He achieved far more than this. Australia had shared the American view about Reuters' possible connections with the British Government. No Australian newspaper leaders asserted this more strongly than the two men of commanding position in the Australian Press whose goodwill Haley had to win: Sir Keith Murdoch of the *Melbourne Herald*, and Rupert Henderson of the *Sydney Morning Herald*. But once that goodwill had been won, technical difficulties of very old standing began to melt away. Haley was the first ambassador for 'the new Reuters': three and a half years later Christopher Chancellor flew to Australia and completed the task.

This was a great rebuilding period in Reuters – the years 1942 to 1945. While vital world relationships were being formed, the Agency went ahead technically and added to the reputation of its news service during a time of total war. The objectives of the new ownership, and the principles of the Reuter Trust, had been validated. And the frequency and ubiquity of the personal missions overseas – undertaken by Chancellor, Cole and Fleetwood-May – showed an impressive energy and determination to expand Reuters throughout the world, despite all the difficulties of war.

All this formed a hopeful prelude to the tasks that peace would bring – the re-creation of the Reuter organisation in Europe and the Far East; the task of meeting the full force of the competition of the American Agencies which would come immediately the war was over; and above all the great responsibility of being the only surviving fully independent world Agency based upon Europe.

But the essential battle had been already won. Reuters had been able to show that it could stand with the American news agencies and share with them a great war achievement – something alien, and indeed incomprehensible, to the totalitarian powers of those days and of today. This was the successful demonstration in practice of the principle that news and propaganda are two separate and distinct things – that propaganda, or 'information', must be left in the hands of Government departments explicitly responsible for it, and that news agencies must be left free, even in war-time, to disseminate unbiased, factual news for the honest information of the people of the world. That this achievement was possible in England during one of the worst periods of the war is a fact worth remembering.

Largely as a result of the policy followed by Reuters and the American news agencies, it is recognised in the United States and Britain that national propaganda is a Government function and not an activity that can with safety be touched by a free Press and its organs, the news services which serve it and which it owns. Presentation of the British point of view, countering anti-British propaganda, is the responsibility of the Foreign Office through its Information Services and the British Council, and the overseas broadcasting services of the BBC. Reuters' responsibilities, and they are very great, lie elsewhere.

19

Co-operation in Europe :
and a Challenge from the State Department

THE FINAL YEAR OF THE WAR BROUGHT A RENEWED PLEA
among the independent world Agencies for removing all barriers to the exchange of news in peace-time. But the plea took
different forms. Kent Cooper, executive head of the Associated
Press, took the lead in the United States. In the event both the
Associated Press and the United Press launched crusades for
international action after the war to ensure world Press freedom. Special resolutions on the subject were included in the
political platforms of both the Republican and Democratic
Party meetings at Chicago in 1944. Freedom of news seemed
to be one of the few things on which both the political parties
were firmly agreed. In September, Congress passed a resolution favouring 'the world-wide right of interchange of news
protected by international compact'. That same summer Kent
Cooper launched a Press campaign in the United States for the
incorporation of a 'charter of freedom for news and communications' in the peace settlement.

In July 1944, W. J. Moloney retired from his joint General-
Managership after thirty-six years with Reuters. He had served
Reuters in Russia, Turkey, Holland and Germany, and had
managed the Agency's affairs in India for fifteen years before
going back to London as one of the chief executives of the
Agency. The Reuter Board now put Christopher Chancellor,

just forty, at the head of Reuters as General Manager and entrusted him with full responsibility for working out the Agency's plans for peace.

In Great Britain there was no public crusade for international news freedom such as took place in the United States. But Vernon Bartlett, a well-known journalist and Member of Parliament, who had himself worked for a short time in Reuters, made a demand in the House of Commons for support of the American movement to abolish the system of Government-controlled news agencies in all countries. 'There is', he said, 'no monopoly more dangerous than a monopoly of ideas, views and news.' Taking a similar line, Christopher Chancellor made the Reuter attitude clear in speeches and lectures given in London during the closing year of the war. A declaration of independence of Government control was written into Reuters' new contracts with other news agencies. The new contracts with the independent European Agencies were now governed by the following preamble:

Both parties to this present agreement declare that they are news agencies serving no other purpose than the dissemination of truthful unbiased news, that they are free from any Government or tendentious control and that the news which they supply to each other shall be compiled and selected purely on its merits as news, and that editorial discretion on each side is free from outside dictation or pressure.

This preamble was accepted enthusiastically by the news agencies of Western Europe.

But there was already a cloud on the horizon. Even before the war ended, the Moscow magazine *War and the Working Class* attacked the American campaign for Press freedom as a trick of the capitalist Press. This attack was an early sign of a split on Press and news-agency principles that was to widen as the political rift grew between East and West.

It was soon clear that agreement on principles was not intended to limit competition between the great international news agencies themselves. The men who controlled these Agencies realised perfectly well that competition was the healthiest stimulus to efficiency, and that lack of it would bring about the one thing they had set themselves against – a monopoly in the channels of news. Both the Associated Press and the United Press were in expansionist mood. Reuters, with the Reuter Trust behind it, could quote express instructions from its newspaper owners: 'that no effort shall be spared to expand, develop and adapt the business of Reuters in order to maintain in every event its position as the leading world news agency'. The conviction that competition throughout the world was of value in itself was clearly to be tested to the full.

With Reuters busier, reporting the Second Front, than ever before in its history, the new General Manager had to take far-reaching decisions, most of them – and all those concerned with Europe and the Far East – acts of faith. The Agency had also to devote much of its energies to North and South America and to continued reorganisation at home.

In the United States, Reuters already had more subscribers than ever before in its history; and an important milestone was reached when Colonel Robert McCormick's *Chicago Tribune* decided to take the service in the summer of 1944. This came after a personal visit by J. Loy Maloney, the *Tribune*'s able Managing Editor, to London to check Reuters' credentials and efficiency. The Agency's service to the most influential newspaper in the American Middle West began the same day that Chancellor became General Manager.

The same summer Reuters strengthened its position in South America by purchasing 'Comtelburo', a private company, founded in 1869, that had had for many years a virtual monopoly of reporting commercial prices between England and South America. Tottering to its fall under fierce modern competition, it was now grafted on to the Reuter commercial services, which took over its name. Comtelburo's part in financing the cost of the general news service became at once important in South America. American competition, and high transmission and other costs, kept full pace with increased revenue from newspapers. A policy of retrenchment was enforced by Chancellor, and concentration on the main bastions of the Reuter service – Argentina, Chile, Brazil – took the place of further penetration into the smaller republics. It remained a source of amazement to competitors that Reuters stayed in Latin America at all; and another milestone was reached when a contract was made with the great Latin American newspaper, *La Prensa* of Buenos Aires.

There was no doubt of the Agency's solid base at home. One of the fears of those who had opposed the sale of the half share in Reuters to the Newspaper Proprietors Association in 1941 was that the London newspapers would fail to give full support to the Agency. The enthusiasm and practical concern of the new Board showed just the opposite.

Soon, as a result of close working relations established between Christopher Chancellor and Edward Davies, General Manager of the Press Association, Reuters became more closely integrated with its sister organisation and part-owner. Jointly, Chancellor and Davies launched subsidiary enterprises managed in partnership, the most important being 'P.A.–Reuter Photos', which has built up since 1944 the greatest Press picture business in the United Kingdom.

Reuters' main energies could now be devoted to the future in Europe, beginning to take concrete shape. Immediately after the liberation of Europe, Reuters set out upon a policy of working in close association with the national European Agencies. Such co-operation seemed to be the healthiest and technically best news system for the newspapers of Europe. But a prerequisite was that these Agencies should be independent of Government influence and fully supported by their countries' newspapers.

The wisdom of basing such a new alliance on definite principles was soon apparent. The European resistance groups had made freedom of news one of their declared ideals in all discussions on the Press during the German occupation. Insistence on these principles now showed practical support of the values for which those groups had fought. In 1939, soon after the outbreak of war, a group of neutral and independent Agencies had established a loose federation, with a view to developing their news services untouched by war propaganda. Their plans had been destroyed by the realities of the German invasion; but, with liberation, the group's spirit was revived. The prime mover of the group, H. H. J. van de Pol, energetic head of the Dutch Agency, emerged from four years 'underground' in Holland to take over his old post. His own natural orientation was towards Reuters. So too was that of the rest of the '1939 group', now composed of the following independent news agencies:

Agence Belga of Belgium,
Agence Télégraphique Suisse of Switzerland,
Algemeen Nederlandsch Persbureau of Holland,
Finska Notisbyrån of Finland,
Norsk Telegrambyrå of Norway,
Ritzaus Bureau of Denmark,
Tidningarnas Telegrambyrå of Sweden.

Of these, Ritzaus Bureau of Denmark is the only news agency in the world, in addition to Reuters, which still operates under the name of its founder: and the present head of the Danish news agency, Lauritz Ritzau, has in his possession a letter written in 1867 to his father, the Agency's founder, by Julius Reuter offering to buy Ritzaus Bureau.

Soon after the end of German occupation, all these Agencies made new agreements with Reuters, within the spirit of the

Reuter preamble declaring both parties' freedom from 'any Government or tendentious control'. In contrast to the pre-war situation, there was now no question of Reuters' desiring such contracts to be exclusive, nor of wishing to limit its allies to the Reuter source alone. This assurance and this spirit were entirely new.

A bold effort by the Italian newspapers to establish a strong co-operative Agency in the place of Stefani, the former State-controlled organisation, had Reuters' influence to help it. In the spring of 1944, as the Allied armies moved north towards Rome, Reuters made its policy clear: it would oppose the revival of Stefani or the creation of another State-controlled Italian Agency; it wanted to carry out the plans of the Italian newspapers in forming an independent news agency of their own. With Reuters' goodwill and with this backing, after endless difficulties, Italy's first newspaper-owned co-operative Agency, Agenzia Nazionale Stampa Associata (ANSA), came into being.

An ardent worker for this cause was Cecil Sprigge, appointed Reuters' Chief Representative in Italy in June 1944. He was an ideal choice. *Manchester Guardian* correspondent in Rome in the 1920's, well known as a lover of Italy and as a devoted student of all aspects of Italian life, he had from the start the full confidence of the Italian newspaper leaders and politicians alike.

The new co-operative Agency was launched in Rome by the twelve then existing daily papers in the capital on the cessation of the official Allied news service in January 1945. It collected and distributed Italian domestic news, and took over the distribution of world news supplied to it by Reuters. By September, its twelve members had grown to ninety-seven, and it had offices in the chief cities of the North. It was largely due to Sprigge's efforts that the North Italian Press linked up with the co-operative after the German collapse.

During the next five years ANSA suffered much from the deep political divisions within the Italian Press. It failed to produce continuity of management, and the working arrangements with Reuters broke down. The Reuter Service now reaches ANSA and its members through a privately owned Italian Agency, founded by Dr. Pietro Cobor and called 'Radiocor', which Reuters has appointed as its agent in Italy.

Many vicissitudes have also marked post-war Agency developments in France. Prospects of the rebirth of a great, independent world Agency, such as Havas had once been, at first looked hopeful. Agence France-Presse (AFP), a new Agency, was created at the end of 1943 from the fusion of two 'Free French' Agencies which had been subsidised – one by the British Government in London and the other by the French authorities in Algiers. The new Agency, although dependent on funds from the French Government, had pledged itself to achieve independence. It had the quickly given assurance of Reuters' support, provided that it gained this freedom and developed under the ægis of the French Press. But early hopes that it would give up its large Government subsidy and join the new alliance of newspaper-owned Agencies were soon dispelled. The first days of the liberation were critical for the French newspapers; financially unstable and politically divided, they were mostly indifferent to the status of their national Agency. A cheap news service was all that they demanded, and they did not care who paid the bill. At the same time, there were clamours on every side that France must have a world Agency, that Havas's old domains must be reconquered. It was a question of French prestige.

Subsequent developments are best explained by quoting a report on the French news agency's 1947 accounts issued in Paris by the 'Commission for controlling the accounts of public enterprises' in 1947:

'The Commission recognises that the institution [AFP] is of public interest, and in particular the Commission agrees that for political reasons the offices of the Agency abroad must be kept going, even if these incur heavy deficits. Hence the Commission does not dispute the principle of a big financial contribution of the State to the costs of the service [of the Agency].'

After expressing some criticism of the system of accounts adopted by the AFP in 1947, this report showed that in 1947 the costs of running the Agency amounted to 797 million francs, while real revenue (*'recettes propres'*) amounted to 310 millions, or only 40 per cent of the total expenses. Estimates for 1949 were that the revenue would only represent 30 per cent of the expenses. For the year 1950 the *Journal Officiel* (August 12th, 1950) gives the Agence France-Presse subsidy as 903,518,000 francs (approximately £1 million at the then rate of exchange).

So the Government subsidy continued. With such backing, a programme was developed of vast extension overseas. When necessary in the name of French prestige, services could be uneconomic. Within a few years, the new French Agency was strongly established in Egypt, South America and parts of the Far East. It commands respect – for it is efficiently run and retains the services of many French journalists of experience and ability. But the French Press has not yet developed a sufficient solidarity or sense of joint responsibility to organise an independent news service of its own.

Since the war, Reuters has in a few years created in Paris a major European base. Here the Reuter Bureau collects the news of France, distributes a basic world service in French to newspapers in Paris and the provinces, and serves as a communications link with the rest of Western Europe. Beginning with a single subscriber in December 1945 – the evening *Libé-Soir* – Reuters now supplies world news to the whole Paris Press. The Chief of the Paris Bureau, Harold King, worked many years in Paris before he went to report the war in Russia in 1942. His staff of fifty is a microcosm of Reuters in London: correspondents, French sub-editors, translators, his own accounting staff. As the Agency's largest office on the Continent, it shows how quickly Paris has again become one of the world's major news centres.

The recovery of the newspaper Press in Western Germany after the war is an impressive story; and the creation and success of the first German co-operative news agency, owned by the newspapers, an integral part of it. Germany now has – in the Western Zone – an Agency untouched by Government influence or financial aid: the channels of news are free. Reuters' co-operation from the first with this new Agency, Deutsche Presse-Agentur (dpa), has led to an increasingly close and cordial relationship, which cannot fail to be beneficial to future Anglo-German relations.

The resurrection of a system of news supply to the German Press had to overcome tremendous difficulties. A highly centralised and efficient propaganda system lay discredited and broken-down; the zonal system of occupation cut across existing communication links; the newspapers themselves were in chaos. For some time, the Allies exercised as strict a control over Agency activities as they did over the Press in general. Then, in the autumn of 1946, the American authorities handed over the news agency they controlled in their Zone to the German newspapers. A year later, the British did the same thing in their Zone. At the same time permission was given for the 'foreign Agencies' – Reuters, Associated Press, United Press, International News Service – to operate in Germany themselves.

Within two years, Reuters, through Alfred Geiringer, Assistant European Manager resident in Germany, had established a strong organisation in Western Germany. For the first time since 1866, three large Reuter offices were collecting and distributing news in Germany: in Berlin, Hamburg and Frankfurt. In the place of the suspicions generated by ten years of bitter Nazi propaganda, Reuters found that it had a vast amount of German goodwill to draw upon. But the time had clearly come for the Germans to distribute their own internal news themselves. In the autumn of 1949, the two German newspaper-owned Agencies, the one operating in the British and the other in the American Zone, were finally fused, to create a new unified Agency, dpa. Owned co-operatively by the Press of Western Germany, it made a long-term contract with Reuters. Its constitution embodied a declaration of independence from Government similar to Reuters' own.

In the same year, Reuters and dpa created in Germany a working partnership in the sphere of commercial news which has successfully cut across national frontiers. Just a hundred years since Bernhard Wolff and Julius Reuter revolutionised the European stock exchanges by transmitting financial quotations along the first Berlin–Aachen State Telegraph, Reuters and dpa, aided by an association of German Chambers of Commerce, set up in Frankfurt a new joint Company with exactly the same purpose. The new Company, Vereinigte Wirtschaftsdienste (VWD), is now the chief commercial news agency in Western Germany; more than that, it already has European importance. Not the least significant factor in the total German scene is the fact that the representatives of VWD's two-third German shareholding majority have expressed a desire that Reuters' one-third shareholding should continue on a permanent basis.

Frankfurt is at present Reuters' chief office in Germany, and once again one of the main communication centres of Western Europe. To the Reuter office in the new city which is growing out of the ruins of the war comes a continuous stream of news from Berlin and Bonn (with their own Reuter offices), from thirty local correspondents in Western Germany, and from the German Agency in Hamburg.

Reuters' new strength in Germany and the co-operation shown by the German Agency are healthy signs. On a day in May 1950, Christopher Chancellor flew to Germany and had interviews in Bonn with Herr Adenauer in the morning and with Dr. Schumacher the same afternoon. On both he impressed the great service to the cause of free news in Europe the German Agency was performing by continuing independent of its Government. It is one of the most encouraging news-agency developments since the war that it has remained so.

The greatest struggle for freedom of news – which means free access to the facts – is being fought in Russia and her satellite States. Tass, the Russian Agency, is an organ of State. A case of libel heard before the English Court of Appeal in 1949 removed all doubts on this score: Tass, involved in a libel action, in England, claimed diplomatic privilege – a privilege granted only to the servants of a foreign Power – and the claim was accepted. The national Agencies of the Soviet satellite States are similarly regarded as performing an official function.

Clearly it is both useless and dangerous to rely on these Agencies for the real facts from Eastern Europe. But ignorance breeds as many delusions as propaganda: it became as much a moral as a professional obligation on the world Agencies to penetrate the 'Iron Curtain' with their own correspondents.

Against growing difficulties, they have done what they could. Expenses have been enormous, both in cable charges and in high costs of living due to artificial exchange-rates: after the sterling devaluation in September 1949, only Reuters and the Communist *Daily Worker* of London kept staff correspondents in Moscow. The Russian censorship is ruthless and arbitrary. In a single month in the spring of 1949 more than thirty separate Reuter cables to London were killed *in toto*; and a large number more arrived badly mutilated, although the deletions were unknown to the correspondent sending them.

In the Balkans and other countries of Eastern Europe, Reuters has made a determined effort to obtain its news firsthand. But it has been a cat-and-mouse game, and a dangerous one. In Hungary, the Agency's local Budapest correspondent – a Hungarian – was, in 1948, found guilty by the People's Court of 'sending abroad tendentious news' in his despatches to London. Two years later, Reuters' staff correspondent in Poland was expelled for 'not reporting objectively'. The American Agencies have suffered similar expulsions from Czechoslovakia.

There is a further source of news from Eastern Europe. Tass, and the national Agencies of Poland, Czechoslovakia, Hungary and the other States bordering on Russia, send out radio services in English and other languages. The Reuter listening-post north of London, which did such good work in the war, takes down these services and sends them by teleprinter to the Head Office in Fleet Street. Such news is then issued by Reuters, but only under its official source, to ensure that there can be no mistake about its origin.

Almost every country in Western Europe now has an Agency owned co-operatively by its own newspaper industry. That in itself is a revolution in European news-gathering: it is also a most important chapter in the history of the freedom of the Press. Never before has world news (outside the Soviet *bloc*) been so free of Government influence in any form; and never before have the newspapers themselves controlled so many of the channels of international news.

What Reuters itself still required was a public and widely advertised assertion of its absolute independence of the British Government. This came by accident and in the most extraordinary way. The old belief that Reuters had some special connection with the Government was dying, but it was dying hard. The *coup de grâce* came unexpectedly and without warning from no less a source than the American State Department in Washington.

In January 1946 the State Department, under the authority of Mr. William Benton, Assistant Secretary of State, issued a booklet – *The Post-War International Information Programme of the United States* – by Dr. Arthur W. MacMahon. A special section of this booklet was devoted to Reuters: within it were grave charges against the Agency. Chancellor at once sprang into action, and in almost every newspaper in the world (including the United States and Canada) Reuters itself became front-page news.

Here is an account of the episode from one of these newspapers. I take at random *The Statesman* of Calcutta, dated January 6th, 1946:

WASHINGTON, Jan. 5. – The General Manager of Reuters, Mr. Christopher Chancellor, tonight challenged in a 3,000 word statement addressed to the U.S. State Department what he deplored as attempts by American officials to 'smear' Reuters as a British propaganda organisation.

The statement was issued by the Department at Mr. Chancellor's request following the appearance of a booklet prepared for publication by the State Department on *The Post-War International Information Programme of the United States.*

The booklet, written by Dr. Arthur W. MacMahon, State Department special consultant, was distributed in advance for release last Saturday, but the release was postponed at the last hour for a week as the result of a strong written protest lodged by Mr. Paul Scott Rankine, Reuters' chief correspondent in Washington, on Mr. Chancellor's instructions.

In the name of 'honesty, decency and fair dealing', Mr. Rankine called on the State Department to delay the release so that 'Reuters may have time to study in detail the allegations and to present documentary evidence in refutation of them'.

Reuters alone of all news agencies was given a special section in a chapter headed 'Press Communications' containing statements by Dr. MacMahon and footnotes from American officials in various parts of the world.

After a point-to-point reply to the allegations, Mr. Chancellor stressed the gravity of Dr. MacMahon's charges, which he said 'impugn the integrity not only of myself but of all my colleagues – professional newspapermen – in Reuters and the British newspapers who own Reuters and are pledged to see that Reuters is conducted in accordance with high principles of honesty and truth in news'.

By a selection of extracts from official correspondence and by innuendoes, he said, Dr. MacMahon had given the impression that Reuters was in some special way associated with the British Government, received special privileges and assistance from that Government and as a result 'conditioned' its news to favour British interests.

'This is not true,' Mr. Chancellor's statement declared. 'Reuters today is owned and operated by the newspapers of Britain, as the Associated Press of America is owned and operated by the newspapers of the USA. It is specifically protected by its Charter of Incorporation, which guarantees it shall have complete independence from Government control and political interest. It has no connection with the British Government and receives no exclusive privileges from that Government.'

In his point-by-point reply to Dr. MacMahon's memorandum Mr. Chancellor dealt with the allegations by American officials in Australia, India, the Middle East and Latin America.

Dr. MacMahon quoted Mr. Nelson T. Johnson, U.S. Minister to Australia, for a statement in October, 1944, that 'to a very large extent news from the USA collected by American news services tends to come first to London where the most important consumer lives, and is thence transmitted through the Empire conditioned by such processes of selection and manipulation as British news agencies such as Reuters give it'.

In reply Mr. Chancellor quoted from a telegram from Mr. R. A. Henderson, Chairman of the Australian Associated Press and General Manager of the *Sydney Morning Herald*: 'Mr. Johnson's statement as far as Australia and New Zealand are concerned is demonstrably false,' Mr. Henderson cabled.

'In the opinion of the Australian Press, Reuters' news services today are comparable to any in the world, and its cover of British and European news is superior to that of any other service – its services are fast, reliable, accurate and factual.'

After pointing out that three American news services are available to the Australian newspapers, Mr. Henderson said: 'If Reuters' service obtains wide prominence it is because, rightly or wrongly, newspapers who pay for the service believe it to be the best. We are satisfied that Reuters' service is more free from comment and independent of Government or other influence than any news service in the world today.'

Mr. Sisson Cooper, Chairman of the South African Press Association and General Manager of the *Argus South African Newspapers,* cabled Mr. Chancellor: 'Any suggestion that South African papers would be content with or tolerate manipulated news from America is a reflection on the integrity of South African newspapers which they all resent.

'Any suggestion that American news is "conditioned" for South African newspapers is untrue, and, indeed, such a state of affairs would not be tolerated by South African newspapers.'

If proof were needed to show that the British Press stood behind Reuters, this was supplied in abundant form when the whole British Press – both in London and the provinces – went into action on Chancellor's behalf. Almost every paper devoted its editorial column to 'the Reuter story', and the same interest and support were shown by newspapers in the British Commonwealth.

World's Press News, trade organ of the British Press, stated on January 10th:

Strong reaction occurred the world over to the charges made in the U.S. State Department's booklet against Reuters and Reuters' forthright rebuttal of those charges.

In the United States many leading newspapers published a summary of Mr. Chancellor's statement and made additional editorial comment. These papers included such leaders as the *Washington Star, Washington Post, Baltimore Sun, New York Times* and the *Herald-Tribune.*

Newspapers in the overseas Dominions, notably Canada, Australia, South Africa and India, as well as newspapers in Europe, also gave the statement considerable prominence.

The most incisive remarks upon the whole affair came from *The Economist.* On January 12th, under 'Reuters versus the State Department', it made this comment:

The most incomprehensible thing about the quarrel between Reuters and the State Department is that it should have happened at all. For it is indeed a curious way for the Office of International Information and Cultural Affairs, an arm of the State Department, to have introduced itself to the world-wide public among whom it intends 'to promote inter-allied harmony and help guard against future wars'.

It is pointless to review again the details of the dispute, which has been amply covered in the daily Press. What remains unanswered, however, is how Dr. MacMahon, one of the Department's special consultants, could ever have got himself into such a spot. For the rebuttal presented by Mr. Chancellor, General Manager of Reuters, indicates that the alleged facts about Reuters are based on rumour, gossip or merely wishful thinking. The explanation given in some quarters that an anti-British flavour to this first booklet *Memorandum on the Post-War Information Programme of the United States*, would put Congress in humour to approve the programme does not hold water. In fact, any explanation based on sinister intent blows up because the inaccuracies were too easy to apprehend.

This strange episode, with the amazing world-wide publicity which it evoked, was of almost incalculable importance in establishing beyond further question or dispute the independence and integrity of 'the new Reuters'.

Three weeks later Chancellor addressed the influential Overseas Writers in Washington and publicly declared Reuters' determination – side by side with the Associated Press – to continue to fight with all its strength to prevent Governments 'moving in on the news'. He flew on to Florida as Kent Cooper's guest. Together they hammered out the final relationship between Reuters and the Associated Press, and a new contract was made based upon mutual confidence and respect and a firm alliance in the world battle for freedom of news. It constitutes the most important agreement for the free and unhindered movement of news in the English-speaking world.

20

The New Commonwealth

IN 1946 REUTERS ENTERED A NEW PHASE IN ITS HISTORY.
A development of far-reaching importance was embarked
upon which may not yet have reached its full fruition.

The health and strength of a news agency operating as a
function of a free newspaper Press depend upon the widest
possible newspaper ownership: this ownership should com-
prise newspapers of every political shade and alignment.
Reuters, by a decision taken in the summer of 1946, carried
this conception into a new and wider field: it decided to extend the ownership to newspapers outside the home country.
Before the year 1951 was reached, the Agency, which was in
1946 the property only of the British Press, found itself
operated and owned in partnership by the Press of the United
Kingdom, Australia, New Zealand and India. This has been
much the most important recent development in Reuters'
history; and already it has had far-reaching consequences in
news distribution throughout the world. Its implications go
further. As Christopher Chancellor told the Royal Commission on the Press in 1948: '. . . it is possible that we may be
starting a new sort of organisation which cuts across national
and political barriers'.

A scheme for a 'co-operative Empire news agency' had been
put forward with enthusiasm before the war by a Canadian,
E. Norman Smith, President of the Canadian Press (the co-
operative news agency of Canada). As a delegate to the Imperial Press Conferences in the 1930's, he made it his chief

251

theme. His plan provoked interest and acceptance in principle, but gained little active support. With the outbreak of war it was abandoned.

There is little doubt that the status of the 'new Reuters', and especially the guarantees and principles embodied in the Reuter Trust, were the key factors that led to the success of the post-war approach to this project. Reuters, now strong and with the British Press behind it, had gained the respect and goodwill of the Commonwealth, and it possessed a world organisation which could readily be adapted to a wider form of ownership. Sir Keith Murdoch, the leading newspaper proprietor in Australia, came to the Sixth Imperial Press Conference in London determined to find a new basis for the relationship between Reuters and the Australian newspaper-owned Agency, the Australian Associated Press. It was he who struck the spark from which came the new Commonwealth conception of Reuters. The proposal itself for a partnership between the Agency's United Kingdom owners and the Australian Associated Press emerged from a discussion between Lord Layton (one of the London Directors of Reuters), Sir Keith Murdoch and Christopher Chancellor at a luncheon party during the meetings of the Imperial Press Conference in the summer of 1946. Chancellor at once said that the idea was practical and that he could put it through if it were sincerely desired by the Press of the two countries.

The partnership now proposed possessed most of the requisites for success lacked by the earlier 'Imperial' scheme. The approach to it was empirical and practical: it would be a natural growth, not the result of an abstract plan; and it found in the Reuter Trust a firm guarantee of those principles concerning news which were close to the hearts of the Australian newspapers. The possibility of this exciting scheme growing into something even more comprehensive became immediately clear as the discussions developed.

The British Press, through the Board of Reuters, welcomed the idea without reservation; and as soon as Sir Keith Murdoch arrived back in Australia, he found that his own colleagues on the Board of the Australian Associated Press were equally enthusiastic.

With this background, the negotiations themselves were quickly accomplished. Immediately the Australian decision had been made, Sir Keith Murdoch telephoned to London asking Chancellor to come to Australia and negotiate a partnership agreement. Chancellor flew out at the end of October, and on November 13th final agreement was reached in Sydney. Ten days later, accompanied by Cole, who had come to Australia to work out the editorial details of the partnership, he met the Board of the New Zealand Press Association in Wellington. On November 26th, New Zealand decided to come into the Reuter partnership alongside Australia.

On December 23rd, 1946, the following statement was issued to the Press of all three countries:

Arrangements have been made under which the Australian Associated Press and the New Zealand Press Association are to become partners with the United Kingdom newspapers in the ownership, control, and management of Reuters.

This follows the mission to Australia and New Zealand of Mr. C. J. Chancellor, General Manager of Reuters, and his discussions in Melbourne and Sydney with the Chairman, Mr. R. A. Henderson, and Directors of the Australian Associated Press, and in Wellington and Auckland with the Chairman, Sir Cecil Leys, and Directors of the New Zealand Press Association.

It is proposed to issue new shares in Reuters to the Australian Associated Press and to the New Zealand Press Association. The Australian Associated Press will appoint a Director to the Reuter Board to represent Australia and New Zealand.

The Australian Associated Press and the New Zealand Press Association, which are newspaper-owned co-operative news agencies, will become parties to the Reuter Trust and will pledge themselves to uphold its terms and principles.

On the same day came a telegram from Sydney:

The Board of the Australian Associated Press has nominated Mr. R. A. Henderson as the first Australian Director of Reuters. Mr. Henderson will represent the interest of Australian and New Zealand newspapers on the Reuter Board.

Sir Keith Murdoch has been appointed first Australian Trustee of Reuters.

The New Zealand Press Association has appointed Sir Cecil Leys first New Zealand Trustee of Reuters.

From the United States, Kent Cooper sent his blessing, and welcomed the partnership as 'a great forward step in Empire journalism: both Reuters and the Australian Associated Press are to be congratulated'.

Editorial comment in the British Press was enthusiastic. *The Times* stated:

The extension is to be warmly welcomed on broader grounds than the professional. A principal link of the Commonwealth depends upon the freest possible interchange of knowledge and ideas among its members; and the best security for this is a well informed Press. Men whose writings in the newspapers can influence the minds of millions of their fellow-countrymen can do a work for unity that is beyond the powers of governments; and any joint organisation which multiplies the occasions of contact between journalists practising their craft in the various parts of the Commonwealth tends to assist that work.

And the *Manchester Guardian*:

The entry of Australian and New Zealand newspapers into the co-operative partnership which owns and controls Reuters is an important event in newspaper history. . . . The link between Australasian and British journalism is notably strengthened, to the good of all the partners.

In the United States, the *Christian Science Monitor* in Boston, using as its caption 'News about News', said:

As some of the 'jewels of empire' seem about to be surrendered by Great Britain, the bonds of voluntary co-operation are drawn closer between various parts of the British Commonwealth. The growing spirit of Commonwealth unity finds its latest expression in the announcement that Australian and New Zealand news agencies are to become partners with United Kingdom newspapers in the ownership, control and management of the great British Agency, Reuters.

This is good news and should make for better news for all those readers who are served by Reuters. . . . And the Australian and New Zealand public will be better able to realise their own responsibilities and possibilities in the Commonwealth and in the Pacific when they are no longer merely at the receiving end of the British news service. Reuters, though a non-profit organisation, will profit from this move.

And the *New York Times* commented:

Amalgamation of the Australian Associated Press and the New Zealand Press Association with Reuters, in the United Kingdom, extends the influence of a strong and independent Press more than halfway around the world.

Only through the freedom of an untrammelled Press can the free nations of the earth remain free. The extension of Reuters to the Antipodes strengthens this influence. . . . Reuters is to be congratulated on its enterprise in knitting the continents together for greater understanding.

The new Reuter Director, Rupert Henderson, said in Sydney that by its seat on the Board of Reuters the Press of Australia and New Zealand would have a voice in the shaping of the Reuter world service. This, he said, was not merely a recognition of the status of Australia in the world news sphere: it was a recognition by Reuters of the growing importance of the Pacific. One of the most important immediate results of the partnership would be the establishment of a great joint Reuter–Australian Associated Press news service in the Pacific.

And in Melbourne the new Reuter Trustee, Sir Keith Murdoch, announced:

From the Australian point of view it is surely right that we should be in a position of responsibility and authority in relation to our basic service of news, instead of being a subscriber, accepting for a fee at some central point what the organisation places on our table. The principle of sharing the responsibility for what we put before the public of Australia is highly important, and I think Australian newspapers have advanced in stature and integrity as a result of the new development.

We are rightly in future in the position of principals. But also we have started a method which will undoubtedly be applied increasingly and over a wide area to British activities, commercial and others, where the Dominions are now called upon to join the Mother Country as partners, instead of their old position of acquiescing subscribers or contributors.

As a tailpiece came a note of cynicism from across the Atlantic. With a smile, the American magazine *Newsweek* printed an article entitled 'For God and King – Reuters'. Reuters, it said, had given a kind of Dominion Status to the Press of Australia and New Zealand:

The first step to remove the Union Jack label which Reuters wore in the eyes of the rest of the world, was taken in 1941, when it converted itself from a private profit-making Agency to a non-profit co-operative. During the War it expanded little while watching the American Associated Press move out with its new world service that challenged Reuters at home and in India, South Africa, Australia, New Zealand and other countries where Reuters had been the dominant service. Reuters has now adroitly taken up the challenge.

This event, which had all the momentum of a new idea, gave rise inevitably to discussion of possible further extensions of the partnership. Interest was aroused in Canada and South Africa; and some newspapers in Great Britain, enthusiastic about a wider Commonwealth agreement, suggested these two Dominions as the obvious next phase in enlarging the Reuter ownership. But the Australian–New Zealand scheme, although coloured by a genuine sense of the great principles involved, was essentially pragmatic – it fitted into the pattern of the existing news relationships and needs of the countries concerned. It was a natural, practical drawing-together of three complementary organisations. Anyone with a working knowledge of news communications and long-standing news-agency alignments would have realised at once that Canada was in a case apart. The traditional channels of news and communications link Canada closely to the United States – and the Canadian news agency to its American counterpart, the Associated Press. There were no partnership negotiations with Canada.

Nevertheless, the Australian and New Zealand participation in the Reuter ownership made a deep impression on the Canadian newspapers and enhanced Reuters' prestige. Today Reuters has a valued agreement with the Canadian Press news agency. The Canadian suspicions of the past are dead and buried. Reuters and the Canadian Press, although technically not partners, are close associates and allies – and this with the goodwill and glad acquiescence of the Associated Press. Ten years ago such a relationship would have seemed revolutionary: at that time Reuters was still deeply suspect in Canada for its believed connections with the British Government, and no direct Reuter service reached the Canadian newspapers. Today Reuters depends upon the Canadian Press for the bulk of its news from Canada, and through the Canadian Press the newspapers in Canada receive Reuters' news.

In 1947 it was made known to Reuters that a number of newspapers in South Africa desired to be associated in the partnership. Discussions took place; but it became clear that the political atmosphere was unfavourable, and it was decided to pursue the idea of South African partnership no further. This implied no weakening in the ties which for more than seventy years had bound Reuters closely to the South African Press. The South African Press Association successfully operates under the ownership of all the newspapers. A delegation of newspaper leaders, representing the Afrikaans and British sections of the South African Press, came to London in May 1949; here, in a spirit of goodwill, they negotiated a new long-term contract with Reuters which cements the relationship between the two Agencies and leaves Reuters as the basic provider of world news to the entire South African Press.

It would indeed have astonished those British newspapers which in 1946 were proposing an extension of the Reuter partnership to Canada and South Africa, had they been told then that on September 20th, 1948, they would be publishing the following announcement:

An Agreement has been made between Reuters and the newspapers of India which marks an important development in the organisation of world news. The Indian newspapers have formed their own news agency, the Press Trust of India Limited. This will be the national news agency of India, co-operatively owned by the newspapers as a non-profit-making Trust with a constitution similar to the constitution of Reuters.

The Agreement between Reuters and the Press Trust of India is governed by a preamble as follows:

'Both parties declare that they are news agencies serving no other purpose than the dissemination of truthful unbiased news, that they are free from any Government or tendentious control and that the news which they supply to each other shall be compiled and selected solely on its objective news value. They have entered into this agreement in full accord and understanding as to the basic principles of integrity of news.

'They have decided that it is right that the internal news agency of India, hitherto owned and managed by Reuters, be transferred to the ownership and control of the newspapers of India acting together through the Press Trust of India.

'Moreover, they have agreed that it is in the best interest of the Press of India, the United Kingdom, Australia and New Zealand that the Press Trust of India should share in the ownership of Reuters and take an active part in organising the collection and distribution of world news in the international field.'

The Associated Press of India Limited, a Reuter subsidiary company which for almost fifty years has collected and distributed the internal news in India, will be transferred to the Press Trust of India Limited.

The Press Trust of India Limited is to become a partner with the newspapers of the United Kingdom, Australia and New Zealand in the ownership of Reuters. It will be represented in Reuters by a Trustee and a Director and it will become a party to the Reuter Trust.

There was a long history behind this announcement. For nearly half a century Reuters had dominated the news field in India. Through its subsidiary company, the Associated Press of India, it distributed to the Indian newspapers the bulk of the news of their own country. For years there had been discussions with the Indian newspapers about the planned transfer of this internal news agency to Indian ownership. Reuters sought the creation of a broadly based newspaper-owned co-operative, with which it could safely deposit the goodwill and organisation of the Associated Press of India and at the same time retain for itself, as the supplier of the basic world news service, a firm and lasting link with the Indian Press. This policy bore fruit: an Indian newspaper-owned independent Agency came into being and it found in the Associated Press of India an organisation and a trained personnel already at its disposal.

In 1947 Indian independence was proclaimed and it was clear that Reuters could no longer remain in control of India's internal news. At the same time the announcement of the Australian and New Zealand partnership in Reuters opened the way to a new, and hitherto undreamed-of, solution to the Indian news-agency problem. Indian newspaper leaders themselves were quick to grasp the significance of this change in Reuters' constitution. Kasturi Srinivasan, President of the Indian Newspaper Society, sent a formal enquiry to Reuters in the summer of 1947: would the Indian Press be admitted to the Reuter partnership on the same terms as Australia? After consultation with the Australian and New Zealand partners, the answer from London was an unequivocal 'Yes'.

The negotiations were long and complicated. There was an acute division of opinion in India. Inevitably, in the exciting atmosphere of newly won independence, there was a desire in many quarters to cut all the old ties with Great Britain; and Reuters, as a British institution, was naturally suspect. More than once the discussions came perilously near breaking down. Finally, in the spring of 1948, the Indian Newspaper Society – after establishing a national news agency, to be called the Press Trust of India, with a constitution modelled largely upon the Reuter Constitution and the Reuter Trust – sent a delegation of newspaper proprietors to London. The Reuter Board, after consulting Australia and New Zealand, appointed a Pleni-potentiary Committee with authority to negotiate a partner-ship agreement. This Committee consisted of Lord Layton of the *News Chronicle* (representing the London ownership), John Scott of the *Manchester Guardian* (representing the British pro-vincial ownership) and Christopher Chancellor, Reuters' General Manager. In the course of the negotiations Scott, owing to illness, yielded his place to W. A. Hawkins of the *Bristol Evening Post*. The London negotiations continued for four weeks. Then the project had to be debated by the Indian newspapers themselves at a full session of their Society in Bombay. The decision was finally made, and in September 1948 the new agreement and the partnership terms were announced simultaneously in India and Great Britain.

The Indian partnership follows the pattern of Australia. The Press Trust of India (PTI) became the owners of the same number of shares in Reuters as are held by the Australian Associated Press. It has the same rights as Australia. The Reuter news service to India is selected and despatched by PTI men who are sent to London, where they work side by side with British and Australian colleagues in Reuters' Editorial Department at 85, Fleet Street. Indians, as well as Australians, are being appointed to important positions in the Reuter world organisation.

The legal formalities took a few months to complete. Once again in the space of two years the Reuter Constitution and shareholding had to be altered. It was not until February 1st, 1949, that the Indian newspapers became legally joint owners of Reuters. Devadas Gandhi of the *Hindustan Times*, Mahatma Gandhi's son, was appointed by the Press Trust of India as its first representative on the Reuter Board. C. R. Srinivasan, a distinguished newspaper publisher in Madras, became the first Indian Trustee of Reuters.

C. R. Srinivasan and his cousin Kasturi, who is the first Chairman of the Press Trust of India, played a major part in bringing this partnership to fruition. In his Presidential Address at the All-India Newspaper Editors' Conference, meeting at Bangalore in May 1949, C. R. Srinivasan said: 'I refer to the formation of the Press Trust of India to take over the distribution of Reuters' service in the country and the coverage of internal news by the Associated Press of India. Negotiations to this end lasted over several years, and final form and shape were given when a delegation of the Press visited England at the invitation of Reuters last year. Under the agreement that has been concluded and implemented the PTI has acquired the qualifying shares to be a partner in Reuters' world set-up and may now claim, of right, a voice in the direction and control of Reuters' organisation. The internal news service has passed entirely into the hands of the PTI, and Reuters has no part or place in it. The arrangement entered into is provisionally for a period of four years, as a sort of mutual try-out in a new set-up, but with goodwill on both sides what starts as a promising adventure will, I hope, lead to enduring association.'

In March 1949, a Reuter 'goodwill mission' flew out to India. It consisted of three Directors and the General Manager.

The Directors represented the partners in the Reuter ownership – Lord Layton, the London Press; Malcolm Graham of
Wolverhampton, the provinces; and Rupert Henderson, Australia and New Zealand. Lord Layton had been in India in
1928 as financial adviser to the Simon Commission: he remembered the hostility that he and his colleagues had then encoun-
tered. But in 1949 the Reuter mission was received with an
exuberance of goodwill and friendship by politicians and newspaper men everywhere it went during its month's tour of
India. The mission met the Indian political leaders in Delhi.
In reply to Lord Layton's comment on the warmth of their
reception, the Governor-General, Mr. Rajagopalachari, said:
'Why should you be surprised? We have lived with the British
for nearly two hundred years. We know your virtues as well as
your faults. There is now no reason for distrust.'   •

The Reuter mission was in India at a moment when a great
decision had to be taken. Was India to remain a member of
the British Commonwealth? It was at this stage, when India's
decision was not yet finally made, that the Reuter-PTI partnership began to figure prominently in the Indian Press. There is
no doubt that Pandit Nehru, Sardar Patel, and politicians and
journalists all over India, were deeply impressed by this first
and concrete evidence of the readiness of a great British institution to work in partnership with India on equal terms. Here
we deal with intangibles. But Lord Layton himself is convinced
that the Reuter partnership played a part in India's fateful
decision, made a month later, to stay inside the British Commonwealth.

The entry of the Indian Press into the Reuter ownership, at
a time when it was still doubtful whether India would remain
in the Commonwealth, was an extraordinary event in Reuters'
history. It was a move in practical internationalism; but it is
to be treated as an experiment during its early years. Like
India's association with the Commonwealth itself, the Indian

partnership with the other owners of Reuters is not immutable and there is provision for dissolving it if desired.

All the parties have faced frankly the difficulties inevitable in this ambitious attempt to fuse into a single organisation such diverse elements. It is recognised that this wider partnership can only succeed if, in practice, acceptance of the basic conception of truth in news transcends the fluctuating movements of nationalism and the local pressures which may in time become evident. It is also recognised that efficiency must come first and that there may have to be some practical limitation to the extension of partnership arrangements in an organisation which depends for its existence upon highly centralised control and a power of quick decision. It is too early at this moment in the continuing story of Reuters to predict the final outcome.

What is abundantly clear is that the character of Reuters has changed. A long road has been travelled since 1915. The 'new Reuters' would not accept any suggestion that it was concerned with the spread of British ideas abroad. It would tell the British Chambers of Commerce overseas to address their representations to the official British Information Services and the BBC. And in a most practical way its international outlook and its independence of Government is safeguarded, not only by the Trust but by the increasingly international composition of its staff. In the huge open editorial floor in Fleet Street are to be seen Australians and Indians selecting and sifting the news; Canadian and American newspapermen in charge of the North American service; and a European news desk partly manned by editors from the European allied Agencies – from Holland, Belgium, Norway, Sweden and Finland and, starting in Reuters' Centenary Year, from the head office of the German news Agency (dpa) in Hamburg – playing their part in making the Reuter service to Europe essentially European.

The new ownership necessitated yet another change in the Reuter Constitution. On the last day of 1950 the following statement was issued to the Press:

In order to bring the constitution of Reuters into conformity with the new Commonwealth ownership, under which the Australian, New Zealand and Indian Press have become shareholders in the Company, Sir Lynden Macassey has decided to resign from the Chairmanship of the Reuter Trust at the end of this year. Sir Lynden Macassey was appointed in 1941 by the then Lord Chief Justice of England as the Independent Chairman of the Reuter Trust when the ownership of Reuters was held in equal shares by the London and Provincial Press of the United Kingdom. The shareholding bodies, the Reuter Trustees and Sir Lynden Macassey have agreed that under the changed conditions today there is no longer any need for an Independent Chairman of the Reuter Trust. The purpose of the Reuter Trust, which guarantees the independence of Reuters from any form of Government control and ensures the objectivity of the Reuter service, remains unchanged.

In 1951 there are eleven Trustees appointed by the newspaper bodies owning Reuters: four represent the London newspapers, four the provinces; one represents Australia, one New Zealand and one India. The Trustees meet once a year to review the work of Reuters in terms of the Agreement of Trust. There are eight Directors: three London newspaper proprietors and three from the provinces; a representative of the Australian and New Zealand Press, and an Indian nominated by the Press Trust of India. There is no Chairman, and the General Manager is directly responsible to the combined Board.

The development of a genuinely international outlook in Reuters has been one of the new Management's chief concerns. It reflects Chancellor's personal outlook and his own beliefs. The Commonwealth partnerships, the new relationship with the Associated Press of America and the Canadian Press, the closer association with the independent Continental Agencies, including the new co-operative Agency of Germany, are the practical expression of this policy. The number of full-time foreign correspondents is being steadily increased, and in this process too there is an international flavour. In addition to implementing the partnership policy by giving important posts to Indian, Australian and New Zealand journalists, Reuters selects Americans, Canadians and others whose capacity as Agency correspondents has been proved.

The intangible result of such a policy cannot yet be assessed in its wider aspect. It would seem that it must certainly benefit relations between the Democracies; it demonstrates a sincere attempt to achieve practical international co-operation through a great British institution. The impact upon Reuters itself has certainly been remarkable: the news service has strikingly improved in efficiency and scope, and there has been a great advance in the Agency's prestige abroad.

But some of the old problems remain. Reuters, although non-profit-making, must still pay its bills: and these bills continue to grow. Everything that goes into the making of a world news service increases steadily in price: wire and radio communications grow more expensive; the costs of a sterling-based organisation financing large overseas staffs in the hard-currency areas mount yearly in the countries where inflation has run wild. Reuters must have its men in the news centres of the world – whether in Korea, Indonesia or Washington – and the bills have to be paid. Expansion of the service during the last ten years has been enormous: expenditure in 1951 is three times what it was in 1941. Reuters' newspaper owners have faced their responsibilities and carried the load: almost every year since the war they have accepted an increase in their annual fees or assessments. But the battle is a hard one and it will always be hard in this international and highly competitive business. The American news services are strong and efficient; and Reuters cannot afford to lag behind them.

One thing is certain. The decision taken during the war to put an end to all Government facilities once and for all has borne full fruit. Reuters' independence is now universally recognised and accepted. And the wisdom of the decision has been appreciated by the British Government itself. In the House of Commons in July 1948, in reply to a question about Reuters' activities abroad, Mr. Gordon-Walker, then Under-Secretary of State for Commonwealth Relations, said this: 'Reuters' tremendous reputation in the world depends in part on its not being subsidised or controlled by the Government, which it has not the slightest desire to be.'

Pursued logically, this principle of independence means that all attempts – however good the motive – to give an international authority power over the world's news agencies must be viewed with suspicion. Freedom of information cannot be enforced from above: it is a trust voluntarily undertaken by those who handle the news. During the past three years, the Freedom of Information section of the United Nations and the Commission on Human Rights have debated draft 'Press Conventions'. These seem at first sight unobjectionable: they include the limitation of censorship, where censorship still exists; the right to correct inaccurate reports; the outlawing of certain journalistic offences. But they have met strong criticism from Chancellor himself and from most of the leaders of the Press in Great Britain, Australia and the United States. Dislike of such powers being given to *any* official authority is one reason for this opposition. But another is the fear that such powers might be gravely misused. Moreover, the draft International Conventions in their present form draw no distinction between the independent world Agencies – the Associated Press, United Press and Reuters – and those used openly or disguisedly as instruments of Government. By treating all alike they would give international sanction to Government propaganda services masquerading as honest news, and would allow

– if not encourage – the State-subsidised Agencies to use privileges, guaranteed in the name of news freedom, for the benefit of the States which sponsor them. It is surely the essence of any international Convention that all parties to it should 'speak the same language', be agreed on the meaning of their basic concepts. Any fumbling over what is meant by the words 'news freedom' is morally and intellectually indefensible.

The Royal Commission on the Press, sitting in 1948, invited its witnesses (if they wished) to make recommendations to the Government for ultimate presentation to Parliament as the basis for possible legislation. The reply of Reuters' General Manager to this invitation was as follows: 'I cannot think of anything. As far as Reuters is concerned our chief desire is to be left alone, to be allowed to operate freely and to develop ourselves.' After nearly a hundred years of Reuters' free development, it was a fitting answer. Evolution from a German émigré's two-roomed telegraph office, reporting commercial news, to a co-operative world Agency, owned by the newspapers of Great Britain, Australia, New Zealand and India, is striking enough. But to the outside world the continuity has been far more important than the change. In a peculiar way, the name is still the organisation.

This is so largely because the 'desire to be left alone' has been the dominant desire. There have been times when it has run low: times of internal crisis, and times when national demands have been insistent. But, even on the occasions when Government was allowed to come nearer than it should have been, Reuters resisted more successfully than the old German and French Agencies. Reuters is now the only survivor of the three private European telegraph companies founded by Charles Havas, Bernhard Wolff and Julius Reuter. It is partly political chance that this is so; partly superior flexibility, a greater power to adapt itself to a changing world. But the Agency still represents the best qualities of the old triumvirate:

their reliability, imagination and enterprise. Much in the modern Reuters the founder would undoubtedly find strange or even alien: its co-operative ownership, its decision to make no profits. But that reply to the Commission on the Press he would have understood. The insistence on being left alone, in a realm where any other attitude must inevitably endanger the integrity of news, would have evoked from him only enthusiasm.

Index